MW00680058

Meet Me On The Mountain

The story of an

immigrant family

in the United States

An autobiography

by Siegfried Robert Hoffmann

Meet Me On The Mountain

© Copyright 1995 — Siegfried Robert Hoffmann, RR 1 Box 135F, Battle Lake, MN 56515 and 1701 Commerce Ave., #64, Haines City, FL 33844.

All rights reserved. No part of this book may be reproduced or transmitted in any form or by any means, electronic or mechanical, including photocopying, recording or by any information storage and retrieval system, without permission in writing from the author. Published by Victor Lundeen Co., Lundeen Building, Fergus Falls, MN 56537.

Cover Photo by Eric Hoffmann

Library of Congress ISBN# CXU-705-020

Printed in the United States of America

Table Of Contents

PREFACE

This book is a culmination of incidents. After the war Helen very rarely, better to say, hardly ever spoke of her experiences. I did not want to question her. I knew she did not want to relive something she wanted so badly to forget. So years and years went by without Helen ever opening up to anybody, not even to me. But once in a while there came a few words or sentences from her that shocked me. In my Prisoner of War years here in the USA, I was protected from the hate people had for Germans. I was shocked to hear some of the things she said. Our children were brought up without knowing what Helen went through, till sometime, maybe around a campfire at our summer house on Crane Lake in Minnesota—I don't remember anymore, Helen started to tell some of these stories. We were all stunned. Everybody listened quietly while Helen poured her heart out. After she finished, we were silent. None of us could immediately comprehend the reality of it ever occurring. The first responses our kids had were, "Ma, we did not know! Ma, why did you not tell us before? We would have liked to have known it sooner." Of course, it was hard to make them understand that for Helen to go through so much and finally tell about it, she needed time—exactly as much time as it took her to finally tell about it.

Later we thought to record it on tape so that the kids could play it back. We could not find time to do that. It started on one of our weekend trips to our summer house. We had a tape recorder running in the car and while we drove, we recorded. Here we found the time to record. Sometimes it was a question-and-answer type of conversation. Sometimes it was in German. Sometimes Helen had to stop and cry when all the memories were vividly coming back. Then there were experiences of my own life on it. And so, we recorded and stored many, many tapes.

One day our son, Eric, asked us for the tapes, especially for those about the time when Helen and I climbed the mountains to get together again. He wanted to put the story in a script for a screen play. Before sending the tapes to him, I played some of the tapes back. Some of it was in German, all of it was out of sequence, some of it without a detailed explanation; what year, where, what place, which we never explained in the recordings. Eric speaks German; but with all the other omissions, it would have been impossible for him to sift through all the tapes and get something down for a script.

When I talked to friends and I mentioned, for instance, that I played in the Sultan's Palace or that Helen climbed a mountain near Hitler's house in Berchtesgaden, it seemed to many of my friends a fabrication. But others had more questions, like why and when and where did it happen. It was important for me to get our life story in sequence and detail to make everybody understand it. As different as Helen's upbringing was from mine, we found a love for each other that binds us together and still endures. Life taught us many lessons—one of them is to make each other's life easier to live; make each other happy and, like a chain reaction, every one around you will be happy.

When we decided to write our story, we thought we had the right plan. First, I had to get all the tapes on paper. This meant listening to all the tapes and writing down everything word by word, sentence by sentence. We suddenly realized how many tapes we had. It had taken me three years to get the main group of tapes on paper. Meanwhile, our normal life went on. I did this in my spare time. Then came the sequencing. Marking everything by number and then transcribing it. By the time I got to the writing part, we were finally in retirement.

We had started to record on tape in 1969 and with the passage of time had forgotten so many details. Many names which I had forgotten in 1969 came back when I read my written copies from the tapes. Some names I can not remember at all anymore. Yes, we are getting old and forgetful. My mother could remember much more detail of our time in Istanbul, and I had all our conversation with her on tape, too.

My mother was 90 years old when she died in 1989 in Niederalm, Austria. I was fortunate to interview her frequently in the years I traveled to see her. Her mind was slowly getting confused. When we talked about past occurrences in Istanbul and Bielitz, occurrences that were not clear in my mind, she remembered everything vividly, everything to the last detail. This triggered my mind and I followed with small details of my own, and suddenly the exact occurrence was in front of us and on tape.

Helen was brought up as a Catholic, and so was I. Her life was surrounded by experiences of church and church life. She and all her sisters and brothers were deeply religious. After the war, her life and that of her family, endured the terrible persecution. She did not lose her faith in God.

I was raised Catholic at home, in the Mission School, and later in the Turkish-German school. There I learned to live with people of different religious persuasion which was the complete opposite of mine. I respected their beliefs but did not accept them. Later on in life, I admired my grandparents Olschowski's marriage. It was an example of how two people who are Catholic and Evangelical can live happy lives together and raise happy children.

Our life story was written for our children and grandchildren. Helen related her life on the tapes with that in mind. In writing it down, I followed her words on the tape exactly. Changing it would have changed her feelings and possibly the truth. Helen learned her first word of English in 1952 when we arrived in this country. Yes, I have to admit it, I failed in teaching her English.

In obtaining dates, times, and years, I relied mostly on my many books and my encyclopedia. I needed more. I needed more detailed information on the dates of the events in Bielitz prior to 1921 and World War I pertaining to Bielitz. When we least expected it, help came. Our son got a contract with the Folger Shakespeare Theater in Washington, D.C., and lived just a block from the Library of Congress. He used the Library of Congress a lot for his personal research, and he asked me if he could help me with obtaining information I wanted. I sent him the dates and the topics concerning Bielitz, and he sent me printouts of all the books available regarding that subject and copies of certain pages of books. When we visited him in Washington on one of his opening nights, Helen and I spent time at the Library of Congress researching. Helen read the Polish books, and I read the books written in German. What we needed, we made copies of, and we made a lot of copies. That gave me the information to finish the book. Thanks, Eric, for your help. May God give me the strength to finish it.

Part I

Helen's Story

Chapter 1

My Childhood

My thoughts drift forward to the day I will die. Will I leave something behind that my children and grandchildren can remember me by? Is there something that will remind them, at least a little bit, of their mother and grandmother? The children do not know much of my life and only the oldest grandchildren have heard some of the happenings in World War II and the time afterwards. I decided to tell them what happened in my life. It may be not too interesting in the beginning to hear of a normal life on a farm, but I had a happy time growing up.

It was the tragedy of the War and the things I had to endure during and after the War that formed me and my outlook on life.

To my children and grandchildren. I am not a writer. I tell my story like I would be telling it to you, sitting next to me. So please forgive my errors and read it and understand it like a story. The only difference is, everything is true.

When Andreas and Marie Urbanke got married, they planned to live and work together and raise their children in God and live happily. They had seven children, happy children, who were raised with love and in return received their children's love. These were my parents.

I was born in our farmhouse in Alexanderfeld, Poland, on May 15, 1922, the sixth of seven children. When my father died in 1924, my oldest sister, Trude, was 9; my brother, Karl, was 8; Rudi was 7; my sister, Mimi, was 6; Viki was 4; I was 2; and my sister, Liesl, was 8 months old. He worked as a tool and die maker in a big machine shop. He worked there every weekday and sometimes on weekends. In the evenings, he took care or his farm work. It was a small farm compared to farms here in the United States. The farm income was not enough to feed a family with seven children.

One of the first events my family told me about was my father's death. It was on a Sunday. He had a lot of hay left on the field when a storm came up. Everybody except the small kids had to work to load the hay on the wagon, and then the cows would pull the wagon to the barn. Then the axle on the wagon broke. My father decided to carry it in himself. He put the hay in a canvas and carried it on his back into the barn where my mother took it from him and stored it. He went back and forth till the wagon was empty. He had to save the hay from getting wet. In the evening, he started to have a terrible headache. My mother called the doctor, but he could not figure out what it was. This was on Sunday. By Wednesday, he had already lost consciousness. His fever kept going higher, and the doctor thought it was typhus fever. The next Sunday he died. The autopsy revealed he had died from a brain hemorrhage. In the strain to bring the hay in, a blood vessel had burst.

My mother had told me much about my father. One day she went with me to the cemetery and she showed me the grave where my father was buried. I was still a very little girl. She met someone at the cemetery and began talking with her. When she turned around, she saw me digging with my hands in the grave. I had dug a deep hole already. My mother asked me what I was doing. "Well, I want to see my daddy," I said. Yes, I wanted to see him again. I was so young.

After my father's death, my mother had to go on with her life and raise her children. She did not intend to part with her children. All our relatives supported her in her efforts. The three youngest children, Liesl, Viki and I, were small and needed care. The three oldest were in school already. Mimi, the middle child, was big enough to help at home and was almost ready to go to school. She went to stay with our grandmother on my mother's side in Alt-Bielitz, where she stayed and went to elementary school. But our mother insisted on raising us together, and we often visited our grandmother and played with our sister, Mimi. It must have been hard for my mother to keep the farm and raise the kids. I don't know how she did it, but we had the greatest respect for her. We all had to pitch in and help.

We lived in the outskirts west of Bielitz, Poland, in a suburb called Alexanderfeld. It was about a half an hour walking distance from the center of Bielitz. I went to the Alexanderfeld Public School for the first four years. The same as all of us kids. Then I went to the Notre Dame Convent School in Bielitz in the center of the town. We walked back and forth to school and to church every day. We walked in snow or in rain. We had no school bus. The first fifteen minutes from home were not paved. It was a dirt road with a little gravel on it. When it was raining, we had to jump over water puddles and our shoes got pretty dirty.

One day a fire broke out. We don't know to this day how it happened. In the upper part of the barn, the hayloft was on the left side and the straw on the right. The straw caught fire. Luckily we saw it in time. All of us doused it, without having to call the fire department, by bringing pails of water from the well outside.

We had another fire at the farm once, but this time the fire department had to come. This fire was set! We had noticed there was somebody sneaking around in the neighborhood and hiding in the fields. My brother, Rudi, came home one day very late; and as he came down the hill and went over the bridge, a man jumped him. This man had his face masked like a mummy—a completely white mask.

Luckily Rudy punched him, and the man started running and got away. It was not more than two days later we saw him hiding around the house again; and before we knew it, the barn and also the house were on fire. He had thrown matches into the hayloft. Our neighbor saw him coming around the house. My mother was alone at that time, so she called the fire department and they put it out.

When you come from town to our house, you turn left down the hill from the main road. To the right from the turn off on the main road is the Exerzier-platz—the training and parade ground of the military. One of the farmers saw this man hiding in a wheat field. He alerted the military and they surrounded the whole field and caught him. We had no more trouble.

I remember our house very well. We had a small farmhouse with a big living room and a big kitchen. We had two bedrooms plus a big hallway. In the hall, my mother had an oven where she baked. In our church, First Communion was always a big celebration for parents and children. The children always went in a group, girls and boys together to the altar. I went to a private Catholic girls school with only nuns for teachers. For First Communion, they always had a big breakfast in the gym for all the kids in the Catholic youth group that me and my sisters and brothers belonged to. We would set up the tables with table cloths and flowers and my mother would do all the baking. She would make sheets and sheets of cakes, like cottage cheese cake, sometimes as many as twenty big bak-ing sheets which we would carry downtown to the breakfast in big cloth baskets. Because my mother was such a good cook, she was always asked to do the bak-ing. She would do all the baking in that oven in the hall.

The oven was made out of special clay bricks. It was very deep with an open-ing that was two feet high and three feet wide. My mother used a wooden board with a long handle on which she would put the baking sheets and shove them into the oven.

First, we had wood burning inside the oven; and after the wood was all burned up and the oven was hot enough, she would put the cakes in. She would put three sheets of cakes in at a time, and they always came out just perfect. There was a special flavor to the cakes when they were baked in this oven. The baking was done by the bricks—special clay bricks that would hold the heat for a long time. Once you heated it up, you did not need a fire anymore. When it got too hot, you would open a small sliding metal slot with a handle on it. Every year my mother would bake all the cakes for the First Communion celebration. People would always look forward to getting some baked stuff.

We didn't have horses on our farm. One time my brother tried to ride on a cow. She had big horns and got behind my brother and suddenly lifted him up with her horns and threw him onto the roof of the shed. That cured him of ever trying to ride that cow again. My mother and the oldest children milked the cows. They had to do it by hand. We did not have any milking machines. When the younger children milked the cows, we'd shoot the warm milk right into our mouths. It was not easy, but we did it.

We had a smoking oven. When we slaughtered pigs, my mother would smoke the bacon and ham herself. She would smoke the meat for days with wood and pine needles, which gave it a terrific flavor. She had a rack across the oven where she would hang the meat for smoking. We did not have to get many groceries. We had the meat. We had the milk, butter, and buttermilk. We baked our own bread and fruit we had in our own orchard. We had a huge orchard with lots of beautiful fruit trees. People would order the fruit from my mother ahead of time to be sure of getting as many bushels of pears and apples and peaches as they needed. We also had lots of raspberries and gooseberries and cherries and all kinds of vegetables. We took very good care of ourselves.

Members of the Catholic youth group would meet in front of the church on Sundays after mass and decide what they were going to do that afternoon. "Oh, let's go out to the Urbankes and play ball in the orchard," was the most common suggestion. And they came out. Boys, girls, even priests played soccer on our huge lawn in front of the house. My mother always had cake or something for people to eat, and we would sit on the ground outside. We also had a beautiful gazebo with wild grape leaves growing around the sides and over the roof. When it rained, we would all run inside and sit on the benches. In the evening we would sit in there and sing. We were seven children, and all my brothers and sisters had good voices and loved singing. So we always sang. Some of us sang alto, some of sang soprano, and the boys sang tenor and baritone. It sounded so beautiful. People on the street sometimes stopped to listen to us. It sounded so nice. Of course, all the Urbanke kids sang in our church choir. My grandfather Borgel was a musician, band leader, music teacher, and played all kinds of instruments.

My grandfather Urbanke died many years ago. I can't remember him at all. He died quite young. I don't remember how old he was when he died. When he died, the farm was supposed to be handed down to the oldest son, like it was always done before. Franz, the oldest, had a good trade making oven bricks and he did not want the farm. My father, as the second oldest boy, inherited the farm and had to pay the other brother and sisters their share of the money the farm was worth. My uncle Franz got permission to build a house on our property. My grandmother Urbanke could live in one room in our house with two of my aunts, who were not married. They were the two sisters of my father that took care of my grandmother. This is an old custom. The parents who give their farm to their children have the right to live in the house till they die. My grandmother Urbanke died when she was 75 years old.

Our house sat on a little hill. Coming down the road from the hill, there was a creek with a small bridge. The road led up another little hill to a larger road which connected to the paved road that lead to downtown Bielitz. On this road from the bridge were three houses close together. In the first house on the left lived my uncle and aunt and five of my cousins. Else was the oldest and then there was Trude, who was my age. We both were in the same class. Then there was Edie (Edward), who was Liesl's age. Then there were two younger cousins from two sets of twins. There was Hansel and Gretel. Gretel died shortly after birth. In the second set of twins, there was Marianne and Josef, but Josef died. On the right side of this street was a farm house. Their name was Piesch. It was a bigger farm than ours.

Right after you passed my uncle's house on the right side, there were trees, bushes and a live fence which was always cut short and nicely trimmed. The same was true on our side of the property. Our house had one on two sides—on the west and on the south side. It was also always nicely trimmed.

When you came to our house you saw the big grass lawn in front of the house, which was to the south. The fields were on the north, the east and the south of the house. The grass lawn was about thirty feet wide and seventy feet long. On the left side was the gazebo. We all loved that gazebo. We spent lots of time there. We ate our meals in there in the summer time. We had company in there. Inside was a big table and benches all around it. On the outside, wild grape vines grew all over it. The vines grew thick green, and it was always shady and cool inside.

Next to the gazebo at the left side was our well. Over the well was a little roof with a winch and a big rope with a wooden pail. We had to get all the water from the well, as we had no pump at the farm house. We were a family of seven children, my father, mother and grandmother but we had practically only three large rooms. In the kitchen we had benches, a large table, and a couch. Liesl and I slept there. All of us did our homework on the table in the kitchen. The baking oven was next to the kitchen.

Besides baking cakes, my mother would bake her own bread. I think my mother made the best bread. Boy, did that bread taste good when it was freshly baked! A little bit of butter on it; oh, that tasted delicious! She made what we called a Blumen Schnitte—a slice of fresh bread, cottage cheese, and butter all around the slice. It looked like a daisy. That's why it is called Blumen Schnitte, flower sandwich. We did not need meat or anything else on it. Sure, we had meat—we had a smoker next to the baking oven.

As kids we worked hard but we had lots of fun, too. We had all kinds of fruit trees in our orchard. I don't remember how big the orchard was. There must have been 40 to 50 fruit-bearing trees and 10 to 20 young trees. We had quite a few trees of every fruit. We had at least 20 berry bushes. My mother sold a lot of fruit every year. People ordered from year to year because they liked the kind of fruit we had. For instance, one pear tree had such juicy pears and so huge—as big as my hand—not the fist, the hand. When the pears were growing, we had to support every branch because they were hanging down so heavily the branches would break off. When you bit into a pear like ours, the juice would run down your face. They were so sweet and juicy!

Then we had the "Grafensteiner Apfel"—the most delicious apples we had. And the cherries—we had a huge cherry tree in the back. Way on top were the nicest and ripest cherries. I always climbed all the way up where the blackbirds came to eat the best cherries. We had walnut trees on both sides of the house, in the back and in the front. In the front, lightning had struck the tree and split it practically in half. If we would not have had the tree, the lightning would have hit the house. It was taller than the house.

We loved to sleep in the hay. Naturally, a lot of our friends loved to do that, too. My best girl friend, Hedwig, often stayed with us overnight. She had a crush on Viki, but Viki was not crazy about her. Whenever she would visit us, she would look forward to sleeping with us in the hay. Viki always tried to scare the daylights out of us. One night Liesl, Hedwig, and I were sleeping in the hay and that stinker, Viki, climbed up from the grain storage area into the rafters. He had a white sheet over him and two flashlights. These were his eyes, and he came out from the rafters and jumped on us. We screamed! We were scared to death! But we paid him back eventually.

We had a pear tree close to the street. One day, Liesl and I climbed up on this tree with our aprons on. We were completely hidden by the branches and leaves. We filled our aprons with as many overripe pears as we could and waited patiently and quietly till Viki came home from school. As he passed by unsuspecting, we bombarded him with all the overripe pears we had. And that was plenty! When he avoided one, he got hit by another one. We had our aprons full. We did not have to pick them, just throw them. We paid him back! It was not malicious—we were brothers and sisters, but Liesl and I were stinkers, too. We had a good time. We were not rich but we had a happy childhood because we had so much fun. Our mother was very understanding of our youthful antics; but when it came to house and family, we all had to pitch in and help.

As you went by the barn on the right side, we had grain bins—wheat, oats, barley and rye. There we also had a room where we flailed. Yes, flailed. Flail? Most people today never had to do that, threshing by hand; but we had to learn to do it. After we brought the harvest in, wheat or oats, they had to be threshed. As soon as we were strong enough to thresh by hand, we were expected to help. Sometimes four of us were doing it, in a rhythm—one, two, three, four, one, two, three, four, and so on. It sounded real good. Naturally we were playful, so we hit each other with the flail just goofing around. Sometimes we hurt each other because the flail would ricochet back and hit you.

My mother always had to hire some outside help. I remember we had a woman helping us for a long time and later we had a young boy. This boy helped us a lot and we liked him very much. He was already working for us when the German troops marched in; but the Germans wanted him to work somewhere else. But he did not want to leave us, and we did not want him to leave. We stuck up for him and he was so grateful. When the Russians marched in and the Communist persecution started, he stuck up for us and for my mother.

I would like to describe how the house looked on the outside. It was white stucco and the walls were very thick. The walls on the houses here in the United States are only the thickness of one brick, and that is the strength of the house. The outside walls of our house were almost a yard thick. We also had an attic and a basement. We kept potatoes, canned goods, and apples in the basement. In the attic, we stored our grain through the winter.

In one part of the attic my brother, Rudi, built pigeon houses. It was amazing how he created these pigeon houses. He loved pigeons. He had a huge collection of all kinds of beautiful pigeons, not just common pigeons. He had studied architecture and was an architect. His uncle, Rudi Borgel, who was an architect too, financed his schooling. My brother, Rudi, built a little house for each pigeon with a bed and fancy furnishings, each different from the other. He really put his architectural ideas into practice in that room in the attic.

Rudi also did all the grafting of our fruit trees. He had his own little garden where he tried out his grafting experiments. When they were bearing good fruit, he transplanted them to the orchard. He also grafted some of the old trees. Some would bear two different fruit.

When I was a little older, I joined the "Marianische Jungfrauen" congregation of our church. Translated it means an organization of "young women dedicated to Mary." We would go with our priest hiking and camping in the Beskid and Tatra Mountains. These were beautiful mountains and we had a great time. Sometimes the "Jungling" organization "young men" joined us. These are the boys. We had a good time. We did not sleep together. We slept in different farm houses, but we played games together. We always had a priest—either Father Sedlarzek or Father Orzow, who would come along. Fathers Sedlarzek and Orzow both spoke German and Polish.

I would like to tell you about Christmas at our house. Whatever I can remember, I will tell you. At first the house was cleaned from top to bottom. Every one of us had a job to do, the boys included. Then my mother started to prepare the supper. In Bielitz it was carp. But these carp were raised in special lakes. Before the lakes froze out, they were drained and all the carp were put in very large, wooden bins in a building with a constant flow of fresh water and regularly fed. The carp were delicious! At that time all Catholics ate fish at Christmas time and the Evangelicals ate geese. My mother breaded and deep fried the carp and she usually made potato salad and one vegetable. As dessert my mother served coffee and many cakes, apple strudel, cheese cake, plum cake or poppy seed cake. And one thing that my dear mother always did after we ate—she would go into the barn to the cows and given them a piece of cake or whatever it was that we had for dessert. She felt they belonged to the family, too, and they should know it was Christmas.

Our Christmas tree was never put up weeks before Christmas, like it is here. It was decorated on Christmas Eve. Because I was so young, my older sisters and brothers got to decorate it. Liesl, Viki, and I were not allowed to go into the living room because that's where the tree was. Everything was always hush-hush! Something was going to happen! We little ones did not know what until we were called into the living room. The door swung open and I saw all the lights and all the glitter; and I stood in awe before the Christmas tree.

Later on we all got to decorate the tree. We decorated it with ornaments, cookies, nuts, dates, all kinds of fruits, and wrapped candies. We would put a string on one end of the candy wrapping and hang it up. When we got a little bit older we put them behind the tree, where you could not see them too well. There we would hang up the nicest candies, the ones we liked the most. While the tree was up and my mother was not looking, we would sneak behind the tree, take the candy out of the wrapper, pack the wrapper up again and leave the empty candy wrapper hanging.

We also had real lit candles on the tree. Only the oldest kids were allowed to light or extinguish the candles. In the early years we had no electricity in our house; but later on, when we had electricity, we still put real candles on the tree. We always cut down our own tree and only just before Christmas.

When we sat down at our Christmas table, everybody was always dressed nice and clean. The boys had their hair combed nicely. On the table, at my mother's left side, was the Bible; and in the middle of the table was a dish with salt and a slice of bread, symbolizing the hope that we would have salt and bread all through the year. We had another dish on the table where everyone would put a coin, symbolizing the hope that we would have enough money all through the year.

We had honey and oblaten, which are thin wafers. First we would say a prayer and my mother would read the chapter Luke 2, verse 1 to 7 about the birth of Jesus. Then we had the "breaking of the bread" ceremony. My mother would put a little honey on one of the oblaten and hand it to the person next to her who would break a small piece off, wish the person silently something nice, and hand the oblate to the next person, who did the same thing. Each person had his own oblate. It was always a very solemn occasion.

When the ceremony was over, the boys were usually already very hungry, but my mother always said a few words before we ate. We were poor and my mother could not afford to buy us any presents. Sometimes we got something from our aunts or uncles or godparents. When they gave us presents, they put them all under the tree. Usually it was something to wear. When we were little we would get some kind of a toy. I don't remember ever getting two toys. I grew up learning that material things don't matter much when it comes to happiness. We were very happy! We never complained.

After the opening of the presents, it was usually pretty late. When we were young, we were put to bed; but we got up soon and we went to midnight mass. I remember some nights when it started to snow, the air was so crisp and clear and it was so very quiet. The snow would just glitter as it came down. The whole world looked like a fairyland. This was the real Christmas spirit—to walk through the snow in the middle of the night to walk to mass. We never missed a midnight mass.

When I finished school, my first job was as a governess in the town of Kalish. They were a young couple. She was Polish and he was Austrian. They were very rich people, and they had a four-year-old daughter whom they wanted to learn German. So, they hired me to be with her, to talk to her and to play with her. I did not have to do anything else but be with the child and be her companion. I stayed with them till 1938 when the disturbances began between the Polish and German-speaking people. The long years of tranquillity between Austrians and Poles began slowly to disintegrate. Austrians were now considered Germans by the Poles. "Down with the Germans. Long live Poland." This kind of slogan was painted all over town.

My mother was often afraid that something might happen to me. She had heard of many people being kidnapped. I was told to come home and got a job as a governess with the Schmeja family, a wealthy local family. His wife had died at the birth of their fifth child. He also needed somebody to be with the children. He had a housekeeper and everything else, but I had to take care of the baby and watch the smaller children. I worked there for half a year.

My brothers, Karl and Rudi, were drafted into the Polish Army. My other brother, Viki, was too young. The Poles sent Rudi back home because he was an architect and they needed him to build up what they knew would be bombed. But they kept Karl. He was stationed at the Polish-Czechoslovakian border shortly before the War broke out.

Karl came home on furlough right before the Germans marched in. He knew what was going on and what he had heard. The Germans, who had already occupied Czechoslovakia, were massing troops on the Polish border. The Polish Army expected that the Germans would attack right where he was stationed. He told Viki that he was going to desert from the Polish Army because he could not shoot at German soldiers. If they knew he was going to desert, the Polish Army would kill him before he could desert. He told Viki not to say anything about it to my mother or anybody else.

A few days later, after Karl had gone back to his unit, Polish soldiers suddenly came and surrounded the house, came in with bayonets on their rifles, holding the bayonets on my mother and asked her where her son, Karl, was. She said, "He is in the service." They said, "He is not. Where is he?" My mother's honest answer was, "I don't know." They kept on questioning her but she really did not know. If she had known anything about it, a change in her face would have made them suspicious. So they left again. Twenty years later at our first family get together in 1963 outside Cologne, Germany, we found out from him what had happened. He swam across the river from the Polish side to the Czechoslovakian side, which was actually the German side where he was welcomed and promptly drafted into the German Army.

The situation with Germany and Poland came to a peak. I heard on the radio that Germany had marched into Poland. We were afraid that we would be hurt or killed by Polish radicals. Karl was a Polish soldier and was not home. Viki was too young to be drafted into the Polish Army.

On the night of September 2, 1939, we were all in our basement because we heard shooting outside. All through he night the shooting continued. Early in the morning on the third of September, it was suddenly quiet. My brother, Rudi, decided to go out and see what was going on. My mother said, "Rudi, don't go, stay here!" Rudi peeked out the door and saw at the distance soldiers crossing our fields, but he noticed they had a different uniform. He called my mother and she came out. As Rudi and my mother were outside, a soldier passed in front of our house and greeted my mother in the Austrian dialect saying, "Greetings, mother, now you will have it good!"

As more and more soldiers came by, my mother called us out of the basement. We embraced the Austrian soldiers who had marched into our area. We were thinking, now the War was over. It was a very bright sunny morning, the right thing to make you feel good. Soon we heard that Russian troops had marched in and had occupied the eastern part of Poland. German and Russian troops now controlled Poland.

To prepare myself for the future, I took night courses in shorthand and typing, but I needed a job to pay for my schooling. In looking for a job, I found one at Molenda, a factory which produced textile goods. First, I worked for awhile on a machine that made material for cloth or coats. One day Mr. Molenda's private secretary asked me to come to the office. She asked me if I would like to work in the office. I had hoped to do that one day, so I happily agreed. I became a typist, stenographer, and switchboard operator.

Mimi got married to Leopold Paulitscke in 1941, and I attended the wedding. We all liked him very well and we called him "Poldi." Not very long afterward, he was drafted into the German Army. It was now just before Christmas 1941.

Our company had planned a Christmas party for the wounded soldiers in the hospital in Biala, the sister city of Bielitz. Mr. Molenda's secretary asked me to help her organize it. We used our own large lunch room and stage at the factory. The tables were beautifully decorated, and we planned to put on a stage show with folk dances, singing, and good entertainment. We had a lot of girls working in our company and the chairs were arranged so that each soldier was going to have a girl sitting to his right and his left. It was one girl, one soldier, one girl, one soldier, all along the tables.

When the soldiers came in the room they were lead to their seats. They were surprised to find an empty chair to their right and left. I remember I had a Dirndl on, the traditional Austrian dress, and was performing on the stage singing and dancing. We were a group of girls performing folk dances, all dressed the same. After the performance on the stage, all the girls marched down single file to the empty chairs. That was the first time I saw Sig. I liked him right away, so I asked him if I could sit next to him. I got the sense that he was very happy about it. We had a wonderful evening. That's how it happened that Sig and I met.

Afterwards Sig walked me home. We said goodbye. We did not kiss. Sig called me a few times at the factory office and then asked me if I wanted to go to the movies with him. By then, I had found out that Sig was not wounded but was, at that time, recuperating from a very bad bout of yellow jaundice and had been in the hospital already for five months. Soon after that Sig was released from the hospital. He went back to the Army, promising he would be writing me.

Shortly after Sig went back into the Army, I entered a nurse's training program from the Red Cross in Bielitz. First, I had training in class and then practical work in a hospital. I was assigned to the hospital in Biala where Sig had been. When the Germans took over our city, it was converted into a military hospital.

When I was working there on the practical part of my nurses training, I met a young man from Bielitz who knew Sig and was a very good friend of his. He was on crutches from a shot in the leg. He fell in love with me and followed me around wherever I went. Whenever anybody was looking for me, all they had to do was look for this soldier on crutches and nurse Helen was not far away. He became a very good friend of mine. We dated off and on, but I told him I loved Sig. Before he was discharged from the hospital, he said he understood. He could not take a girl away from his best friend.

I saw Sig only one more time. It was on Christmas Eve 1942. At that time, I did not know the circumstances of how he had come home for Christmas and for only 24 hours. It was Christmas morning and we were coming home from church. As I looked up the hill toward the Exerzierplatz, I saw a uniformed man coming down the hill. It was snowing and my sisters and I could not make out immediately who it was. But to me it looked like Sig, so I started to run down the hill from my house. We met right at the bottom of both hills at the bridge and embraced each other. He met some of my brothers and sisters and my mother. He invited me to his house for Christmas dinner, which in our country is at twelve o'clock noon.

At the dinner I met Sig's sisters, Brunhild and Erika, and we celebrated Erika's engagement to her boyfriend. Afterwards we all went to the railroad station to see Sig off. Sig was so shy. He did not want to kiss me in front of all the people. Sig's sisters, Brunhild and Erika, tried to push us together and they said, "Come on, give her a kiss. Giver her a kiss." So Sig finally gave me a big kiss. I remember it so well. Brunhild and Erika and her boyfriend walked me home. We didn't know that it would be 1947 before we would see each other again.

Chapter 2

Drafted As A Nurse Into War

After my training in the military hospital in Biala, I was sent to Brealau in Silesia, Germany for the rest of my training and my exam. It was called the "Mutterhaus," the main hospital of the Red Cross nurses—the Augusta Hospital. Before I took my regular exam, all of us nurses were told we were drafted into the German Army Nurses Corps and would go through a fast "Blitz" exam.

Those of us who passed this exam were sent right away to a field hospital close to the Russian front line. They needed nurses on the front. They needed nurses in field hospitals. We could hear the rumbling of the fire of guns and the explosions of bombs in the distance. It was in the Ukraine, east of Poland, and was called Truskawiez. It was a spa, a resort town. It was a small town with beautiful houses. The German Army had taken over the spa and converted it into a hospital. The spa consisted of many small houses that were made into hospital rooms. One house was made into an operating room. Each nurse had one house to take care of depending on how seriously wounded the soldiers were. If they were very badly hurt, you got more help. I was so young and inexperienced, but I was not afraid of the work.

In the meantime, the Russian front came closer and closer. We were told they would get us out by train so we would not fall into Russian hands. So they put us on a train. The soldiers were left in the hospital. I don't know how many miles we had gone on the train before it stopped. The railroad tracks were bombed. Big holes covered the tracks. We could not go any further, so we had to go back again. We were regularly bombed and we could hear the shooting at the front; that's how close we were. They tried to protect us as best they could. That lasted for about two weeks before the Russians were pushed back again. We repaired as much as we could on our field hospital and kept on working there. Yes, we all—doctors, nurses and orderlies had to repair the damage.

Christmas was getting near, and I was told I would go on furlough. I will never forget it in all my life. I came home! It was Christmas 1943. It was so wonderful to be with my mother, my sisters and my brother, Rudi. We were worried about my brothers who had been drafted into the German Army. My brother, Viki, had already been drafted into the Germany Army and wounded in the face. Sig was a Prisoner of War in the United States and he wrote me letters at my field post number, which were strictly censored by the United States and by German censors. From my brother, Karl, were some letters I read. All in all it was a very good feeling to be home again, away from the terror and fear of the War.

I was supposed to report back to duty on New Year's Day at 5 o'clock in the morning at Truskawiez. I took the train from home. It was close to Truskawiez when suddenly the train stopped. We heard voices outside yell "Everybody out. The train does not go any further. You'll have to find your own transportation."

It was New Year's Eve and it was getting dark, so I went to the military headquarters in this town and asked them if there was any kind of transportation going in the direction I had to go. They said there was a a truck leaving, but they were going only so far and then I would have to find my own transportation. I thought well, as long as I go forward, I'm fine. So I got on this truck and after many hours of driving, they stopped and told me they didn't go any farther and I should again find my own way.

By now it was night. They told me there was a train depot not too far and there I might try and catch a train to Truskawiez. They also told me that if I crossed the market square, not to get scared because the authorities had been hanging people there constantly and there may be some hanging there now. We were told, as a safety rule in the military, not to walk along the houses but in the middle of the street.

I was carrying my suitcase as I slowly approached the market square, walking in the middle of the road. Suddenly, I saw ten people hanging. They were partisans, who would now be called guerrillas. You can not imagine what this did to me. I was a young girl, twenty years old. My heart was in my stomach. I tried to stay as far away as I could from the posts where they were hanging without walking along the houses. Suddenly, there came a truck with drunken soldiers in it, screaming and hollering and singing. They stopped and told me to come along. I asked them what direction they were going. They told me a certain direction, which was towards Truskawiez.

I did not care that they were drunk as long as I could get away from this scary market square. I threw my suitcase in and got into their truck. After I was on the truck they began to make advances toward me. I was so scared. As soon as the truck slowed down at an intersection, I threw my suitcase out and jumped off the truck. They kept on, roaring and howling as the truck sped away. I don't think they even noticed that I was gone.

There I was, in the middle of nowhere with my suitcase, wondering how to get to the depot. I walked. I had to keep going. I finally made it to the depot, but the train was delayed. I had to wait. When it finally came, it had no windows. They had all been shot out. That's how I made it back to Truskawiez. When I reported back in the office late, they understood. It was New Year's morning. I will never forget that New Year.

The learning experiences I had in the field hospitals in Truskawiez and later on in Olmuetz, Czechoslovakia are so different from that of a regular hospital. I consider this the time I really grew up. We had left Truskawiez, really retreated with the German troops, but were always close to the front line. As a nurse I worked many times in the operating room. At first when you help a doctor in amputating a limb, it is emotionally shocking for a young woman. Later, when you do this day in and day out, sometimes twelve to fourteen hours a day, you just want to hold out physically. You don't want to make a mistake.

The actual nursing itself was very rewarding. Bringing a person back to health again, especially when he's lost his limbs or will be disabled for the rest of his life, required all the skills of good nursing. I nursed them back to life—a life they gave up on. The hardest thing to do in the hospital is to stay with a dying person in his last hours of life. They trust you. You are the mother they are longing to be with. If they know that they are dying and they are not in pain and conscious, they want the nurse to let their mothers know certain things or don't want their mothers to know certain things. Why does every dying person think of his mother before he dies?

After he dies you have to write to the next of kin about his last hours or minutes of life. And you can not generalize it, you have to give details about the last moments of his life. You know it is a grieving mother or father or brother or sister. I always kept that in mind. It is someone who loved him who is grieving, maybe a fiancé or a wife or any of his children. Many times I stayed in contact with these people long afterwards. You care for your patients like you hope to be cared for yourself. And you always know that your own life may suddenly end.

One day I got a letter from my brother, Viki. He wrote from a military hospital. He had been wounded for the second time, again in the head; but he wrote he was doing all right. I knew how soldiers wrote. They don't want their own relatives to know how bad it is. So I wrote him back asking him to tell me the truth. "I can take it," I wrote. "I am a nurse and have seen many head wounds." I was expecting the worst.

When I got his letter he wrote me not to worry, he would look even better now, and he had a dimple in his cheek. I was not sure if I should believe him. I never found out the actual truth till we met him with Sig and Brunhild in the Alps at the Stahlhouse. The first time he was wounded, the shot went through his lower jaw and out the other side of his upper jaw. This time the shot went through his cheeks; in from one side and out the other cheek. He could not open his mouth very far and had a tough time chewing his food; and sure enough, he had a cute dimple in his cheek.

In Olmuetz I got engaged to Sig. Yes, I did. Of course we did it by mail. Sig and I were corresponding by Prisoner of War mail. The censors did not cut out this part. Sig had to write on special letters made to help censors. Anything Sig wrote in a special POW letter was first censored by United States officials. Anything the censors objected to was cut out of the letter without Sig ever knowing it. The letter was then sent to Germany, where the German censors cut out any-thing objectionable to them. As a Prisoner of War, Sig knew the rules. There was hardly anything ever cut out of his letters. He could send only one letter every month. One month he sent one letter home, the next month he sent a letter to me.

As a Red Cross nurse, I always had a military mailing address, just numbers. Even if I was moved from one town to another I got the mail, sometimes three or four months late. Sig really never knew what was happening to me. It was just generalities the censors allowed me to write. I never knew where he was or what camp he was in. I wrote regularly to some code numbers or letters only the post office in the United States knew. My mail went the same way, first to German censors and then to United States censors.

Now, getting back to our long-distance engagement. It was Sig's wish and mine to become engaged. It was easier for me to deal with the many proposals I got while dating to say I was engaged. But I needed to have a visible sign of my engagement. I had a silver chain which a jeweler made into a ring for me. Very plain, but it helped me through the long and tough years of the war.

It was by my regular nursing duties that got me my most faithful followers. I was always joking and had a happy face. That's what the patients wanted—some-body that treated them with fun and jokes. I teased the patients but I had to ac-cept teasing myself. That is why I had so many happy admirers. I was the person they first saw every morning when I turned the lights on and woke them up. Also I was the last person they saw turn the lights off before they went to sleep. This was a joyful time for me, to be with them and make the daily hospital routine a delightful experience. I was also a mischief maker. Yes, I instigated many things to bring life into the hospital.

I had one patient on crutches. When he came back from being out late at night, he had no regard for the other sleeping patients. He sat down on his bed with such a loud noise that everybody woke up. One time when he was out again, I removed the middle part of the 3-part mattress and replaced it with a wash ba-sin of water and covered it with a sheet. Everybody knew about it but him. When he came back to his bed and sat down with his usual loud noise, he sat down on the water basin and got all wet. All my other patients enjoyed it. From that time on he quietly came to his bed and never made noise any more.

One time I had a patient who always tried to kiss me when I changed his ban-dages. I had a trick up my sleeve for him. I bought a pacifier and put it in mus-tard. As he approached me to kiss me again, I stuck the pacifier in his mouth. At the same time a doctor came in. When he heard what I did, he laughed out loud. The patient never tried to kiss me again, but he was not mad at me. He took it as a joke.

At the beginning in Olmuetz, we were far from the actual front line. But the Russians kept coming closer and closer till one day we had to get our patients ready for transport to the rear. Transportation was almost always in cattle wagons. For wounded soldiers, nurses, or hospital staff they painted a big red cross on the wagons. We loaded all our patients on these wagons, gave them extra bandages and medications, and some orderlies went with them. Three weeks later, we left. The whole hospital was shipped to Prague.

The hospital there was an old building converted into a field hospital. I don't know what it was before. It could have been a school. There were six huge rooms with bunk beds. We had to stand on a chair to take care of the soldier who was laying on the top bunk. We had to do all the bandaging and treatment standing on a chair or a ladder. The room I took care of had 18 beds.

I had a day off and was not in the hospital when a transport of wounded soldiers came in. When I arrived for work the next morning and did as I always did in the morning, I turned the light on and said, "Good morning, guys." Suddenly I heard from all sides, "Sister Lene, sister Lene, come here, come here. Oh, so good to see you again." These were the patients I had in Olmuetz.

They had arrived four weeks after departing. They said they had been pushed onto a dead track and left there the entire time. They had received little care from the few orderlies they had and the condition of the wounds was unbelievable. Most had gangrene. When you opened a cast, the puss would just ooze out. I had to do all the opening of casts, and it was an awful-smelling job. It was good to see these guys, but can you imagine living so long with so little care and holding on to your faith and hope.

With these men was a Lieutenant whom I had taken care of in Olmuetz, as well. He was so happy to see me. He was married and had two children and was the nicest guy I ever met. He was ordered to be transferred to a different room for officers, but he refused to go. He insisted on staying in my room and being taken care of by me. They let him stay.

One day we heard that the Russians were coming closer and closer but there were no plans to evacuate us again. We were told instead to go to a warehouse not far from our street and take whatever we wanted, instead of leaving it for the Russians. So we, nurses and orderlies, went to this abandoned warehouse and there found chocolate and coffee and desserts—stuff we had not seen all through the War. We packed whatever we could carry on our backs and brought it back to the soldiers.

The next morning we heard the Russians had taken Prague. The German soldiers had left us. Everybody said the War would be over soon. We were now thinking of where to hide the chocolate and coffee and all this good stuff. Each room had a fireplace. It was clean and had not been used for some time. We decided to hide it in there, where we stacked it up as high as we could. Some of the soldiers had it under their mattresses.

The next day, it was very quiet. We could not hear any shots or other noises from the street. We were scared and did not know what was going to happen. The doctors and head nurses told us to keep calm and not say anything. We did not realize how bad it would be. We could not hear what was going on outside. All we kept doing was taking care of the wounded.

It was about noon the next day; we just had lunch when suddenly Russian soldiers came in. They were pretty decent. They did not mistreat us. They went through the rooms, looked at us, did not ransack anything, and they went out again.

It was some days later that I and another nurse were called into the office. Russian soldiers were sitting there. They had gone through our files. They said we would be separated from the others because we were not German citizens. "You will be released," they said. I thought, this is fine. I have not heard from my family for over a year. She and I were taken out of the hospital room and down the street. There was a whole line of Russian soldiers guarding some nurses which we had to join. We were marched through Prague. People were standing on the street, spitting at us, screaming at us, calling us German pigs and things like that.

They took us into a huge building where we saw all kinds of different prisoners—women and children. We were told to take care of these people. There were a lot of pregnant women. One told me she had been raped by a soldier. All of them needed immediate care by a doctor. Babies were being born and we had nothing to help them with—not even food, no baby formula, no milk, no diapers. We had our white nurses aprons, which we tore apart and made diapers out of. The little children kept crying constantly. They were hungry or sick.

Some of us nurses had some emergency medication like aspirin along, which helped a little bait. A lot of women had menstruation problems and terrible pain. Some had stomach illnesses. All I could do was try to keep them calm. We all were so scared. It was such a nightmare.

The next thing I remember was some time later. Despite years of trying to remember, I can not recollect anything in between the time in the women and children's building and when I found myself in the streets of Prague. In my hands I had some discharge papers from the Russians, but I still had my German Red Cross nurse's uniform on. I did not want to have anything that told people I was a Red Cross nurse because I was afraid I would be captured again.

First, I went to a public toilet some place and threw my nurse's cap away. My Red Cross brooch I threw into the Moldau River. I still had on my gray uniform, gray blouse and boots. It must have been September. I met a woman on the street, a German, who gave me a blouse. It was a colored blouse so I didn't look like I had a uniform on. My thoughts were all about what to do now. I had a piece of bread in my pocket, and this food I was going to keep for an emergency when I didn't have anything to eat.

I wanted to go home. The train was the only possibility. Maybe I could jump on a train some place. I walked to the train station. There I saw a transport train with refugees. I thought maybe I could mingle with them. Maybe I could get some place towards home. I was longing to see my mother and my family. I spent days and days at the railroad station. Transports with refugees came in and left Prague. I ran to all the incoming transports to see if any of my family or relatives were on board. I heard people were fleeing Bielitz and every place else. Maybe I would find somebody, but I never had any luck. I don't know how many times I ran to the station in the hope of finding somebody. Finally, I got on a transport and left Prague.

After some distance, I don't know how far or the names of any towns, the train came to a stop. It was dark outside. I heard women scream and Russian soldiers yelling and screaming. The Russian soldiers got on the train and raped the women. I was scared. I jumped off the train. It was pitch dark. Only the outline of a forest was visible in the distance. I ran as fast and as far as I could and hid in some bushes. I was scared stiff and crying and wondering what to do now. I didn't know where I was, what I was going to do now or where to go. I knew I had to know where I was first.

I waited until morning. I was cold and freezing and it started raining. I had no raincoat, no jacket. I was hungry, but I did not touch my emergency piece of bread. I started walking, some place, any place, to find people and ask them where I was. I could speak Polish, so I used the Polish language to ask people where I was. As I came to a town, I saw German people working on the street repairing bomb damage. They had a swastika on their back or their arm. Some were on crutches. I was so scared and so numb.

My hope to see home again seemed to vanish. But I had to keep on going. My hunger kept me from thinking straight. I tried to eat grass. I saw farmers harvesting potatoes, so I stole some potatoes and ate them raw. I stole kohlrabi and carrots and other vegetables and ate them raw. There were days I don't know how I survived, but I kept on going. I got on a train again some place and I rode this train for a while till I came to Dziedzic. In Dziedzic, I got out and I was standing on the station platform trying to decide if I should walk or ride the train again.

I knew it was about half an hour by train to Bielitz. I saw a German woman with two little kids. They were shivering and the one little girl said, "Mommy, I am so hungry." The mother had tears in her eyes and she said, "Honey, I don't have anything I can give you." I don't tell you this because I want to brag or anything. I just want to describe what happened, how people were starving. I searched for the emergency piece of bread which I had in my pocket now for a long time and gave it to them. These kids, the way they grabbed this bread and ate it, I suddenly felt no hunger anymore.

I got on a train to Bielitz. I remember sitting in this train. There were no windows and it was raining. The wind was blowing the rain into the car when I arrived in Bielitz at the depot. I had decided not to go through town but around it. I vaguely remember what roads I took. I got to the Exerzierplatz and I saw the house. Yes, the house was still standing. When I came to the house, it looked abandoned.

I walked into the house. It was quiet. Nobody was around, at least I didn't see anybody. I did not know if anybody was still living here, if my mother was living. Should I have knocked on the door? Suddenly, a door opened in the hall and my mother came out. She came out from the little room my grandmother used to have. She looked at me and I looked at her. She did not recognize me. I had an old pillow case covering my head from the rain. I looked so dirty and filthy. My hair looked like strings hanging down. She looked at me again and I said, "Mut-tele, Muttele." Finally, she recognized me and I ran to her. When I was in her arms, I broke down and cried and cried.

Chapter 3

The War And Suffering Are Over But Not For Me

I don't know how long I cried in my mother's arms. All the fear I had carried all these days I let go. I let it go out with my tears. Finally I got hold of myself and I could talk. We both started talking. She told me that Rudi had been taken away by the Russians. She did not know where he was. Liesl and Mimi had been taken away, too. Mimi's husband, Poldi, was a prisoner of the British, but nobody had heard from him. From my brothers Karl and Viki, who were in the German Army, she had not heard anything for a long time. Trude lived where she used to live in an apartment with her little baby, Brigitte. Rudi's wife, Lizzi, with her young son and daughter and her mother, lived in Biala some place.

My mother told me of the people who had taken over our house and the orchard. They were Poles who came from the area the Russians took from Poland. The Polish government sent them. They allowed my mother to stay in one little room of the house where my grandmother used to live. That's the only room she was allowed to use in her own house.

She had to work on her own farm for these people. She was not allowed to go into the orchard to get an apple or any other fruit. Everything my mother had planted, she was not allowed to touch. No berries and no eggs. An apple tree my brother, Rudi, had grafted was bearing its first apples. My mother wanted to find out how they tasted. She had some in her apron when the Polish woman appeared. She made my mother drop every apple she had in her apron.

I lived in my mother's room for maybe two weeks when the Polish woman insisted that I go and register. She was afraid she might get in trouble for hiding German people. So I went to the mayor's office and I registered. I showed them my papers, especially my discharge papers. That was in the morning. In the afternoon two Polish militia men with bayonets on their rifles came to my house and said I had to go with them. I said, "Why? I haven't done anything." My mother fell on her knees and begged them not to take me. She told them that I was the only one of her children she had left now. It didn't help.

They took me along to the mayor's office. There they asked me all kinds of stupid questions and then put me across the street in the basement of a house. There were chickens kept there and it was filthy. In one area was a wooden trough for pigs. The door was locked behind me and nobody told me why I was put there or what was going to happen. I sat in this basement and cried my eyes out. I was hungry and thirsty, and nobody came to look after me. After two days of having nothing to eat or drink, they let me out again. They said I could go home.

I found out the reason I was released was that my mother had begged the Polish people who ran our house to tell the authorities they needed me for working. So these Poles took some sacks of flour and other items to the mayor's office and asked for my release. I went home and had to promise to come in every day and register. They were afraid I may run away. They told me what office to go to every day and register.

The next day I arrived, as I was told, and thought I just had to write my name in and go home. I saw a lot of people standing in line. When I asked them why they had to stand in line and wait, they told me a commissar runs the mayor's office and you have to register with him. So I waited till my turn came. I was led to a room where this Polish commissar was sitting with a man from the Polish Militia. The commissar began to ask me all kinds of questions. "You are a Nazi, aren't you?"

I said, "No, I am not a Nazi."

He tried to make me admit to things that were not true. He tried to put me in places I never was. He tried to make me lie and make me admit guilt for things I never did. To him my papers were all fake. He spit in my face and the Militia man slapped me many times. I don't know how long that went on. More questions and more questions. Then they said, "Go home."

The next day the same thing again. A few times the Militia man held his pistol to my head and I heard a click. I told my mother what had happened and she said that tomorrow she would come along. The next day she came along, but they did not allow her to come into the building with me. She sat out by the street in the ditch and waited to see if I came out or not. There were a lot of people who came out and were led away by two Militiamen to go to prison or concentration camps. I was kicked and beaten day after day to get a false confession out of me. That went on for about 2 ½ months.

One day before I was supposed to go again, they came to my house and took me and my mother away. They did not allow us to take much along. They took us and put us into the Alexanderfeld School. Many people were gathered there and I wondered what would happen to us now. Maybe they would deport us like they had done to so many people. Then suddenly my sister, Trude, came with her little baby, Brigitte. Lots of people we knew were there. I counted. In that one classroom were about 300 people, and there were many more classrooms full of people.

The Militia who watched us were young Polish kids, and the people were mostly little children and older people. Most of the younger people were already taken away, like my sisters Liesl and Mimi. Some grandparents had their grandchildren with them because the mother was already in prison. Soon typhus fever broke out in the school. The older people got it first.

They separated the sick people and put them in a shed next to the athletic field. We used to keep our school sports equipment in there. They put some straw on the ground. There was not even a floor, just dirt. That's where they kept the sick people. Sometimes they had a blanket.

Then they told me since I was a nurse to take care of them. With typhus fever you have diarrhea. I washed their clothes and their bodies. Whatever I could do, I did; but I had no medication. I had nothing to give to these people.

This went on and on. I was desperate and tired. During the day we had to stand in line for interrogation again. There was a hallway leading from one building to the next and that's where we always stood for interrogation. There were no windows in it. All were broken. That's where Trude's little girl got meningitis. After Trude's interrogation she was told she could go home. My mother and I were kept there.

Once they called me in the middle of the night and said I should come because the sick people in the shed needed me. My mother said, "I will go with you. I am not going to let you go alone with them." She was sleeping on the floor and got up and went with me. The militia did not figure that my mother was going to come along. They were really mad about it but they didn't say anything. When I got to the shed everybody and everything was okay. Nobody had asked for me.

The Militia was just trying to get me alone. They got so mad, cussing and swearing. Suddenly when I was back in the room with my mother, a shot rang out. Somebody had shot through the keyhole into the room and hit a little boy who was sleeping in a stroller. He was shot through both legs. I don't know if they were aiming at me—if they wanted to kill me or what. There was a terrible panic! I looked to the boy. He was in critical condition and I said to the Militia, "This boy has to go to the hospital immediately. Get an ambulance and get him to the hospital."

"We are not going to call an ambulance for you," was the answer they gave us.

So I said, "We are going to make a stretcher and we are going to bring him to the hospital!" I was really furious. They let us make a stretcher. We put a blanket or two together, put the little guy on it, and walked out of the school and down the street to the hospital.

The next day we found out the boy had died. This little boy was with his grandmother. His mother was in a concentration work camp. In three weeks about 18 people died. We still stood in line every day for interrogation. Finally they let me and my mother go. Some of the people from the school were later put on transports and shipped out. We don't know to where they were shipped.

After I got home, I went over to see Trude. Little Brigitte had meningitis very bad already. Trude had a female doctor who came a few times and gave Brigitte some shots. One morning I came over to Trude's again, and Brigitte was throwing her little head around. With meningitis, you have terrible headaches. Trude had put pillows all around the little crib so she would not hurt herself. Her head was just flying back and forth and back and forth.

She started to get weaker and weaker, and I knew that she could not last much longer. Trude insisted on going to see if the doctor could give her something or could come out and give Brigitte a shot again. I told Trude, "Don't go. It's no use. Stay here." Naturally, a mother does everything to help her child. She went, and while she was gone, I held little Brigitte in my arms as she died. Brigitte had passed away just 15 minutes before Trude came back. It was terrible. I will never forget the look in Trude's eyes as she took her little girl in her arms and cried quietly.

The next day we went to get a coffin. We could not afford a mortician or a mortuary. Trude and I went downtown and bought a small, white coffin. On the way home with the coffin, we stopped at the church and asked Father Sedlarzek to come to the cemetery and bless the coffin. He agreed. We came home, put the little body in the coffin, put it in the stroller, put flowers around it, and pushed it to the cemetery. People stopped along the street. Some of them laughed, some of them spit at us, some felt very bad. I can't imagine what it did to my sister, Trude.

When we came to the cemetery, the priest was there already, waiting for us. My mother was at the cemetery, too. We blessed the coffin, said a prayer, and we lowered it into the grave. That's how we buried our little Brigitte. She was 16 months old.

Trude's husband, Hans, was in the German Army and had been missing in action since 1944. When they met, he was a seminary student studying for the priesthood. Right after he was drafted into the German Army, Trude and Hans decided to get married before he had to report. The day after they were married, he went into the army. She never heard where he was missing, only somewhere in Russia. He never knew he had a daughter.

Trude's brother-in-law, who was in a concentration camp in Myslowicz, smuggled out a letter to his wife in which he said he had seen Liesl and Mimi in the camp and she should let us know about it. That's how we found out where Liesl and Mimi were.

In a nearby camp was Lizzi's mother, too. Lizzi had a little baby, Anne, and one day the Militia came and tried to arrest her and bring her to a concentration camp. Her mother said to them, "You are not taking away the mother of this little baby. I'll go in her place," she said. So they took her mother and put her in one of the camps near where Liesl and Mimi were. Her camp was one hour away from Liesl and Mimi's camp.

We also heard that you could bring packages to the prisoners, so we decided we would try to do that. My sister-in-law, Lizzi, and I spoke Polish very well; so we made packages of food and clothes, bread and butter, a blouse—things like that—and took the train to the prison camps.

First we went to Liesl and Mimi's camp and then to the camp of Lizzi's mother. The camps were rows of barracks with barbed wire around them. No towers, but heavily guarded. The guards were mostly Militiamen positioned on the outside of the barbed wire fences. We had to hand the packages over the guards, but we never knew if my sisters got them.

Trude's brother-in-law smuggled out another note in which he told us how to smuggle letters into the camp. We folded letters and put them into the bottom fold of the paper bag, but Liesl and Mimi didn't find them. We marked the bag to tell my sisters that there was something else in the bag that they should look for; and sure enough, they found it and sent us out another slip of paper. It was in Mimi's handwriting. She wrote that Liesl was very ill with typhoid fever and if we hoped to see her alive again, we must try to get her some medication and a pillow. Liesl had deep sores —bedsores, from lying on a flat board.

That's how we conversed, by hiding little slips of paper in the folds of the paper bag. First we sent her the pillow and then we got in contact with a doctor and asked him if he would go into the camp and check on Liesl and give her the medication. He said he would try and they allowed him to see her. We paid him what we could.

One time Mimi wrote that she got the bread but no butter. We found out that the guards who check the packages take out whatever they want. The next time we made a package, we cut a big hole in the middle of the bread and filled it with butter. Maybe they found the butter, but they did not bother to scrape it out. That's the way they got the butter they needed.

Soon, we did not have any money left to buy food for the packages and pay for the transportation, but we still had some clothes we could sell on the black market. It was risky to do that. If they caught you, they put you in jail immediately. The clothes we had were the few we had hidden from the Russians. After I had come home, the Russian soldiers came many times to our house and ransacked our room to find valuables. What they wanted, they took. They would hold their pistol on us and turn the room upside down. Yes, they were Russians. The Polish Militia was not allowed to do that sort of thing. The Russians could do anything they wanted.

So, we hid our clothes and whatever else we had all over the house—in the attic, the barn, or in the hayloft. Even the people who owned our house could not find it. We got what was left in our hiding places and sold them on the black market. With this money, we paid for the trips, for food and doctors' bills, and the packages.

After awhile Liesl got better, mostly through constant care by Mimi. Mimi herself had typhoid fever but not as bad. Every morning Mimi went to the barrack where Liesl was, washed her, fed her, and then went to work outside the prison. In the evening when she came back from work, she went back to Liesl's barrack and washed and fed her again. That's why Liesl is still alive today.

Mimi told us many years afterwards in 1963 that Liesl was semiconscious to completely unconscious for almost three months. After Liesl could walk again, she wrote in one of these paper bag message slips for us to come to this certain hill by the barbed wire and she and Mimi would try to come as close as they could so that we could see them. Lizzi and I went there and saw them. We could not recognize their faces! But they were waiting for us, so we knew it was them. Liesl had lost most of her hair. After awhile, it grew back.

When she got out of the prison camp, she was completely gray. Mimi's illness was not as bad. She did not loose all her hair. When the doctor had visited Liesl in the camp he always gave Mimi a shot, too.

From the time we found out they were in the camp, we tried to get them out. Robert was Liesl's fiancé. He had been drafted into the German Army; but nobody had heard from him till one night, at my mother's room, there was a knock at the window. It was late—11 o'clock or so. It was Robert. He came home. He was in civilian clothes he had picked up some place. After the end of the War, many men from Bielitz who were drafted into the German Army wanted to come. If they were seen wearing a German uniform, they were arrested and shot like so many young men were. We feared for him. We told him he could not stay here and we told him what had been happening to me here. For him, being in the German Army, it would have been even worse. He had an aunt who lived in Bielitz, who was married to a Polish man. So he went there and stayed with her.

Because Robert had gone to Polish schools—high school and college—he spoke Polish without an accent. It was perfect Polish. He went to the police in Bielitz and applied for job in the Polish Militia and got it. Because of his higher education he was advanced quickly. As soon as we knew where Liesl and Mimi were, we told him. He immediately began looking for ways to get them out, without raising any suspicions.

We got in touch with Father Kasperlik and Father Orzow, our church leaders, and got them involved, too. Both priests had known Robert, Liesl and all of us for a long time—ever since we were kids. It took a long time—many affidavits, a lot of documents which completely contradicted the Polish Communist documents. Finally, the day came. Liesl and Mimi were released. Fifty to sixty people daily were now dying in their camp. One uncle of ours died there, too, without Liesl or Mimi ever seeing him in the camp.

In the meantime Robert got transferred to Breslau, where he was in charge of all the paper work for the transports to Germany. He took the job so he could get his fiancé and her family out. Liesl went to Breslau to stay with him. He got the forms, release papers and so on, for Lizzi and her two children; Guenther and baby Anne; Lizzi's mother; Trude; Mimi; my mother and I. He arranged all the papers; and one day he wrote us that he had everything ready. He told us to take only the things we could carry.

Secretly, we got our clothes together and snuck out of our homes at four o'clock in the morning. At the train depot we stayed separate, not talking to each other as if we were strangers. We all went by train to Breslau. Robert hid all of us in his small apartment. He hid us till the transport was ready to leave. Suddenly we found out that he did not have all the paperwork. He would have to smuggle us into the transport. Liesl, of course, had her papers.

Whenever people came to his apartment and wanted something from Robert, we all hid in closets. We were jammed together in different places and often were afraid that the little kids would cry or say something. That would have blown it. One day, two Militia men who were working with Robert, came to his apartment. We were hiding when little Anne started to cry. Lizzi held her hand over her mouth till the two men left.

Finally, the day came that the transport was going to leave. We had a little hand wagon where we put our things together and pulled it to the depot. The train was already standing, assembled from all kinds of cattle wagons. Robert had called in sick to his superior. He told him he hurt his leg and was limping. He even made an appointment with a doctor. He was in civilian clothes and said it was better and safer for him not to be seen at the depot. We did not see Robert when we left the apartment. We had the papers. Robert was normally responsible for inspecting the train and for the train departure. We saw other Militia organizing and arranging the seating in the cattle wagons.

We noticed that Liesl was very nervous. Every few seconds she looked out the cattle wagon door toward the train depot. As the train slowly left the Breslau station, she was still looking out the door in the direction of the rear of the train. Suddenly she cried out, looked at us and said, "Robert just jumped on the train." She had recognized him when she saw a man limping next to the tracks who suddenly jumped on the last wagon. She said she knew he would have to do that. If they found out what he did, he would be shot. He had to get on the train at the last second and hope that not too many people saw him.

Now he was on the train. Liesl knew he was not safe till the train crossed the no-man's land at the border into Germany. The train did not stop till it was on German soil. As the train stopped at the many stops on the way, Robert slowly worked his way forward to our wagon. There was a silent embrace. Maybe the War was finally over for us.

Chapter 4

Heading West

The train was heading west for all of us into an unknown future. We were free but did not know what lay before us. We spent two or three days on the train. These trains, at that time, had the least priority, and many times we waited on side tracks as other trains were let through first. We had some food for the little ones but not much for us. Lizzi had some milk she had gotten in Breslau. We didn't have food from the Red Cross or any relief groups, but we were so used to being hungry we did not think of food. All we were thinking was "Are we going to be safe or are we going to be caught again?"

Our concern was for the little kids—that they wouldn't be hungry—and for us, being safe and not having to worry anymore. Even long after we crossed the border, we still did not believe we were in Germany, in the western part of the country. We hoped the Russians and the Polish Militia could not harm us anymore.

The biggest relief for us came as the train rolled into German cities, and there were people standing at the depot who offered the people in our train shelter. Some even had jobs for them.

The cattle wagons emptied more and more. For us, it was Alfeld where the train stopped. Alfeld is near Hannover. Some of the people got shelter there, but we were driven to Grünenplan about 50 km from Alfeld. In Grünenplan there were volunteer villagers waiting for us who offered us shelter and jobs. Grünenplan was a very small village. The villagers who were in charge of organizing our resettlement did not want to separate the families, and there were quite a few people in our family. One family took my mother, Trude, Mimi and me. Liesl and Robert went to a different couple. They hoped to get married in Grünenplan and later on they did.

In the beginning Lizzi and the kids were with us. Lizzi's mother was resettled in Alfeld, so she moved on to Alfeld. We had one little room, right under the roof in the attic. The roof was slanted and that made the room much smaller. We had a couch, a table, and a little stove so we could cook. I slept downstairs in a different room, but spent the rest of the time up in the attic.

We tried to get jobs. Trude got a job in the office of the local glass works, where they produced and cut glass. They also made mirrors and eyeglasses. I also got a job there cutting out eyeglasses, not prescription grinding. It seemed everybody in Grünenplan worked in the glass factory. The village could only exist because of jobs at the glass factory. Robert got a job as an electric meter reader.

Grünenplan was a very pretty village, a very friendly village. The main road went through the middle of the town. All along the road were nice, little houses. It was very hilly. In the back of the houses, right and left of the street, was the most beautiful forest. It looked like the village was built in the middle of the forest. On the edge of the forest were paths for walking and bicycling. There were many raspberry and gooseberry bushes, and my mother and Trude often went berry and mushroom picking. I did not dare to pick mushrooms because I didn't know which were edible and which were not; but my mother and Trude knew. Liesl and I learned from them. Many times they brought home a meal for us.

My mother cooked for us on that little stove. We got by. It was very tough in the beginning because we did not make much money. In the factory, we got minimum wages; but we were used to cutting corners. Liesl did not have a job in Grünenplan because she had not lived there long enough. Mimi found her husband, Poldi. Before Poldi was drafted into the German Army, they had agreed that in case they lost contact with each other, they would write a family they knew in Berlin. When Mimi came to Germany, she wrote them. Luckily, this family knew where Poldi was. This is how they found each other. Poldi was a POW by the British and after the War worked for the British Army. They adopted little Ernst.

We had lived there for a year when I suddenly got a letter from my aunt. She wrote me that some time ago when she was in Salzburg, she saw an ad in the newspaper there. Somebody was looking for me. She did not know where I was or who the person was who was looking for me. She sent me the ad that she had cut out. It was from Brunhild, Sigi's sister, saying only that she was looking for me and gave her address in Salzburg. I wrote to Brunhild to try to find out if she knew anything about Sigi. I had not heard from him since I was at the hospital in Olmuetz as a nurse. That's where I had gotten my last letter from the POW camp. After I wrote the letter, I waited anxiously every day for a letter from Brunhild.

I will never forget when I came home from work one day and asked my mother if there was any mail for me. She said, "No."

Her face had such a sly and devilish expression that I said to her, "Come on, Ma. I can see on your face you are lying. Give it to me." After more denial, she finally gave me the letter. It was from Sigi. He had been released and was in Salzburg. That's how we found each other.

I wrote back right away. He suggested that we meet somewhere at the border; but the borders were closed, and nobody was allowed to cross. He wrote me that up in the Alps was a lodge, and the border went right through the lodge. It was high in the mountains. I would have to climb, which I had not done since I was a student in Bielitz. We had not seen each other for four and a half years. We did not know if we felt the same way about each other. This lodge was called the Stahlhouse. My brother, Viki, who was in Linz, Austria, would climb up with Sigi.

The date for the climb was set. Liesl and Robert were going to climb up with me. But Robert could not get away from work on that day, so Liesl and Robert decided to come a day later. First I had to find out exactly where the Stahlhouse was. I inquired at a travel agency, and they told me to take a train to Berchtesgaden and from there to take a bus to the town of Königsee.

The day of the climb arrived. I had left Grünenplan very early, traveling from northern Germany to southern Germany to arrive early in the morning in Berchtesgaden. When I got to Berchtesgaden, I inquired again at a travel agency. They told me there was a marked trail going up to the Stahlhouse from the town of Königsee, but they had no maps of this area for me. Looking up at the high mountains I said, "Oh, my God! How am I going to make it?" I looked at my wooden sandals, the only shoes I had. Shoes were rationed, and I could get only one pair of shoes a year. I was scared stiff. I had never climbed such high mountains before. Without a map but with a prayer in my heart, I started my climb from Königsee.

It must have been 9 o'clock in the morning when I started. With my knapsack on my back, with something to drink and a few sandwiches, I started climbing. Right away a steep path greeted me, and it got steeper and steeper. My wooden sandals broke so I took some string, wound it around, and kept on climbing. The string slipped off, and I had to repair it many times. The trail was poorly marked.

Sometimes the markings were on rocks and hardly visible. My feet were bleeding from the sharp rocks, and once or twice I got lost because the markings were so bad. I was praying and I was crying. I was scared of getting lost again. But I did not give up. I just kept on going.

The wooden shoes and steep path caused me to stumble many times. I was all scraped up and my knees were bleeding. I climbed all day long. Occasionally I sat down and rested for a while. I did not meet any other people on the trail, only a fox and some other animals. It was a beautiful day. The sun was shining, and it was still pretty cool. It was 5 or 6 o'clock in the afternoon when I reached a shelter house on the German side. I sat down and said to myself, "What now? Is he going to be here? Did he have a rough time climbing up, too?" I went into the German shelter house and asked if it as possible to get to the Stahlhouse. They said there was a wire fence and a gate about three hundred yards away, over the hill.

So I climbed the last little hill and saw the wire fence, gate, and the Stahlhouse before me. The gate was open. I sat down on a rock and waited to see what was going to happen. I waited quite a while, always looking toward the Stahlhouse. Suddenly, I saw somebody come out of the Stahlhouse wearing short pants. I looked and looked and thought it must be Sigi. He looked around, and then I started calling, "Sigi." He looked and called my name. We started running toward each other, and we met right at the open gate. That's how we met again after four and a half years. For me, it seemed as if we had seen each other just a day ago.

We walked hand in hand to the Stahlhouse. I saw somebody else coming towards us—my brother, Viki, and Sigi's sister, Brunhild. We hugged and kissed, and then we sat down inside the lodge to eat and talk. Sigi wanted to know why I came alone and why so late. He almost gave up on seeing me. They had an easy climb up the Austrian side in the beginning and only later it became very steep. They all had mountain climbing shoes on. I explained to them that Liesl and Robert were coming the next day. We could not get a room in the lodge anymore; they were all filled up, so we took the hayloft.

We did not sleep all night. We talked and talked. We were not tired. The next morning we all went for a walk. There was snow all around us. Sigi had brought some cherry or strawberry syrup, so we got some clean snow, poured some of the syrup over it, and had delicious snow cones. Soon Liesl and Robert arrived, and we had a great time together. We took pictures together and then came the time to say goodbye again. It was very hard for me, but Sigi said that he would try to get the papers ready soon so we could get married.

Going downhill is normally much harder than going up; but with my sister and brother-in-law along, it was easy. Everyone was in a happy mood. We all went back to our daily work at our new home in Germany.

Sigi went to work on the papers for a marriage permit and wrote me letters about his efforts. One day he wrote he was having difficulty getting an entry permit for me to come to Austria. The Austrian government absolutely refused to allow anybody into Austria. He wrote he was trying to get this entry problem solved. In my village of Grünenplan, there were a lot of people telling me they didn't think he was going to get married to me and that he had a lot of other girls in Salzburg. My landlord, who had an eye for me anyway, was saying I was foolish to run after a man when I could get any man here in Grünenplan, including him.

Suddenly came a frightening letter where he said I would have to come across the border illegally; but as soon as I was in Austria, it would be legal to get married. I did not understand this. In the next letter he wrote that there was another lodge in the mountains where the border goes through and asked me if I would be willing to come across the border illegally. I was worried about it, but Sigi said that this was the only option he had left. As long as we could be together, that's what I wanted. So, I agreed and I wrote back to him. Soon he sent me instructions from a friend of his who knew all these problems and would help me to come across the border. The name of the lodge was the Purtscheller House, and he wrote that I would have to go to Berchtesgaden again and find my way up from there. He said that Brunhild would climb up with him from the Austrian side.

This time when the date of the climb arrived, I was prepared. First, I had strong leather shoes and rain gear; and in my knapsack, I had lots of emergency items to help me in case of trouble. And, of course, food and drinks.

My sister, Liesl, promised to come along. The day arrived and Liesl and I, after saying a long goodbye to my mother, took the train to Berchtesgaden. I was leaving everything I knew behind and risking all in a trip which I did not know how it would end. But this time, I had more confidence in me. I felt it would be nothing like what I had faced in the War or in the camps or when we came across the border from Breslau. All these times flashed by in my mind. I told myself if I had endured all that in Poland, this climb up the mountain was not going to be that tough.

It was the beginning of October 1947. In the town of Berchtesgaden, we again asked a travel agency how to get to the Purtscheller House; and again they said they had no maps, but the trail was marked and we should take the bus to the Berghof on the Obersalzberg. We were happy that the bus trip would make our climb easier. The bus took us up a very long and winding road; and as we went higher and higher, we thought that this would be a nice way to travel. The bus soon stopped at the end of the line and we got out. There were no buildings there and no ruins, but we found the marked trail again. Later on I learned that the Berghof on the Obersalzberg was Hitler's home away from Berlin.

We did not meet anybody on the trail; and as we climbed higher and higher, it got tougher to breath. We had to stop more often to rest. My feet were not getting bloody this time, but we were getting tired. But when two persons are climbing together, it is easier for both of them.

Liesl was such good company for me. It was also easier to find the markings on the trail. The trail kept getting smaller and smaller. The trail was, at first, about 3 feet wide; then it was hardly 2 feet wide and getting smaller. There were quite a few drop offs that gave us a chill when we looked down. These were paths for people who knew mountain climbing; but for us, it seemed constant dangers were lurking all over. But we were young—I was 24 years old and Liesl a bit over 22 at that time.

When we saw the Purtscheller House in the distance, we got fresh energy; but we were still quite a way off. When we looked up, there were all these high mountains staring down at us.

We had all the instructions from Sigi, and on our climb we went through them time and time again. One instruction was not to talk to Sigi or Brunhild. Behave as if they were strangers. We were only to give signs to them that nobody else could see. Liesl and I went over the instructions, but we could not imagine how it would work. There were many people at the Purtscheller House when we arrived. This time we made it up in only three hours.

It was not hard to follow the instructions till we saw Sigi and Brunhild. I could not say hello nor look at them, even when they passed by me. But all this was necessary. I picked up a sign from Brunhild that told me to follow her to the toilet. There, we quickly exchanged our clothes. She gave me some identification papers to stay in Austria and we left the toilet separately.

What I did not know was that the mountain police were watching every one coming from all the different trails, from the time you start climbing to the time you arrive at the lodge. They watch you with binoculars from hidden spots, some high above the lodge. They identified you by the clothes you were wearing. They knew that who comes up on one trail has to come down the same trail. The mountain police did not sit around at the lodge. They just came down from their hiding place for a drink of beer or some food. They were in uniform and you could spot them easily.

It bothered me tremendously that I had to pretend not to know Sigi or Brunhild. Suddenly Sigi gave me a sign to follow him. I had already said goodbye to Liesl and I worried how she would manage, going back alone. I picked up my knapsack and went outside. Sigi was already far ahead, so I followed him as he walked farther down the trail to the Austrian side.

After we both crossed over a hill, away from the trail, Sigi stopped and we finally embraced. Suddenly, Toni, an Austrian guide and mountain climber, appeared out of nowhere. He had been watching and directing the whole thing without Sigi or Brunhild knowing where he was or what he was doing. He said, "So far, so good." Then he told us the rest of the plan. He said we should keep walking in small groups, occasionally changing the people in the group. He told me to walk with Brunhild for a while and then with Sigi. Brunhild was already ahead of us. Toni said that when we came to the end of the climb, he would give us instructions again. He left and vanished in no time. Sigi told me Toni could climb up and down the mountain two or three times while we went up and down once. He never used the marked trail where everybody goes, so you never saw him.

It was fun going down with Sigi on the Austrian side. In the beginning, the path down was only a trail; later on, it became a road. We caught up with Brunhild and I walked with her for a while. We met a lot of people going down, but they never saw me walking with the same person.

As we came close to the foot of the mountain, Toni appeared again. He had been down and was coming up again. He told us that down at the bridge before the railroad station were mountain police checking everyone's papers. There was no way to go around it. He said he and Sigi would go first, then I, and Brunhild last; and he said to pretend not to know Brunhild. This gave me the shivers. What if they check my papers and see I don't have an entry permit? What would they do? We were so close to being together again for good.

I was very far behind Sigi and Toni, and there were other people between us and the bridge. I could see Sigi show them his papers and point to where I was coming. Sigi went through, but Toni stayed and showed the police something and was still talking to them as Sigi kept on going to the railroad station. As I approached the policemen and was going to show them my papers, Toni was showing them pictures of his family and his kids and talking to them in the Austrian dialect. They were laughing. I showed one of them my papers and as he looked at them, Toni told the policemen a joke. I told him that my husband had everything else and had gone through already. The policeman nodded and laughed at Toni's joke and let me through.

Slowly, trying not to show excitement, I walked toward the railroad station. When Brunhild arrived at the bridge, the mountain policemen checked her papers thoroughly. Brunhild went through, too. Toni was already at the railroad station. At the station we still could not openly embrace. We still had to play the role of strangers, even on the train to Salzburg. When the train pulled into the Salzburg station, I got what I was waiting for—the hugging and kissing, and hugging Toni, the man who directed everything. He refused any money. He did not want anything. He said, "Sigi is my friend and I had to help him." We thanked him many times.

I will stop here and let Sigi tell his story, including the climb from his side and all that he had to do to get us finally together again.

Part II

Sig's Story

Chapter 1

My Childhood

On June 8, 1921, in a suburb of Bielitz or Bielsko (the Polish name for the town), I was born as the firstborn child of Josef and Martha Hoffmann in the house of my grandparents, Johann and Angele Hoffmann. A year before, in 1920, the Bielitz area still belonged to Austria. After World War I, the Allies ordered French and Italian troops into the disputed area. In Bielitz were Italian mountain troops. In a plebiscite, this area was handed over to Poland despite a German-speaking majority population. In the Treaty of Versailles, the border of Poland was finally established.

Our farmhouse was a two-story house with sturdy thick walls. My father was the youngest of five children and my mother the youngest of seven children. As soon as I was old enough to understand, my parents told me that at the time of my birth an airplane flew over the house. This is a common occurrence now, but in 1921, it was a rarity. I did not understand the significance of this and I had to endure many jokes like: "The stork didn't bring Sig, an airplane dropped him over the house." Later in my life it had more significance to me. In 1924 my sister, Brunhild, and in 1925 my youngest sister, Erika, were born.

We kids had lots of fun on our grandparents farm. My grandparents had cows, chickens, geese, a ram, and a dog. They also had a lot of fruit trees and strawberries; and my grandmother sold many of the fruits, vegetables, and eggs in the town market. I was their first grandchild and they loved me very much. When my sisters were born, they shared their love equally among all of us.

My grandfather, Johann, was a farmer and a carpenter. Next to his farm he had a large carpentry shop where he would mass produce a wide array of items. He was very ingenious in what he did. He would get ideas for items that could be made out of wood and mass produced them. He introduced a simple pinball machine with a bell in the middle and small nails for the pinball to bounce off. He called it Tivoli and mass produced it. He made a double-sided rocking horse with a seat in the middle, beautifully painted and mass produced it. These sold very well. After awhile he changed the design and made double-sided swans with a seat in between and this rocking swan sold even better.

Another thing he made was a carrying seat for a baby. He made it out of drilled wood with a strong rope through the wood. Two people could carry the baby between them or you could carry the baby alone on your back. The great part was this wood rope combination could be easily folded together into a small light bundle. For fun he made kites, mostly the box type, covered with impregnated cloth. The kites were very stable and could fly very high.

One day he was experimenting with an idea to put candle-lit Chinese lanterns on the corners of his box kites. On a breezy night he let them fly. To his surprise the Chinese lanterns did not burn up. That night he flew this kite for a very long time. The next day the newspapers reported that many people had seen lights in the sky, waving back and forth, and nobody could figure out what it was.

Like so many people at that time, you had to be your own doctor. My grandfather, Johann, never went to see a doctor. He had all kinds of herbs and roots and made his own medicine. My father learned to make some of them and gave them to us kids. I especially remember the cough syrup. One layer of chopped onions, one layer sugar, one layer of chopped onions, one layer sugar, and so on. Let it stand for a few days and drink it. The best cough syrup and darn cheap, too!

My grandfather, Johann, was a Socialist, despite the fact that all his children were raised Catholic. My father told me that one time, on a clear night full of glittering stars, my grandfather had my father and I, a four-year old boy stand next to him. He pointed to the heavens and the stars and said, "There are many worlds like ours out there and there are many people like us on these worlds. One day we will get to know these people from another world." I don't know if my father believed in that and I never remember my grandfather saying that to me, but I was reminded often that my grandfather believed in that.

The grandfather on my mother's side, Andreas Olschowski, was in charge of the maintenance department at the big vocational campus. It was an engineering school, trade school, management training school—that type of higher education. My father and all his brothers were educated there. My grandfather, Andreas, lived on the campus. He and his family were the only ones who lived there. My mother and all her sisters and brother were born and brought up on this campus. Imagine, six girls and one boy living with all these young men on campus. No wonder all the Olschowski girls married highly educated men.

As a young child I would visit my grandparents and play on this campus. The fence around the campus was a very peculiar one. It was a small stone wall with a small wooden fence built on top. I learned to jump the wooden fence after climbing over the stone wall. For some reason, this fence stayed in my memory.

After my sister, Erika, was born in 1925, my father decided to travel to Turkey and build the first hat manufacturing plant in that country. He had acquired the knowledge through his schooling and working, and he had the money. My father explained it this way to me. He had read in the newspaper that the new President of Turkey welcomed foreigners to come to his country and help him to reform and change Turkey into a modern republic. My mother's sister, Mitzi, and her husband, Karl, and their children already lived in Turkey. This was my uncle, Karl Beck, who had come to Turkey to install textile machinery built in Bielitz. The Turks liked him very much and offered him the job of running the factory. Eventually he brought his wife and children over.

It was my father's intention to go to Turkey with a German fellow, who was supposed to help him run the plant. My father had the idea that a hat manufacturing plant was of utmost importance to Turkey because of the law forbidding anyone to wear a fez. The moslem "fez", as a strict rule, was worn constantly, never taken off. Even in their mosques they had to wear it. I guess the only time they took it off was when they went to bed. After a while, because of the constant wear, they would be full of sweat and were very disease ridden. Turks who were educated in western universities objected to constantly wearing the fez. As a symbol of their religion, they had to wear it, but they objected for hygienic reasons.

The President of Turkey, Mustafa Kemal Pasha, was committed to bringing Turkey along the path of western civilization. He decreed that the wearing of the fez was forbidden; and after twenty four hours, anyone seen still wearing a fez would be hanged. Hat manufacturers from all over the world emptied their inventories and shipped it to Istanbul, where they sold the hats for a big profit right off the dock. My father wanted to get permission to build the plant and start construction and about a year later, come home and pick up my mother and us.

When my father arrived in Istanbul (in the old times called Konstantinopel) they were still hanging law breakers or fez wearers on the light posts of the Galata Bridge, which crosses the Golden Horn. When the posts were full they would cut the bodies down and hang more. This was the only way the moslem followers could be shocked into abandoning this symbol, the fez, which in fact was very unsanitary. Kemal Pasha, the president of Turkey, also decreed that women were not allowed to wear their veils anymore. He did not dare to hang women, and the moslem women wore veils for a very long time afterward. It was at the beginning of the westernization of Turkey.

During the time my father was in Istanbul, according to my mother, he had to fight a lot of red tape. For instance, he had to sign a contract with the government agreeing to hire a large majority of Turkish employees for his plant. Due to the large unskilled labor force, it would have been difficult training all these unskilled people and still keep the plant running full blast.

It was 1926 when my father returned from Turkey and told us he had the plant almost built. He also told us that in the meantime, he had opened up a shop in an exclusive area where he was selling new hats from every manufacturer in the world. His partner stayed behind and was running the shop.

On his trip to Bielitz he had an unfortunate accident. The oceanliner from Istanbul to Varna, Bulgaria, sank in a heavy storm in the Black Sea. The lifeboat he was riding in was often swept with the ice cold waves of the Black Sea. After landing at the shore, the survivors had to wait for a long time until an emergency train arrived. After he was on the train, he discovered the train had no heat. That's where he got his chronic bronchitis.

My father and the whole family took the train from Vienna, Austria to Varna, Bulgaria. I believe it was the early days of the Orient Express. I was five, Brunhild was two, and Erika was six months old. My mother often told me that I was up every night looking out the window to see the lights of the stations as we passed through and watch the activity in the stations where we stopped. From Varna, we took the sister ship of the one my father came over on, which had sunk, and we arrived in Istanbul.

We lived in an apartment and my mother had a young girl named Antoinette, who took care of the house and us children. My mother was surprised to learn that this girl could not cook. She did not know anything about taking care of a house. We kids liked her, so my mother kept her on for our sake while my mother cooked, washed the laundry, and did all the housework. We lived on a dead end street. There was no traffic so we played in the street. I learned the languages my playmates spoke—Greek, Yiddish, French and Turkish. I remember a boy by the name of Philip who was my best friend.

My father and his German partner got together and ordered the machinery for the plant and my father gave him the money to buy them. However, the German fellow got sick and was sent to the hospital. When my father went to visit him in the hospital, he was gone. He had skipped the country, as sick as he was, with all the money my father had given him.

My father informed the police, even the International Police. They located his mother in Germany, who was very poor, and found out he had arrived there but died shortly afterwards. No trace of the money was ever found. The police found out that a male nurse in the hospital had helped him to leave Turkey. So, suddenly my father was broke. Our parents kept this news from us for many years but slowly they did reveal it to us. My father had said to me, years after the incident, that his determination to stay in Turkey grew stronger. He felt if he could not be the first hat manufacturer in Turkey, he would be the first hat repairman. So he opened a hat repair shop on the Yüksek Kaldirim, a very busy and popular business street in Istanbul.

In 1927, I entered a mission school called Saint George College. It was run by Austrian priests, Notre Dame nuns, and private teachers. It consisted of a school, a church, a hospital, and a girls boarding school. One thing I do remember well are the first teachers I had—Pater Dworczak, the principal of the St. George College, and Pater Siegfried. Right from the first grade I had to learn German, French and Turkish.

The Turks, at that time, used the Arabic letters which go from right to left. In the second grade, our Turkish teacher started to teach us Turkish with our western, the Latin alphabet. Little did I know that the President of Turkey himself went from school to school instructing the Turkish teachers to switch to our Latin letters. You may not believe me, but some of us students were smarter than the teacher. We found we had to correct the teacher over and over because we had been raised with that alphabet and the Turkish teacher had just learned it during the school vacation. In the third grade I found I had a problem learning Turkish grammar. There was no grammar developed yet. Besides that, the Turkish language was going through a "de-arabization"—removing Arabic words from the language and replacing them with English, German and French words.

Once my father had opened the hat shop on the Yüksek Kaldirim, we moved to a different house behind the store. We could play on the sidewalk in front of my father's shop. We played mostly hopscotch. We had a lot of Greek, Turkish, Spanish and Portuguese friends and learned to count in all these languages. We even learned enough to converse with the kids our age. But the sidewalk was constantly being used by people who would walk right on our hopscotch pattern and bump into us when we were playing. Some, of course, were my father's customers. Some were tourists visiting Istanbul. Some were the regular traffic on this always busy street.

My father learned to speak Turkish very fast. Besides learning to speak it, he had to learn how to conduct business in Turkey. I remember my father telling me that he had to cater to the customer. If a wealthy Turk entered his store, he would not talk business right away. My father ordered coffee from the coffee shop. Luckily, coffee shops in Turkey are on nearly every street corner. During this conversation, he would talk in polite words, mostly very personal talk, about family or politics. My father would sit together with the customer and drink Turkish coffee. After a long private talk, the customer finally talks business with you.

One day a well dressed Turk came into the shop. Right away, my father called down to the coffee shop for two coffee and sat down for the common, polite, personal talk. He was surprised to discover he was talking to Ismet Inönü, the private secretary of the President of Turkey. After the coffee and the talk, the secretary brouight in 10 or 12 hats of Kemal Pasha for my father to repair. Over the years, Ismet Inönü came many times and after sitting down for coffee and talk, brought the President's hats for repair. After Mustafa Kemal Pasha's death in 1938, Ismet Inönü became the President of Turkey.

My sister, Erika, who was not yet in Kindergarten often played with the boy whose father had the pharmacy right next door to my father's shop. Both were the same age and played so nice together. They usually played on the street but were always in calling distance. My parents were worried about children commonly being taken by strangers and vanishing without a trace. My sister, Erika, was light blond and really stuck out in a crowd. One day she came running into the shop saying that a man passed by and gave her all kinds of kisses. This scared my parents tremendously but they did not know what to do. The two children played so harmoniously together and watched out for each other that my parents thought they would be safe.

One time they were playing together, my mother called them; but she heard no response. She went out on the street to find them, but they were nowhere to be seen. Suddenly, my mother remembered the stories of the vanishing children. Scared, she ran next door to the pharmacist. Now both were on the street looking in all the places they might be hiding. Nothing. No sign of where they might be. My mother and the pharmacist had no other choice but to go to the karakol (the police station).

The police asked all kinds of questions—what clothes were they wearing? Where did they play? And so on. And then the police, in civilian clothes, with my mother and the pharmacist, spread out in different directions from the karakol. My mother and one policeman searched on the Yüksek Kaldirim and below.

They headed closer to the harbour area where the Galata Bridge starts and where all the big overseas ships are docked. And here, on the waterfront, she saw two little children walking hand in hand—laughing, happy, and unmolested— Erika and the boy of the pharmacist. They did not know that they had done anything wrong. My mother could never understand how they crossed the streets with heavy traffic and nobody stopped them and reported them to the police. Besides all the fear and nightmares my mother and the pharmacist had, now they had to go to the police station and explain to them why the children did not know better.

My father was not satisfied with the school curriculum. In the fourth grade I transferred to the Turk Alman Ticaret Mektebi, a German-run private school for the rich population of Turkey. He knew the tuition fee would be higher; but with three children in the same school, it would be cheaper and not too much hardship. Because of having three children in school, the parents were also on the school board.

Around that time we moved to a new apartment next to this school. My mother could look directly into the school yard from her window. All of us kids played there. My friend Philip and I, with my sisters, were the only kids allowed to play in the school yard after school hours. One day in school, I was confronted by some older students and warned not to play with "that Jewish kid, Philip, or they would beat me up. I did not know what they meant, but I was scared. Philip went to a different school. I did not know why it made a difference that he was Jewish. Without telling anyone, not even my parents, I went to Philip and told him I could not play with him anymore and why. We both cried. We parted and never saw each other again. Many years afterwards, all these events had more meaning to me.

One problem the school board faced was the children not eating enough. Many got neither breakfast at home nor anything in school. My mother's suggestion was *why not serve milk*? My mother knew a German farmer who made cheeses who was glad to bring the milk to school. My mother worked as a volunteer in the basement serving the milk every school day at 10 o'clock. We could drink cold or warm milk and I help my mother serve. It did not cost the children anything.

In comparing the students of the two schools I attended, the Mission School had youngsters from many nationalities who were poor. We had a few black children there but we were all treated the same. In the German school were youngsters or many nationalities, but these were the children of ambassadors, doctors, Turkish government employees, and once in a while refugees from countries like Russia. There were a lot of refugees who were rich. The refugees on the street were poor—in some cases beggars and could not afford this school. The teachers in the German school also treated every nationality the same. The teachers were very well educated professors with many advanced degrees.

What impressed my parents was the teacher's ability to teach the subject very understandably and to effectively help the students who did not get it the first time. I was very weak in math and did not understand much; but my math teacher knew my problem, and in a short time I could follow with the rest of the class.

My music teacher was Theodor Jung, a famous composer. He was German and he composed, among other music, the Turkish National Anthem. To this day I still can sing it. He also composed many sound tracks for Turkish movies. My father and mother were in the choir that sang many of the Turkish songs for the movies. I liked him very much. Every music class was held in a big room called the Aula. He had his piano there and played excerpts or a main theme from symphonies, operas, and operettas. He also played the music of other composers who used the same theme or a similar one. I was not the only one who listened quietly. Everybody was always very quiet. That's where I developed my appreciation for music.

In gym, we actively pursued all kinds of sports you see now only in the Olympics. I was in a boxing program, too. There the parents had to give written permission. In the fifth grade I took English and in the sixth grade I took Latin.

Even as I was learning German, Turkish, French, English and Latin, I also wanted to learn the customs of the people, how they live.

One day I was visiting a Turkish school friend who lived in one of the suburbs of Istanbul. I had my parents permission to travel. Outside of my friend's house, I looked up at a building where all the windows had iron bars in front of them. There were women at the windows. I asked my friend what these women were doing in jail. He laughed and said, "These are my father's wives and this is his harem." When I came home, my parents had a hard time explaining a harem to me. I thought I understood but actually, I was too young.

Turkey has a tropical or subtropical climate. I remember only one time snow falling on Istanbul—the first snow in forty years. The people in the streets did not know what to do about it. Some of them ate it. "Like Mana from heaven"—it had to be food, they thought. But, for us kids, it was nothing new. We knew snow. The hope of making a snowman was soon gone as the little bit of snow melted.

We always celebrated Christmas the way we did in Bielitz. On December sixth, St. Nicolaus Day, Santa Klaus came to us. He was clad the way we in Bielitz remembered it—as a Bishop with a Bishop's hat and staff. In Bielitz, Santa Klaus always came with the Krampus, the devil. Santa Klaus would ask the parents if the child was good or bad. If the parents said the child was good, the child got some cookies, candy, or chocolate. If the parents said the child was bad, then Santa Klaus asked the Krampus to do his job. Krampus always had a rod or a switch along with which he slapped you, more symbolically than actually, and you did not get any goodies. Not getting any goodies hurt more than the slap from Krampus.

In Turkey, St. Nicolaus came on the sixth of December and was clad the same as in Bielitz. He was very gentle to us kids. If my mother said we were not good, Santa Klaus reminded us to follow God, be on the right path, and help your parents. We always got some goodies and there was no Krampus and no switches. And always, when St. Nicolaus came, my father was not home. He always came back after St. Nicolaus had left. Over the years, sitting on St. Nicolaus' lap, I noticed in his face a remarkable resemblance to my father. In a few years I knew it was my father. When I had discovered that my father said, "Be quiet. Don't mention it to your sisters."

The highlight of the Christmas time was the actual celebration. My parents always used to have specially raised carp for Christmas, but my father could not find carp in Istanbul. So he went to the bazaar and bought a goose. On Christmas Eve, the table was festively decked. We had a small plate on the table where everyone put money—a few cents or a nickel, not more. We also had a plate where my mother put salt and a slice of bread. Where my father sat was the Bible. My father would read the Gospel from Luke. He thanked God for everything He had done for us and asked Him for His blessing on the food. My father remembered all our relatives and friends and also remembered all who had died in the past year. Then he broke the Holy Bread—little wafers. We kids even got one to break.

This ceremony was handed down from generation to generation. Everyone we know who is from Bielitz celebrates Christmas this way. After opening the present, one present only, we went to the midnight mass in the St. George Church. We always had a Christmas tree, but we never saw the tree till Christmas Eve. My parents decorated the tree without us present. When the time came for us to see the tree, my father rang a little bell and called out in German, "das Christkindl ist hier (the Christ child is here)." When we entered the room, the beautiful candle-lit tree was a great joy for us. We also had a Christmas tree in school, in the church, and in the hospital—in fact, wherever Christian people were gathering. But no electric lights or decorations on houses. After all, Turkey is a Moslem country.

Friday is the day everything closes, like Sunday in the western countries. On this day my parents would go with us into the country, and many times we would have a picnic somewhere near a brook. My father would search under the banks of the brook for fish. He used his hands only. If he caught a fish, he would throw the fish on shore and we had to catch it. Sometimes he would throw out a snake or a crab.

Many times we would take the ferry boat from the Galata Bridge to some lovely, quiet bay on the Bosporus. There my father did the same thing, try to catch fish by hand in the holes along the bank. We had many fish fries in the evening. Sometimes we slept in a tent along the shores of the Bosporus. There also were two beautiful beaches with very fine sand where we, as a family, often went. Miles of sand. Clean sand. No trash or cans. No bottles or cigarette buts. Now I remember the names—Floria and Moda.

In 1930 we found a Polish town on the Asiatic side of the Bosporus. Its name was Polones Köy. The first time we were there we thought we had been transported to Europe. The houses were the same style as the houses at home. The soil was rich, fertilized with manure. They spoke Polish and German there. We had fresh milk, fresh butter, butter milk, and fresh baked rye bread—things we never saw in Istanbul. We often stopped in this village. I remember my father carrying Erika on his shoulders because it was so far to walk to Polones Köy from the ferry station on the Bosporus.

My mother received a letter from her sister, Mitzi, who lived in Kayseri, Turkey. She asked my mother to pick up her three youngest children. They would be coming by train. The trains coming from the Asian part of Turkey, called Anatol, stopped at the train depot in Haydarpasha. We and our mother went by ferry, crossing the Bosporus to the train depot in Haydarpasha, to see our cousins arrival. We had never seen them before. We kids were dreaming about how much fun we would have playing with our cousins. When the train pulled into the station and they got out, we were shocked. We could not speak to them in German. They only knew Turkish. My aunt had entered them into the Mission School of Saint George College and they were staying in the boarding house of the school.

I wrote before about us playing in front of my father's shop on the street. My father had hired two people, one was a Turk and Josephine was a Greek or Armenian seamstress. My mother also was an excellent seamstress and she taught Josephine to sew the inside silk lining, the inside leather band, and the outside band and bow of the hat. It was a standard style at that time. My father and his Turkish employee worked on the chemical cleaning and the refinishing of the hat, which meant steaming, applying some finishing chemicals (appreture) to the hat, and putting the hat into a large drying chamber. This helps the hat to hold up in rain and snow.

When my parents were in the shop and we were not in school, we would play outside on the street. The street was always full of people. Some were merchants walking by and shouting out whatever they had to sell. I remember the men who came by and shouted "sal-ep, sal-ep". They would carry their goods on a long round bar around their shoulders balancing the items with the two ends of the wooden bar. One was a mangal, a glowing charcoal stove, and on the other end they had cups and spoons, the dry ingredients and some more charcoal. They would sell a thick, soupy, sweet brew made from the roots of salep. We kids liked it very much and it sure cured our colds fast.

In a taped conversation with my mother when she was 86 and I was 63, she reminded me about the donkey's milk. These men came by with their donkey and shouted "donkey milk, donkey milk". They would milk the donkey right in front of you. My mother told us that donkey milk was very nutritious and good for us, but we could not stand the taste of it. My mother was very insistent that we drink it. She would put the donkey's milk into our regular milk glasses; and after the first swallow, we knew right away it was donkey's milk and could not drink it. My mother thought that after a swallow here and swallow there, we could finally like it, but we never did.

One day, a young man stopped in front of us while we were playing in the street and said he heard us speaking German. He asked us where our parents were and we told him, inside this shop. He introduced himself to my parents as Alfred Reitenbach, 16 years old, from Helenendorf in the Caucasus in Russia. We got acquainted with him and he told us his life story. Thus started a remarkable friendship. He spoke a perfect German. His ancestors had come to Russia by invitation of a Czar many years ago. In my research, I could not find any period in the history of Russia when that sort of thing occurred, unless perhaps, under Catherine the Great. They came by ox carts, hundreds of them, got land and settled. They farmed the land the way they had learned it in Germany and became prosperous.

When the Communists started their "kolkhos" system on the farms, we call it a collective farm now, these German farmers resisted. Their lifestyle of free enterprise and voluntary help of your neighbors was in direct conflict with the Soviet system of no property ownership and laboring for the state. So the powerful Soviet government destroyed the German farmers. They took their farms away and forced them to be part of the "kolkhos" system or killed them. He and his sister were the only ones left of the village of Helenendorf. When he was fifteen he decided to flee.

He fled his village through Russian Georgia, then through Armenia into Tabriz, Iran. From Tabriz he fled to Turkey. It took him a year to do that. He was working for a Turkish-German wine company who had their store just a few shops away from our place. His parents were killed when he was ten years old. My father accepted him into our family. Now again, he had a father and mother and I had an older brother. He called my father, Dad, and my mother, Mom, and whatever our family did he was along with us.

On our Friday trips, fishing in the creek or on the ocean banks, he would enjoy catching the fish my father threw on the bank. He went swimming with us at the beach, he lived in our house and ate the food my mother prepared for us, and he loved it. After losing almost everyone in his family, it was nice to be part of a family again. He told us that many times. He had a brother and two sisters now; and for me, it was great to have an older brother to look up to.

Chapter 2

Life In Turkey

In the taped interviews with my mother, she recalled many of the happenings of that time; and of course, that made me remember a lot, too. Here are some of those stories.

My mother often went to the open market in Istanbul which was at the end of the street car line. This market was like the flea markets you find here in the states. We went mostly for fresh vegetables, and she took us children along. A lot of Turkish women also went shopping there with their children. The women were always clad in their standard black clothes and wore a veil. Sometimes they were completely veiled with only those black shinning eyes looking out. My mother could never learn Turkish, so she was always talking to us in German.

One day, it must have been school vacation time, we went to this market. Next to us was a Turkish woman, walking with her little girl. She must have been my own age—eight or nine years old. I noticed her blond hair and I mentioned it to my mother. Suddenly, the Turkish woman and her daughter stopped, and the Turkish woman spoke to my mother in German—something like—it is so nice to hear German again.

My mother was surprised and happy to hear her speaking German. She told my mother her story, a story repeated many times in Turkey during this period. She was a young German girl who had studied at a university in Germany. She met a young Turkish student, fell in love and got married. Her knowledge of Turkey was what she had read in *"A Thousand And One Nights"* , all fairy tales. When her husband went back to Turkey he, of course, took her along. To her surprise, she immediately had to wear drab black Turkish women's clothing and a veil and had to live in a harem. She was not allowed to talk to men or foreigners and not go where she wanted. My mother was the first foreign women she had talked to since she had arrived in Turkey many years before. There was nothing her family could do to help her. Her husband had neglected to tell her that being a European does not exempt you from the Turkish law, which was Moslem law as well.

At that time, the Turkish government under its first democratic president, had to move slowly in the enforcement of the law. The blond girl was her daughter. Her name was Cemile, pronounced Dshemile. I got along with her very well, as did my sisters. Our mothers also got along very well and were best of friends till we left Turkey, and they lost contact with each other . But this story is very much intertwined with another.

My father had met many people enduring hardships. He knew a refuge from former Czarist Russia who must have been a person with some degree of wealth. He was working as a porter in a hotel; but times were rough for him, and he wanted to sell some jewelry to my father. He showed my father a bracelet, excellently crafted in gold, which interested my father very much. He wanted to buy it as a present for my mother. The price was very high. My father made an agreement with the porter so he could save up the money, and the porter would hold on to it till my father had the money.

My father saved and saved, and once in awhile stopped at the porter's house to see the bracelet, to get more incentive to save. One day he got the money together, paid the porter, and brought this fancy heavy gold bracelet home and gave it to my mother. When my mother saw this beautifully-crafted golden bracelet, she was very excited and happy. My father wanted to put it away for safekeeping, but my mother wanted to show it to her friend she met at the market at the end of the street car line.

The next day my mother and I went with the streetcar to the market to meet Cemile and her mother. I had partially forgotten what happened, but my mother remembered every moment of it. Soon after she had shown the bracelet to her friend, some gypsies appeared. There were always gypsies at this market. One girl wanted to read my mother's palm and tried to take her hand. My mother said "no" and pulled her hand back; and soon afterwards, I heard my mother cry out that her bracelet was gone. My mother was shocked and crying, but her friend had good sense to call for police. She spoke Turkish and acted as the interpreter.

We had to go to the Karakol (police station) , where my mother filed a complaint, explained the circumstances, and gave a description of the gypsy girl. Right away the police went looking and soon after they dragged the gypsy girl in. Of course, they did not find the bracelet on her and she denied she stole it. My mother and her friend had positively identified this women as the palm reader. We children were led out of the police station and told we had to wait outside.

Inside, the police started beating, kicking, and interrogating the gypsy girl over and over again. The girl was crying and bloody. My mother and her friend saw everything. The police did it right in front of them. My mother cried and pleaded with the police not to beat the girl anymore. The police asked her if she wanted the bracelet back; and my mother said "yes", but not by beating the girl. Then the police said that if my mother would withdraw her complaint, they would stop. My mother said it was a hard decision because she knew how much that bracelet had cost and how long my father had been saving; but she could not stand to see them beat the girl anymore. So my mother said, "Yes, I withdraw my complaint. Don't beat the girl anymore." She left the police station on the arm of her friend and said she had felt as though she had been beaten herself. For me as a child, it was terrible to see my mother cry; and that day always sticks in my mind. When we came home, my father saw my mother's face. He knew that something had happened, and when he heard, he was shaken. He remembered diligently saving for a beautiful present that was gone in an instant. But, as my mother said on the tape, he never accused her of losing his gift.

One time the German Hospital made a gingerbread Hansel and Gretel house. To us children, it looked huge. First it was on display, and then the school decided that the only family with three children in our school should receive it. In a lovely and festive ceremony, we received it. Afterwards, the problem was how to bring it home. Somebody with a car offered to bring it home. It was so gigantic that we even had lots of problems putting it into the car. We had so much to eat that we gave most of it away to other children.

In 1984 I asked my mother how she baked in Istanbul because I never saw an oven in any of the places we lived. She said people had no ovens because there were bakeries all over the town. On almost every street corner was a bakery and all you did was bring your cake or bread in, tell them how long you wanted it to bake, and then pick it up. That simple. This leads to another story.

I liked my math teacher very much because he made understanding math so easy for me. One day I told my mother that it was the math teacher's birthday, and I heard him say how much he missed good home baked cakes. My mother said she would bake a cake for the teacher. My father wrote a small poem, I recited the poem and gave him the cake. The next day all hell broke lose. All the teachers lived in a separate house next to the school, and a cake like the one my math teacher got was hard to keep a secret. The smell alone gave it away. Soon every teacher wanted a cake and was willing to pay any price for it.

My poor mother agreed, and even asked what kind of cake they wanted—cheese cake, plum cake, apple strudel, or poppy seed cake. All the cakes my mother always made for us, she would make for the teachers. The teachers' admiration for my mother's cake was overwhelming. They said they had never eaten cakes as good as my mother's. Jokingly, they were saying they would go on strike if my mother stopped baking.

My grandfather Johann Hoffmann died on May 12, 1930. He was 70 years old. A few years later I found out what had happened. He never saw a doctor and did not believe in doctors. He cured himself with his own medicine made from roots and herbs. One day, after a stubborn cold that would not get better, he agreed to see a doctor—the first doctor he ever saw in his life. Soon after he received the injection from the doctor, he died. All his friends thought his body could not except the medication.

Religious education in school was non-existent. My mother, being on the school board, got a program through where the students had religious education on a voluntary basis after school hours. Our Catholic teacher was Pater Dworczak, my first teacher and principal of the St. George College. His bearded face and his soft voice made an imposing figure to me, but his catechism teaching did not address the new students who were influenced by socialism, communism, and other radical ideas. They were many clashes in class were Pater Dworczak would be unable to explain the stand of the Catholic church. I had to do it as clear as I could understand it. I came to the aid of Pater Dworczak, but I was a kid myself.

I became more and more aware in school that so many ideologies were floating around with different nationalities and that people sometimes would divide into camps. We had strong Moslems who were, in themselves, split into many groups. Then were the socialists, coming from different nations with their own shade of socialism. Then the Czarists, with their different classes, followed by the communists with their many different attitudes. The Greeks and Turks hated each other, and many other groups and classes each felt they had a right to distrust or even hate each other. The Nazis were not making any loud noises, not yet.

It was exciting for the school and for me when an announcement came that the school planned to build a glider and volunteers were welcome to work on it. This was the thing for me! A glider! We would construct a glider, a real flying plane, that somebody could sit in and fly. I guess it was 1932 when we started to build it in the attic of the school. The attic was big and had many windows and good lighting. I lived close to the school and could work on it with my teacher long after everyone went home.

I must have been the youngest of the students, being that I was in the fifth grade; and we had twelve grades. Learning aerodynamics, airflow on wings, and building a plane from balsa wood and impregnated paper was the foundation for my wanting to fly model air planes.

The glider was finished. We had to break a wall and a window in the attic to get the wings and the fuselage of the plane out. It was brought to the airport and assembled on a nice day, with a big crowed on hand. It was pulled by a regular plane to a certain height, the cable released, and it flew—beautifully, circling the airport and gliding back to the spot it took off. It was a great triumph for me to see something fly, and I had participated in building it. The newspapers reported the next day that it was the first glider ever flown in Turkey.

When school vacation arrived most of my classmates spent it somewhere in Europe. Children of ambassadors or doctors could afford expensive vacations. There were many children who could not afford to leave Istanbul, and who did not have an opportunity to go on a vacation. The school offered these children a chance to go, for a month or so, to Germany to live on a farm with temporary foster parents. In 1932, I went to Germany and stayed on a farm in Sehnde, in northwestern Germany. I remember it was a large farm with all kinds of machinery and horses and many cows. It was a completely different farm than my grandfather's in Bielitz.

In 1933, I again went on a trip to Germany, paid for by the school. This time it was to the outskirts of Dresden, where I lived with an older couple who had a sheet-metal shop. I learned to ride bike and learned to play soccer.

My happiest times were when I read books. Our school library was extensive. Travel books were my favorite. "Gulliver's Travels" and Mark Twain's books were very familiar to me, as well as "Don Quixote and Sancho Panza." Of course, they were in German. As a boy I was raised on Western movies and I liked the Western books most boys at my age read—the Karl May books. The German author, Karl May, must have written over 50 books, half of them about the early West, the other half mostly about travel in the Orient. In most of his Western books he had heroes like Old Shatterhand and his Indian friend, Winnetou, and Old Surehand and Old Firehand. These were white people who were living Christian lives and Christian ideals, and who wanted to live in peace with the Indians. His hero's principle was no killing, except in absolute self defense. My Western movie hero was Tom Mix. In comedy movies, I loved the French comedy team of Pat and Patachon. I also enjoyed Laurel and Hardy, Charlie Chaplin, and others; and as a youngster, I loved to see Tarzan movies.

I can't think of a better time than now to tell you about my experiences in the Sultan's Palace. The deposed Sultan of Turkey had two palaces. One was on the European side of the Bosporus, which was gradually opened up to the public and tourists. The Bosporus separates Europe from Asia. There was another palace on the Asiatic side of the Bosporus that was abandoned since the end of World War I, which hardly anyone knew about. It was a very beautiful, impressive-looking palace but very hidden behind trees.

A very close classmate of mine told me that his parents had rented this palace from the Turkish government. He wanted me to come out to this place and play with him. His father was a German doctor named Rabenschlag, who worked at the modern German hospital in Taxim next to all the embassies. His mother was a nurse there, too. My parents hesitated at first to allow me to travel alone on the ferry so far. It was quite a big trip for an 11-year-old school kid on an hour-long ferry.

I traveled with my friend and his parents the first few time, and later on I traveled alone. As a student, I got reduced fare tickets; and I spoke Turkish, so I could read the new Turkish letters (Latin) better than most Turks. I remembered the right ferry line number and knew where the Bosporus crossing ferry would stop. Nothing to it.

The first time I saw the palace with my friend and his parents, it looked very formidable and majestic from the outside. Inside, many walls were cracking and falling apart. The many ponds and fountains had big carps swimming in them. I learned that goldfish turn into carps when they get older. On the left, after you passed the entrance, was a special park. It contained rare and beautiful plants and trees, but now they were overgrown and wild like in a jungle. It had very high trees that were covered with long vines. My friend called this "the Tarzan Park" and tried to swing from the trees. Then I tried it. Like Tarzan, we were swinging, higher and farther, from tree to tree. We could have played in there all day if we wanted.

In the back of the palace was a huge meadow. We never even reached the end of it. I assume it must have been fenced in. Cows and bulls once had been grazing on this meadow because there were many skeletons of them all over the area. We assumed they died of thirst or starvation. In seeing all the horned cow heads we got the idea of putting the cows heads on poles, putting these poles in a circle, and dancing "Indian style" around them. Nobody could see or hear us, not even from the palace. We were in our own world, playing Indians and cowboys, exchanging roles in a very pleasant manner. My friend's parents worked on the palace, making some of the rooms more livable. They only saw us when we came to the palace to eat. We would tell them what we did and what we had experienced; and after eating, we would go out to play again. These were dream times! Dreams came true for us kids. We were two eleven-year-old kids who lived our dreams, if only for a short while.

One of the questions I had for my mother was about my father's customers. As kids we didn't think about that at all. We would play or have homework to do. She said the best customers were the Jewish customers. They were very proud of the new hats they would wear to the temple. The poor Turks wore many kinds of cheap hats, but only the rich Turks bought hats from my father. The Jewish customers liked my father very much. His name, Josef Hoffmann, made them believe he was Jewish. No matter how many times he said he was Catholic, they would insist he was more like one of them. They insisted on seeing him in the temple. One day he agreed to go. He liked it and went again and again, despite everybody knowing he was not Jewish. My mother recalled that she accompanied my father to the temple many times, too.

My mother worried that I was not growing fast enough. She thought there was something wrong with me. She brought me to Doctor Adosidis of the Saint George Hospital, our family doctor. After many tests, he said something about my metabolism and recommended a wine cure. I don't know how old I was—10 or 11. My parents had no idea where to go for a wine cure.

My parents asked Alfred, who was still working for the Turkish/German wine company, if I could get a cure at the company where they made the wine. He said "yes". In a week he would be back there and I could start my cure. He would take me along. Once there, I started eating grapes and drinking wine with my regular meals for two weeks. I had very good meals, but going twice every day through the huge cellar where all the massive, bulky wine barrels were and tasting a little bit of each barrel always brought me into a joyful mood. Alfred was always with me, so I never got drunk. The final result was I did not grow faster—I just like wine very much.

Not long after that Alfred got a job as a sailor on one of the German oil tankers—the Amrun. The ship was traveling from the Mediterranean, through the Dardanelles and the Bosporus, into the Black Sea, and back. Every time his ship stopped in Istanbul and he had time, even for only a day, he would stop and see us. We had moved again, this time into a multi-story apartment building overlooking the Bosporus. From our window we could see if his ship had arrived, but many times we would not be at home. My mother and Alfred had agreed that if he arrived at the port and we were at home, we would hand a long white bed linen from our window. He could see this bed linen easily with binoculars and would come to see us.

We kept up this practice till we left Turkey for good. He switched ships for a while and worked on the sister ship of the Amrun—the Usedom. Always, when his ship stopped in the harbor and we put our bed linen out, he would stop to see us. My parents were his parents. My sisters and I were his sisters and brother. My father said many times that because of Alfred's ordeal in his early life, he grew up faster and was better equipped to live in our world.

In January 1933 we received news from Bielitz. My grandfather Andreas Olschowski had died on January 23, 1933. He died peacefully at the age of 72.

One thing I would like to point out to my readers—in order to understand life in Turkey is when you have a shop in Istanbul, you work right at the display window. No matter what business you are in, baker or hatmaker, you actually work in front of people. They watch you and they see all the moves you do, but they don't understand the purpose of all these movements by your hands. My father was a good hatmaker or "shapkaci" in Turkish. Every move of his hands had a good reason and was taught to him in school. The chemicals he used were measured and calculated to do the job, which was a good looking hat that withstands weather.

In a short time all along the Yüksek Kaldirim new hat shops sprang up, all having a big sign outside reading "shapkaci" (hatmaker), and they had business. Soon, my father had people coming into his shop with a hat that looked more like a rag and claimed my father ruined their hat. Of course my father knew there was no "appreture", no final finish on the hat. My father had to point that out to these people that it could not have been a hat he produced. It was one of the many new shops that had opened up.

Two important things happened in the last years before we left Turkey. With all the foreigners coming in and building new businesses, many Turkish people felt left out of the business boom because they did not have the fundamental knowledge to create a business. Many Greeks were living in Turkey, especially in

Istanbul, who held all kinds of jobs. This formed a hatred between Turks and Greeks that grew to the point where the Turkish government closed their businesses down and expelled all the Greeks. Then came the next government decree—buy only Turkish items, only things produced in Turkey. The slogan was "Turks only buy Turkish wares". This law caused big worries for my father. His quality standards were high. He only bought imported material. The inside leather, the inside silk lining, the outside ribbons or bands, and the imported hats—all were the best available from Europe. He was worried he would lose many customers. He was sure he would lose the business from the President of Turkey.

To my father's surprise, the private secretary of the President of Turkey stopped at my father's shop. My father was scared but felt he had to be open and tell him the truth. After the courtesy cup of coffee, he told him frankly that he could not make his hats with Turkish products. The secretary, Ismet Inönü said, "Good, that's why I bring you the President's hats for repair. He wants the imported items." My father was astonished but happy. He could not believe that the law of the land did not apply to the President.

But the peoples' voices were strong. All the government measures did not create enough work for the Turks, and the government declared that only Turkish people could have jobs and that foreigners would have to leave the country. This included my father. One of the provisions of the law was that you could not take your money out of the country. You could buy Turkish products with your money and, at least this way, take some of your money home. That's what my father did. He bought Turkish and Persian rugs—good ones, and a lot of them and shipped them to Bielitz.

Finally, in 1934, we went home to Bielitz again. To save us money for the trip home, I went to Germany again during school vacation. From there I went by train to Bielitz. My parents and my sisters arrived later. I remember on my train ride, I could not communicate with people. I came through Katowice, Poland, and everybody spoke Polish. Not knowing Polish made me feel like I was a nobody, like I did not exist. Everybody ignored me till I arrived in Bielitz. There everybody spoke German. My grandmother Hoffmann was waiting for me. She could not believe how tall I was. It was a happy reunion. On the way through Bielitz, I saw a familiar fence. It was a stone wall with a small wooden fence built above it. Somehow I always had that fence in my mind. I did not know why I remembered it. My grandmother said, "This is the fence around the Vocational School Campus." And then she said, "You came here to visit your Grandpa and Grandma Olschowski." Now I remembered jumping over the wooden fence. Now I knew I was home.

Chapter 3

Back in Poland

I left Bielitz when I as 5 years old and I was 13 when I returned. Slowly memories of Bielitz returned, with the help of my Grandmother Hoffmann. She pointed out so many places where I had been, what I had seen, and the memories returned. I did not remember my grandmother's house anymore; but as soon as I stood before it, the memories came back. My Grandfather Hoffmann had died in 1930, and I did not remember him anymore. The carpentry shop on the farm was still there, and it looked fairly new to me.

After the death of my grandfather, his farm was divided up between his children. We were sill in Turkey at that time. Each one received an equal part, but my father received the farm and the surrounding buildings and orchard. Each of the other children received only land, which was now used as pasture for my grandmother's cows. She had three cows and would bring them to pasture herself. She was 67 years old at the time I came back and was bringing the cows out to pasture twice a day, milking them, making butter and buttermilk, harvesting the fruit from the orchard, getting the eggs from the chicken coop, and bringing all that twice a week to the market in Bielitz.

At first, my father looked over the job market but found it hard to find a niche for himself in the textile industry. He was selling off his carpets and making good money, even when he had to travel to meet customers for his carpets.

My Grandfather Olschowski also had died a year before we returned. He was 73. My Grandmother Olschowski was still living. My mother, my sisters, and I visited her many times. She lived in a private house now. She had many of her children, including my mother, help her in her old age. She was 76 years old and died at the age of 79.

I was 13 years old and big enough to help my grandmother. In the morning, I had to bring the cows out to pasture. Yes, I was a cowboy now—a real cowboy! The cows were chained together at the horns. I would walk in between the cows, where the chain was, and control them. For a while we had three cows, two to my right, one to my left, and the chain was long enough to control them. I had to watch out that they didn't get spooked by a barking dog or by bees and run off. If one was grazing too fast, I had to control it by pulling on the chain to the head. They got used to grazing together and adjusted pretty well to each other.

After a while, it became a boring chore to walk constantly back and forth over the pasture with them. They got adjusted to you and you had to get adjusted to them. I was all alone on the pasture and would sing mostly loud, melodious songs. Suddenly I would hear some of the songs from other cowboys on the neighboring pastures. I spent hours doing nothing but singing and thinking. It was a great time to let my mind wander, to think about so many things. I'd bring the cows to the pasture in the morning and bring them back at noon for milking. In the afternoon I'd go out with them again and bring them back in the evening for milking.

I never had to do the milking. My grandmother was the only one who milked the cows by hand. I helped in the barn. My grandmother would churn butter daily in the old butter churn—of course, by hand. I can still see my grandmother going twice a week to the market. Sometimes she had a little hand cart full of stuff for the market. She was always dressed like the other farm women of that area. Only by the scarf, the "babooshka", could you identify her. She pulled the cart up the hill and then the long way down to the market in Bielitz and back.

Finally I met all my uncles and aunts and all the male and female cousins and the many distant relatives I had. I never realized I had that many relatives. In Istanbul I had none—only my cousins in the St. George Boarding School, but we seldom saw each other. Here I had so many. It took some time to remember all the names.

I'd like to describe how my grandparent's property looked at the time I lived there. The military garrison was outside the city limits. Next to it was the non-commissioned officer's building. We could see these buildings from our house. From there a street led downhill till it crossed a creek. There were no houses on this street. Past the creek the property began and the street continued. First was our farm house. Later on, some of my uncles built houses on their land. My grandparents' property was on the east side of the street, and it continued along the street till it ended in a deep ravine. To the right, or better said, to the east was the train station Obervorstadt (Bielsko Gorne).

Right after the station the railroad tracks began to climb and turn. I stood many times on top of the ravine looking at the locomotive struggling to pull the train from a standing start at the station to the climbing bend and often slide all the way back to the station and try again. Freight trains had it especially tough.

I took this train many times to see my cousin, Robert Olschowski, who lived only three or four stations away. He was one year older than I and was a good skier. Skiing was new to me, so I was glad to learn to ski from him. In turn, he learned how to fly model airplanes from me. Rubber bands were the only power source we had at that time. My planes were sailing planes. A little wind was enough to launch them from a hill and fly and sail for a long distance. Robert loved pigeons and had built extensive living quarters for his pigeons right above his father's garage. His dream was to become a forest ranger.

Once in a while we heard from Alfred. He wrote us that because he was a German citizen, he was drafted into the German Navy.

It was a tough period of adjustment for me. I knew French, Turkish, English and, of course, German—but not a word of Polish. Because of this, I did not get accepted into these schools. I was tested by different schools; and the tests showed that my education was so highly advanced, I would have to go to the schools which would not accept me because of my lack of Polish. So, I had to go to the last grade of elementary school in order to learn Polish. My parents also worried about me not being able to continue my English and French. To keep my French, I needed only French conversation. My parents decided to pay for my continued French education by hiring a French teacher in town, where I went faithfully for years to continue speaking French and keep up my large French vocabulary.

I finally was accepted into the German Evangelical School for Boys. The girls school was just adjacent to the boys school. They had good teachers, but all the subjects they were teaching I had taken years before. I knew the answer to all the questions the teachers asked, but I was not allowed to raise my hand. All the subjects were familiar to me, with the exception of "Polish History", which was taught in German. I became a nuisance in class. I was just bored. I was put on the last bench of the class where I could do whatever I wanted to, as long as I did not disturb the class.

My biology teacher did not agree to not let me participate in class. He was interested in my life in Turkey and wanted to know all about it. So, in biology, I had to often come up to the teacher's desk and tell the class about my life in Turkey. I noticed that the whole class was quiet. Everybody was listening. Everybody had their eyes focused on me.

I was talking from the point of view of a young boy, and that's what interested everyone. I talked, for instance, about playing cowboys and Indians and Tarzan in the field and garden of the former Sultan of Turkey. That our whole family went camping by a bay on the Bosporus. I told them about the classmates I had. One was the oldest son of the Grandvesir of Istanbul. Others were sons of Pashas and former employees of the Sultan. I told them that some of my mother's friends lived in a harem. I doubt they knew for sure what a harem was.

I had lived all these boyhood dreams and experiences, and I told them to my classmates. There were transformed into another world and loved it. Everybody told me it was their best class. The experiences of life in Turkey you could not find in a book. It was interesting for the biology teacher, too. He liked me very much. I got good grades from him, but I did not contribute much to biology. At least the class leaned about life in a different country of the world, and that was interesting for them.

I had another great teacher in our school. He was my math teacher. He was Jewish and a very fine person. We had a bully in our class, a big tall guy whom you did not dare to get into a fight with. Math was one subject I was good at. Normally I was not called on to answer; but if the teacher needed help to explain something difficult, he would ask me to do it. One day this bully wrote something on the blackboard that was very offensive to Jews, but he had no time to erase it because the math teacher came in.

The teacher did not see who wrote it but he tried to find out. One student pointed the finger at the bully. This bully stood up mad and said it was not him but Sig who wrote it. Nobody stood up for me and my denial did not help. My teacher came to me and said he was shocked to find out that I did it. Whatever I said did not make a difference. The teacher was convinced I did it. Nobody was willing to stand up to the bully. I don't know why this bully had put the finger on me. He may have been a coward and did not want to stand up for what he did.

I had a lot of friends in my class. Viki, Helen's brother, was in my class at that time but I did not know Helen yet. I had many friends who wanted to learn more about life in Turkey. Some friends wanted to get to know my sisters, who were in the school next to ours. We did not have too many Polish students in our class, mostly German-speaking students.

The school taught Polish but they made an exception for me. In the Polish class I did not participate by talking, just listening. I had Polish history and cultural development in German. In Polish it was difficult for me to pronounce words with sz or cz. This was so different from all the other languages I knew. Most of the languages I knew had their origin in Latin, or some of the words had their origin in Latin. Suddenly I had to learn a Slavic language. In the beginning it was very hard for me, but I got it slowly. I knew how to pronounce some words probably in a very strong German accent.

Our farm was close to the Evangelical church in Alt Bielitz. Each Easter morning a band would play in the bell tower, right under the steeple. It was the famous Borgel Band. They would play hymns and folk songs. The sound filled the valleys of Alt Bielitz and the surrounding area. If the wind was strong, the music faded in and out. If there was no wind, you could hear every note. These were wonderful and beautiful times. We would listen to this music that flowed to so many suburbs. My father knew the names of the players, which did not mean anything to me till much later when I met Helen. It was Helen's grandfather, George Borgel, who lead the band and her uncle, Hans, played in the band. They were Catholic. So what? They were praising the Lord and made everybody happy at Easter.

Not far from the Evangelical church was the small Catholic church of Alt Bielitz, the St. Stanislaus Church. In 1935, the St. Stanislaus Church in Alt Bielitz celebrated the 800th anniversary of its founding. It was a very big and important event, and Catholics from far away came; and the Catholic youth organization erected a 20 foot high cross on top of the Alt Bielitz Anhoehe (a high hill overlooking the Bielitz skyline). Helen was in the group who erected that cross.

I normally went to the big Catholic church in the town of Bielitz. It was the St. Nickolaus Church where I was baptized and it was a carbon copy of St. Marks Church in Venice, Italy. That was the church that Helen and her brothers and sisters attended and were singing in the choir.

After elementary school, I had to plan for my next schooling. Industry at that time was mostly textile oriented. Everything from making textiles for cloth or felt, to building the machinery to make it, were in this town. My father wanted me to go into textile machinery manufacturing. He had a lot of friends who helped me to get into a program where I could get a fast apprentice training through all the stages in the manufacturing process and which would end with my engineering degree.

I started to work at Gustav Josephy's Erben, a manufacturing plant where my Grandfather Hoffmann had worked and many of my friends worked. Later my sister, Erika, would work in the drafting department. My confirmation sponsor, Robert Pudelek, also worked there as an engineer. I had to sign a contract with Gustav Josephy's Erben, where I agreed to learn the trade from the beginning as an apprentice to the engineering degree and spend a minimum of one year working for them as an engineer.

My lack of knowledge of the Polish language was slowing me down. I knew my subjects well, but somebody in class had to translate for me what the teacher said. When the teacher asked me to tell the class what the result of my homework was, I could not tell them because I did not know the words. During the day I worked as an apprentice, and in the evening till late at night I went to pre-engineering classes. On top of that, I had to go to pre-military training from the school. Everybody had to go. I was trained to march to Polish commands, shoot rifles and throw hand grenades—all the things you have to do in the military. I felt I was playing war. I had never used a rifle before or even had a rifle in my hand before. We also had to take an oath to defend Poland in case of war.

My studying did not leave me with much time for helping my grandmother. First I could only help her one time a day, getting the cows to the pasture. She now had only two cows; but she still brought them out to pasture, milked them and went twice a week with the produce to the market. My sisters had their own problems with school and could not help with the cows, but they helped as much as their age and strength allowed.

By this time my sister, Brunhild, had entered the School of Commerce where she learned everything from typing to shorthand, bookkeeping, and managing a business.

I joined a group of young people. They were named the "Wandervogel"—a group of hikers and skiers who loved the outdoors. This organization was founded at the time this town was Austrian by the grandfathers and great grandfathers of the group that existed at that time. Their fathers, grandfathers, and great grandfathers had built scores of lodges and cottages with their own hands intended for the use of the Wandervogel members only. Any time you went into the mountains, you had to get the keys for the building. It was meant for Wandervogel groups only. I wanted to hike and ski, and the Beskid Mountains were an idyllic place to do that. It was a very active group of people.

Just before I joined, the Wandervogel and the Guttempler had joined together. Through this joining together of two youth groups, it became a group abstaining from drinking and smoking. They were very environmentally conscious and were the first organization to lead in environmental causes. They did not care what religion you were—Catholic, Evangelical or Jewish. We all loved hiking in the mountains, the singing and camping, sports, and the skiing in wintertime. Now, any free time I had was spent hiking and skiing in the mountains. But there was not much free time for me.

Gustav Josephy's Erben was a union shop. We had a German Socialist union as our main union but a Polish Communist union was trying to get a foothold in this factory. I had to attend many union meetings, in which the Communist union got stronger in their demands and more violent. It was vicious at these meetings. The violence was shown in the beating and clubbing of the German Socialist union members.

I got really scared when I saw all that happening at the meetings. The Communist union turned to violence because, in my opinion, their revolutionary ideas were that they needed violence to eliminate people who were in the way to where they were going. The Socialists were a lot milder in their violence, but they were defending their point of view very fiercely. I knew our German Socialist union representative well. Later on when the German troops had marched in, to my father's surprise and to mine, he had become the head of the Gestapo. I only knew that from my father many years later.

Once in a while Alfred wrote us. The latest we heard from him was that he was now in Peenemunde, a harbour town in the Baltic Sea, where he was teaching U-boat crew men how to escape from a sunken U-boat.

I have read lately many books about the development of the Bielitz area. It is hard to condense all this in a story. For the sake of explaining the next happenings, it is important to do. It is from the book "Geschichte der deutchen Sprachinsel Bielitz (Schlesien)" by Walter Kuhn. It was published in Wurzburg, Germany, in 1981 by Holzner. It is in the Library of Congress.

The development of Bielitz as an area began around the year 1260. It took long years to develop as an area of settlement and village development. I saw a document in the Melk Abbey in Austria in 1980 from the 13th Century, where the people in the Bielitz area had asked some neighboring lords or dukes for schooling and protection. In the second half of the 15th Century, Bielitz became a border town of Silesia against Poland. The villages east of Biala belonged to Poland. The earliest written history of this development was documented in the 14th Century, which shows already a closed community which had German laws. In 1526, the Sudeten area with Silesia became part of Austria. Bielitz now was a border town of the Habsburg Reich against Poland; while in the south, the border was threatened by invading Turks and Kuruz. After 1742, Bielitz was the most eastern border town of Austria and remained as part of Austria till after World War I. Through the Versailles Treaty and connecting treaties, in a 1920 plebiscite the Bielitz area was handed over to Poland.

In Bielitz, a lot of people did not speak Polish. These were mostly older people who were not going back to school and never intended to. People who worked in public offices had to speak Polish and German. You had to speak Polish if you had business dealings with the Polish Federal government. In the market place in Bielitz one could hear Polish and German. My grandmother spoke Polish and German. If you were bargaining with people, you had to know both.

In certain shops nobody spoke Polish. These were old shops which already existed before the plebiscite of 1920. These people spoke German in the Austrian time and the Polish government did not mind them still speaking German. These old shops were serving many of the same customers they had in the old Austrian time. These customers were getting older and they liked the old stores and the storekeepers.

In the time before 1920, the town of Bielitz was considered a jewel in the Austrian empire. It brought higher education to all the people in this region. The aim of the old Austrian Empire was to unite people through education, regardless of nationalities. There was tranquillity and understanding and intermarriage between Poles, Austrians, Germans, Czechs, Slovakians, Hungarians and so many other nationalities.

My own opinion of the politics of the old Austrian Empire is mixed. It was a nation with different nationalities living close together. If it ever could be ruled harmoniously, it would have to be with mutual respect for each nationality. Austria's claim, never conquered or fought to achieve the Empire is shallow, considering that kings, queens, dukes, and other lesser monarchs were hardly the representatives of the people.

Let me continue with my life in Poland. My grades were fine. I learned a lot and fast, but my knowledge of the Polish language did not catch up with my other subjects, especially in my pre-military training. My classmates had to help me and cover up for me. One day we were called for a two-week training in a town deep in the eastern part of Poland. This town is now part of Russia. My father was worried because he knew this area. He knew if they found out I could not speak Polish, I would be treated as a person who refused to speak Polish.

The anti-German sentiment by now had become anti-Hitler, anti-Nazi sentiment; and not speaking Polish was equivalent to being a traitor or a spy. A lot of my classmates were going with me to that "Obuz" (camp), who knew of my problem speaking Polish. They told me not to worry. So I was shipped by train to the camp and worried what would happen.

Our training consisted of lots of marching, shooting on the rifle range, cleaning up the barracks, barrack inspection, rifle and uniform inspection, and singing. Some of the songs cussed Hitler and compared him to a bitch. They had to be sung very loud when we marched through that little Polish town back to our barracks. I did sing loud but when I was asked something, I did not answer. When my friends noticed I did not answer, they answered for me. They said I was retarded, weak in my head, and things like that. I never said a word all the two weeks. I guess that saved my life. When I came back to Bielitz where everybody spoke German, I felt free again.

Hitler's troops marched into Austria in 1938. Because Bielitz was a former Austrian town, a lot of people were initially sympathetic to that, but not with the idea of Hitler's army controlling the country. My father was sympathetic to the Austrian Army. He as a sergeant in the Austrian Army in World War I; but as Hitler's troops marched into Czechoslovakia, it was clear to·most of us that Hitler's aim was revision of the Versailles Treaty. He wanted to regain all the territories that this treaty had taken away from Austria and Germany after World War I.

These events were not only seen as dangerous for the government of Poland, they were seen as dangerous to the Polish people in the street. The anti-Hitler and anti-Nazi sentiment turned into full-blown anti-German sentiment. The Polish people saw a war coming.

I and many of my friends believed we did not want to lose our own culture. We were not willing to give up our Austrian identity, but we surely did not want a war to break out over our territory. We wanted to live in peace. We already had the feeling that Germany may march into Poland. The Polish government had this belief months before it happened. There were fortifications built around the town to the west—bunkers and pillboxes for the defense of the city. They cut down beautiful and majestic trees and parks were dug up and made into fortifications.

We started to dig trenches all around our factory, which was a big complex with many buildings. We had to dig out these trenches deep enough for a man to stand and shoot, lined with wooden frames and sandbags. This was done under the control of, what we were told, three Polish officers. They were all in civilian clothes. They all had pistols in their hands and would say, if we did not work hard enough, we would be shot on the spot. They would walk on top of the trench, aim the pistol at our heads, and shout at us.

Everybody from our plant was working in the trenches. From engineer to apprentice, they all had to work. With the shovels in our hands, we tried to figure out what we would do if these guys began to shoot us. We planned that the first one will be hit on his knee cap with the shovel, the other one would be hit with a shovel of dirt in the eyes, and the third one would be pulled into the trench and there we would kill him. It was an awful idea to kill somebody, but we could not stand to see them with their pistols waving in their hands, walking up and down on top of the trench and pointing the pistols at our heads. We kept thinking—now he is going to shoot us. This is the end for me. Every one of us was afraid. Who will be the first one to be killed by them? It was one episode in my life where I still shudder just thinking of it. We finished the trenches without incident.

Alfred wrote us that he wanted a combat assignment very badly. He was sick and tired of teaching Navy men how to escape from sunken U-boats.

During the last weeks before the German troops marched in, we got leaflets which told us to join civil defense. They wanted people to become air raid wardens. In the area where our farm was, I was the only young man who was willing to do it. In fact, my father suggested it, knowing from his experience in World War I how important civil defense and air raid protection was, so I agreed to join. They had a meeting where the things I had to do were explained to me. I had to wear an armband indicating I was an air raid warden. I had to observe and report where the planes were, how many, what kind and so on, and told what to do if bombs fell and where to report it.

It was the last days of August 1939. I had a bicycle which I used to go to work and to school. It was registered with city hall, like all bikes were. I got a letter to report in the morning on September 1, 1939, to city hall in Bielitz with my bike. Refusal to come would be interpreted as refusal of doing your civil duty and will be punished. I found out friends of mine all had received letters, all approximately my age, all had bikes, and all were supposed to come to city hall on September 1, 1939. My father said, "Be careful. There is something going on if they ask you to come with the bike. I can't figure out why, but there must be a reason why they asked you to come." I was worried to leave my post as air raid warden. I was the only one in that area. My father said, "You better report, otherwise they will hunt you down and you will be put in jail."

September 1, 1939 arrived. In the morning hours I was getting my bike ready for the trip to city hall when suddenly I heard airplanes flying into our area. Then I heard anti-aircraft guns shooting at them from the fortifications all around us. We heard on the radio that Germany had invaded Poland and General Rydz Smigly, the head of the Polish government, had said the Germans will not get even a button from our uniforms. I knew they must be German air planes. I looked up at the spectacle in the air, at the anti-aircraft shells exploding. The planes were flying very high. Suddenly my father came running out of the house screaming at me, "Get in the house! Do you want to be killed by the flak pieces coming down?" It did not dawn on me that all the anti-aircraft flak came down after exploding and you can get hurt or killed by the shrapnel. I told my father I had to go to city hall. He said, "Wait till this thing is over. Don't go now." The planes were probably observation planes since no bombs were dropped.

After the planes were gone, I took my bike and went to city hall. When I arrived I saw a lot of trucks there, all kinds of them. People were loading these trucks with city hall documents. A lot of my friends were loading the trucks. I left my bike outside and went inside city hall. I was told by a man to whom I showed the letter to go and help load the trucks. I asked him, "What do you want me to do with my bike?"

He said, "Leave it outside."

As I was leaving to go help my friends loading the trucks, I asked this guy angrily, "What do you want me to do first? I am an air raid warden. I have a job elsewhere and you want me to do a job here. Which one is more important?"

He looked at me, looked at my armband and said, "You are an air raid warden. Go, you are not needed here. But I do requisition your bike." I asked him if he could give me a paper stating that he requisitioned my bike. He signed on a little piece of paper that he did requisition my bike, and I took off. I looked at my friends and waved, not knowing that this was the last time I would see them.

What happened to them I will never know. They left with the trucks on the Polish retreat. Were they bombed by German planes or killed by Poles? We never heard from them anymore. Being an air raid warden and having my armband saved my life; otherwise, I would have been with them. Strange how fate turns everything around. Being an air raid warden was going to be dangerous. Now it saved my life.

When I got home my father was listening to the radio. He said that Hitler had marched into the Polish corridor, the northern part of Poland. In our area, near the border town of Teschen (Cieszyn), heavy fighting was going on at the Jablunkau Pass. Nothing else was happening near us, at least in the area we could see.

In connection with this Jablunkau Pass, I like to tell you from reading books about it, what actually happened at that time. The Germans had assembled mas-

sive troops at this point of the border. They had to face the heavily fortified
Jablunkau Pass. The Germans attacked the pass from three sides. A frontal attack
to keep the defenders occupied with the defense and two pincer attacks right and
left of this pass, where they used Austrian mountain climbers from the famous
Edelweiss Division. While the defenders were busy defending the pass, the mountain climbers climbed right and left, almost unseen by the defenders, through the
mountains and finally attacked the defenders from the rear. Of course we did not
know that at that time. On September 2, 1939, the pass was already wiped out.
There was hardly any defense by the Polish troops from there to Bielitz. The
Polish troops were in retreat.

The next day, September 2, 1939, still nothing happened around us. The city
was quiet, almost paralyzed, viewed from our area.

On September 3, 1939, it was awfully quiet in the morning. Going uphill
right above our street was the garrison where the Polish cavalry was stationed.
The first building facing our street was the non-commissioned officer's building—a modern building where all the sergeants and their families lived. We
could easily see it from our house. Normally there was always lots of activity;
but on September 3, 1939, it was very quiet.

My father and I went up the street to see what was going on. In the first building everything was abandoned. We kept on going to the open gate of the garrison.
Every building, every stable, everything was empty. There was an eerie quiet
emptiness we could feel. We did not know what had happened or what was going
on. We went further up the main street which came from the west. We saw
German military vehicles coming down the street. People were standing at the
side of the road and some had flowers.

When the troops came closer, we heard them speaking in the Austrian dialect
and they had an Edelweiss badge on their uniform sleeves. They were from the
Edelweiss Division and they came down the old Kaiser street (Emperor Street),
past a little monument which still stood in front of the Alexanderfeld School. The
German inscription told of the day and time the Austrian Emperor, Franz Josef II,
stopped and was greeted by the people of Bielitz and the school children of
Alexanderfeld offered him flowers. This had a very sentimental effect on all the
people. Our town, being a former Austrian town, felt happy that it was Austrian
troops that liberated them, not German troops. Sometime later, we knew how
wrong we were.

We realized the townspeople did not flee from the coming troops. They were
all hiding. Now they all came out with flowers, candies, beer and wine—whatever they had to thank the soldiers. The Polish soldiers and their government had
fled and also the radical Poles were also gone. Some Poles who had lived under
the Austrian Emperor Franz Josef II were there cheering the Austrian troops.

Talking to people, we heard what happened the night before. Massacres had occurred all over town. In their frustration that they had to leave the town, all the radical elements got together and went house by house, dragged people out and killed them in front of their houses. They clubbed them to death, beat and kicked them to death, or shot them. One of the first ones they killed was my former biology teacher, a person loved by every one in our town. He was a good teacher, but he probably had certain enemies who hated him.

I found out other shocking news. A very good friend of mine, Hans Jenkner, was killed. I don't remember anymore what he was, either an electrician or telephone repair man. On the night between the second and the third of September 1939, he was sent from his company to repair some wires. He was working alone on this line when he was confronted by a group of radicals who were defending some area. They probably mistook him for a spy, so they murdered him. The next morning some people found his mutilated body. It was a great shock for me.

Part III

Years in War

Chapter 1

World War II

For the world, the Allied Declaration of War was on September 3, 1939. For us in Bielitz, it was Liberation Day. Some people spent the first few days at the cemetery, burying family members or friends. The main train line goes through a tunnel under Bielitz to avoid heavy traffic on streets and roads—especially the heavily traveled road from west to east. This was the retreat route of the Polish troops. To stop the advancing German troops, the Polish Army blew up the tunnel through the city. The main streets were not damaged. Everything else was heavily damaged. It did not slow down the advancing German troops.

The irony is that Communist Russia marched into Poland from the east a few weeks later. The big, mighty Nazi Germany and the big, mighty Communist Russia carved up Poland between themselves. In a secret agreement between German Foreign Minister Ribbentrop and Russian Foreign Minister Molotov, Poland was divided up between them. When the German troops marched into Poland we, the population in Bielitz, knew nothing of all this secret agreement.

The population had thought that Austrian troops had marched into Bielitz, despite the fact that they were all wearing German uniforms. Behind these troops came regular German troops and officials who took over the government. They were judges, mayors, and other officials necessary for running a town. Most of them were Nazis that were not needed or wanted in Germany and were released from their jobs to become judges and mayors in the occupied territories. The Austrian troops were just pawns in all of this and had nothing to say or do. Germany was ruling everything.

Our hope for the good old times under Austrian rule had vanished. Before we knew what had happened, one radical group had vanished while another radical group had taken over. It shocked the population. For instance, the new government issued ration cards. They rationed the food according to your beliefs and your race. If you were a German or an Austrian Nazi, you got ration card #1—the best ration card you could have. Ration card #2 went to Germans and Austrians without any political affiliation. These meant less rations. The next cards, #3, were for people who were half-Polish and half-Austrian or German. You had to fill out a form to get ration cards.

Soon there was no classification for Austrians anymore, just Germans and Poles or Czechoslovakians. Austrians were regarded as Germans. When it came to the time when they asked you, "What are you, German or Pole?", many people did not know. They had intermarried, spoke German and Polish, and were at a loss to define what they were. They got #3. If you were a Pole, you got #4. If you were Jewish or part Jewish, you were classified #5—the smallest ration you could get. If you were Jewish, you had to wear a Star of David on your clothes at all times and work on the streets, removing rubble from the blown up tunnel.

Under the Austrian Kaiser, Franz Josef II, the Jews were given a rightful chance to live. Even under the Polish government the Jews had their own businesses, their own factories, their own soccer team, Hakoa, and they played other teams in the leagues. Now they were treated as misfits and criminals.

My father had a lot of friends in the group of Jews working in the rubble. Some were owners of factories and business friends, and some were just old school friends. They suddenly lost everything. My father told me that when he passed them while they were working in the rubble, they would plead with my father to help them. He could not stop and have a conversation with them or he would be immediately suspected of trying to help them. So my father devised other ways, mostly with trusted friends, at night somewhere where nobody could see them. He came to the conclusion that the only way to help them is to have a way to get to their properties confiscated by the Nazis. So he tried to become commissioner for confiscated properties. He was a well-known citizen in the community, and a lot of people trusted him. I found out some of it many years later.

All political parties, other than the Nazi party, were dissolved. All the youth groups were dissolved and their properties confiscated and handed over to the "Hitler Jugend" (the Hitler Youth organization). The Wandervogel had many lodges and shelter houses, many built in Austrian times. Now they were going to take all this away from us. We had one last meeting of the Wandervogel before we were to hand them the keys to all the properties. The Wandervogel leaders proposed to join the Hitler Youth in order to have something to say about the disposal of our properties. Many opposed this idea. Many of us in Wandervogel believed we could change the Hitler Youth. The decision was made. We would hold on to the keys and join the Hitler Youth.

Barely six months after the Germans had marched into Poland, I was told by the factory where I worked that I would be drafted into the German Army. One day when I came home, there was a letter ordering me to report for physical examination. My father hoped that they wouldn't take me and I thought I would be too short and would be declassified. The day of the examination came. After first telling me I was too short, the draft board reversed itself and said I was okay. So I was drafted into the German Army.

I was quickly sworn in and had to vow to obey the Fuehrer. I as ordered to report for boot camp in Berlin. Many of us rookies were from Bielitz. When they handed me the uniform, the smallest size was too wide and too long. I could almost wrap it around twice. They sent me to the tailor shop to have it altered. The tailor told me that there was no way to tuck everything in or shorten the jacket without shortening the pockets, and it was against regulations to do that. He only made it one inch shorter and tucked a little bit in on the sides. When I got back to the sergeant, he sent me back to the tailor because it looked as if nothing was done to it. The tailor tucked in another half inch. I looked awful!

Now came the actual boot camp training. We had a drill sergeant who was from the original hundred thousand man army the Germans were allowed to have after the Treaty of Versailles. We had heard of the German drill sergeants, but this was not drilling—this was torture and inhuman behavior. We were constantly shouted at, but we got used to it. Marching and running with your clean rifle and full gear, up and down the field. We got used to that, too. What we could not get used to was running and crawling all day in the field and trenches and then stand for rifle inspection. If you failed rifle inspection you got another two or three hour punishment exercise on Saturday, while other companies stayed in the building and relaxed.

Almost everybody failed these rifle inspections. So on Saturday, the whole company was back for punishment exercises. This went on week after week, and it always seemed to be our company. It became a contest between us in the company and the sergeant. It seemed as if the sergeant was there to break us physically. We were all sure of one thing—if we saw action, the first shot would be fired into the sergeant's back. Every one of us was willing to do it.

When we got gas masks, we had to try them out in the test chamber. You had to adjust the straps to fit your face. Everyone's mask fit but mine. After adjusting the straps to the very end, I had half an inch of space on the right and left of my cheeks. My sergeant said we would see how it worked in the gas chamber. I told him that's too late. He only shrugged his shoulders.

The time came to go to the gas chamber, and I again showed my gas mask to the sergeant. He again said we would see in the gas chamber. After we went in the chamber, we were told to pound on the door if we couldn't stand it. As soon as the tear gas was released, I could smell and feel it and my eyes teared. I looked for the door and pounded wildly. They let me out and I cried and shouted at the sergeant, "I told you so!"

This time he took a look at my gas mask and noticed the space at the sides. He said there was nothing he could do. These were regulation masks. When I asked him how to protect myself he said, "You will be the first to die." When I protested he said, "So what."

On one of these Saturday punishment exercises, we had our gas masks on, and for hours were marching up and down the field and through the trenches. One by one men collapsed and were brought to the infirmary, but the sergeant kept on hounding us. It was hot and humid. We had just finished goose stepping in front of the sergeant for half an hour and now we had to hold our rifles stiff-handed in front of us or side ways. We could not even do it for a few minutes. The sergeant screamed his commands, cussing at us and saying he would get us Polaks and Austrians cut down to size. He would make Prussian soldiers out of us, no matter how long it took.

There were now only four men left on the field—the three strongest men from our company and me—the shortest. Everyone's gas mask was tight but mine was not. I could breath. There we were standing, holding our rifles, following the sergeant's order. It must have been pathetic to see. We were on our last strength. I hardly moved the rifle. I heard the sergeant shouting but I hardly reacted to him. I did not want the sergeant to break me, neither physically nor spiritually.

I did not see what happened next. I was too intent on staying upright and not collapsing. From the infirmary building came three soldiers—a captain, a lieutenant and a staff sergeant. The captain stopped in front of us. He relieved our sergeant of his duties, and the staff sergeant took over command of us. We were sent back to our quarters. What we did not know was the infirmary was filling up with all the rookies which brought our captain, the company commander, to the infirmary. By questioning the rookies, he found out that this occurred regularly every Saturday. That's when our sergeant was relieved of his duties. He was later demoted to private and transferred to another outfit.

I had written about this incident to my mother. She must have taken the next train to Berlin. The next day I was told to get into uniform because my mother and sister were at the gate. What I did not know was that my mother appeared at the gate and demanded to see me. They told her that during rookie training there would be no visiting rights granted. She demanded to speak with the officer of the guard, or my company commander, or his superiors and so on. She refused to leave until she had spoken to the highest in command. Finally she got somebody to listen and I was told to meet my mother at the gate. When I went through the gate and say my mother she shouted, "Sigi, what did they do to you?" My sister, Brunhild, snapped a picture.

I looked very bad with my long uniform. I must have lost some weight, too, so the uniform actually looked longer. She insisted on taking me out to feed me after my "starvation". The guard at the gate did not allow it since I was still in rookie training. Again she insisted on talking to an officer till she got a leave for me, even for just a few hours—enough time to stuff me with food. I was instructed by the guards not to mention to anybody that I had gotten leave.

After boot camp, some men were chosen for training as sharp shooters, machine gunners and so on. I was asked about my education and my language skills. I told them I knew French, English, and Turkish, hoping to become a clerk. They decided to put me into motorcycle training. The first day I was full of expectation till I saw the motorcycle. It was a big, heavy motorcycle with a side car to train in. Everything went fine. No problem on the streets, except that it was kind of hard to turn. I managed it.

I then had to go into field training, which was a problem. With my light weight, I bounced up and down and could not control the motorcycle. I was taken off that training because I had tipped over so many times. I could have killed myself, but luckily I did not get hurt. My new training consisted of machine gun, mortar and rifle shooting. Oh yes, and marching, marching, and marching. Marching was no problem for me. Even in full gear, I could march for miles and hours. In boot camp I had learned to harden my feet for marching; after all, I was in the infantry. But, it was as a clerk that they wanted me. I could do a lot more as a clerk than outside in the field. Later on they put me in the mail room. Picking up mail and sorting it was my job from that time on.

Chapter 2

The First Action

On May 10, 1940, Germany marched into Belgium, the Netherlands, and France. We were stationed in Dueren by Cologne and were on alert, but saw no action. Some days after that we went by train and then by truck into the war zone. We were ready for action but we were never used. We followed the route of the retreating British troops and saw the tragedy of war first hand. As far as you could see the streets were lined with British military vehicles and equipment, either abandoned or destroyed. The British soldiers defending them or fighting in them were still there. Dead. Killed by bullets, shrapnel. Or bombs. They were not removed for burial because there was no time for that.

The fighting must have happened shortly before. People were there, mostly Belgians and Hollanders, snapping pictures. It was terrible. Finally we reached Dunkirk and the English Channel. On the spot where the British troops had been evacuated, probably during low tide, the coast was lined with vehicles covered with water. They formed a long line of cars and trucks way out into the ocean. The high tide had flooded in now and you could only see the tops of the vehicles sticking out of the water. Bodies were washing ashore everywhere, mostly British.

There were German burial units working constantly, but they could not keep up with the bodies washing ashore. People from the town were snapping pictures and selling them. There were pictures of bodies hanging out of trucks or tanks. Some photographers must have made a bundle selling these pictures as souvenirs. War is death for one person and profit for another. This was just the beginning of my experience. Over the years this idea of death and profit no longer bothered me. It became a part of life I grudgingly accepted.

We were stationed on the coast in Belgium and were quartered in houses which the owners were forced to evacuate. I was put on guard duty, guarding ammunition depots, our quarters, and headquarters. You guard, you sleep, and after a little time for yourself, you go on guard duty again. You have to always be alert. Guards often got killed by snipers. People could sneak up on you and cut your throat or stab you before you could shoot or shout. Ammunition depots were prime targets. We knew we were not a friend in this country. We were their enemy.

We were stationed in an area where planes, returning from air raids over Germany, dropped any unused bombs left in the bomb bay. They could not land with any bombs in the bomb bay. They probably were supposed to drop them as soon as they were over water; but sometimes, when it was cloudy or at night, they had no way of knowing for sure if they had reached the English Channel., That's when the bombs hit us.

Ever since we had crossed into Belgium, I had thought about the plane flying over our house when I was born. I was thinking—I was born with a plane flying over me; maybe I will die with a plane flying over me. Here on the coast, this thought occurred to me more often, whenever bombs were dropped short of the water and hit us. We could tell they were not aimed and hardly ever did any big damage. They usually fell on the beach or into the dunes without doing much damage to persons or property.

One day I was standing guard and I heard the returning planes again. At that same time my relief, a very good friend of mine, came and took my place. As I walked away, a bomb hit the spot where I had been standing and blew my friend apart. It knocked me down, but I was not injured. All the years of the war, the shock of this made me wonder—am I supposed to die when a plane flies over me? Why was I spared? All through the war I wondered why did somebody else get it? Why didn't I get it? The fatal bullet! The death!

Chapter 3

Greece

We left the English Channel and were stationed elsewhere. Our unit was out-fitted with tropical uniforms. The ones that Rommel's Africa Corps would later wear. We did not know what to think of it or where we were heading. We had shorts and heavy winter coats. We also had some long bands that you were sup-posed to wrap around your belly three or four times. It was like an abdominal bandage. With these and some more strange items, we got on a box car train for Greece. Somewhere in Greece we transferred to trucks and soon we arrived in Athens. From there we went to a peninsula where we were stationed.

Now we knew why we had shorts and winter coats. The days were really hot and the night awfully cold. I was standing guard constantly. We were attached to a medical unit; and over time, I met and got to know all the doctors and medics. One medic was a young Catholic priest, Father Jungst, who was our priest. We had no chaplains. At Sunday mass we had a double altar outdoors where, on one side, the Catholic priest and on the other side the Evangelical minister said mass—sometimes both at the same time, and you could hear both of them.

One morning, as usual, I was standing guard at the gate. Every morning our chief doctor, I believe he was a colonel, went out in his car. I had to present arms and open the gate. This one morning he was early because I was still wearing my winter coat and had not changed to shorts. He looked at me from his car and said, "Soldier, come over." So I came over. He said, "Lean forward." So I leaned for-ward. I was almost nose to nose with him when he asked, "Where is your officer of the guard?"

I said, "He is inside the guard house."

He said, "Call him out." I went back to the guard house and called him out. He came right out and the doctor told him, "Relieve this man immediately. He has yellow jaundice. Let him report to my infirmary. I will be there waiting for him." He turned his car around and went back. I was relived of duty and reported to him. He gave me a thorough examination, urine and blood test; and I was sent to sick bay. Thus began a fateful odyssey in my life. It contained very bad days, almost death; but it also contained the highlight of my life.

I never noticed I had yellow jaundice. Now that I think back, I had yellow fin-ger nails. The white in my eyes was yellow and nobody, not even I, noticed it. In our sick bay were isolation rooms. I was put into isolation and only my doctor, the colonel, saw me. For treatment, I had to swallow salt water. I was given some salt to dissolve in water and drink, nothing else. No food for weeks. I got worse. I was passing blood in my urine, and my whole skin became yellow.

Shortly after I had come to sick bay, another guy from our outfit came in with yellow jaundice. He had been driving around in a military Volkswagen without a coat and without the abdominal bandage on his stomach. The nights were so cold. He was in the room next to me and got the same treatment as I, but he could not stand to drink the salty water. I was very conscientious about taking my saltwater, despite often vomiting in the beginning. He could not stand the salt-water and the hunger.

Finally we got something to eat. First, it was biscuits for two or three weeks and then we switched to more solid food. It was bland and tasteless. I remember comparing it to plain sugarless ground wheat dissolved in warm water. For at least two months we got only that and the salt water. I felt an improvement in me, but the guy next to me got worse. He was brought by military ambulance with our doctor to Athens; and after a few days, I heard he had died.

I got better. After four or five months, I was told I would be going home to re-cover. I left for home with the strictest dietary rules. One was absolutely no fatty foods. When the train pulled into the depot in Belgrade, our train was swarmed by merchants trying to sell us anything we wanted. They were selling Serbian or Croatian sausage. One soldier bought some and offered some to me. I took only a small piece, thinking that this little piece could not harm me.

As the train kept rolling toward home, I was dreaming of eating my mother's homemade food. It had been a long time since I had seen my family. The last time I saw my mother and sister was when they were in Berlin. I could hardly wait to see them again. What a great "Wiedersehen" I had with them, but the re-union was only for one day. The next day my father noticed I had yellow finger-nails and the white of my eyes were yellow. I could not believe it. I was passing blood in my urine again. My father said I should go to the military hospital in Biala. He brought me there immediately. He found out that an old school buddy of his, Doctor Hahn, was in charge of the hospital. He asked him to take care of his son.

I was put right into isolation, similar to our Intensive Care Units today. I was between life and death for at least two months. I got the salt water treatment again, but I also got daily shots. I don't remember anything during this time. I did not recognize or knew any of my visitors. Doctor Hahn was constantly watch-ing over me, as did the many nurses I had. Slowly, very slowly, I got better. From this time on I stopped smoking and drinking completely. I was in the Biala Hospi-tal for six months. Doctor Hahn said those shots saved my life. That will teach me never to eat Serbian sausage.

Chapter 4

How I Met Helen

Around this time, the wounded in the hospital who could walk were going to an appreciation dinner for wounded soldiers, organized by the Molenda factory. I was one of them. This was my first time out of the hospital. I was still on a strict diet, but the hospital trusted me. As we entered the Molenda dining hall, everything was beautifully decorated—the hall, the stage, and the tables. The seating arrangement was one soldier, one empty chair, one soldier, one empty chair, and so on, all around the tables. I was wondering what in the heck was going on when the ceremony began.

A long row of girls marched in and sat between the soldiers in the empty seats on one side of the room. Nobody sat next to us in our area. Then another group of girls marched up to the stage. After the welcoming speeches of Mr. Molenda and other persons, the girls on the stage began to dance. These were folk dances. Right away, one girl attracted me. Her face was beautiful. She danced so lively. She was like a rose in a bunch of daisies. Nobody was sitting in the empty seats next to us, and I said to the soldier next to me that it would be nice if that girl would come down and sit next to me.

After the dancing, the girls on the stage formed a line and came down. Every girl followed the line and stopped by an empty seat in front of them. That girl from the stage, the one I was infatuated with, sat down next to me. Like destiny, there she was. Nobody directed her to my seat, unless you believe in God and you say it was His doing. She sat right next to me and I was a happy as a lark. We introduced ourselves. Her name was Helene Urbanke, her first name ending in an e and her last name ending in an e. More about the e later. We had a great time that evening, really great time. This girl had the cutest face. She had the cutest lips. Anyway, that's how I met Helen.

I asked her out, but she was working during the day; and in the evening, I had to be back in the hospital at an early hour. A date was not easy to arrange. I met her sister, Liesl, who worked in Biala. She arranged for us to meet on dates to the movies or for a walk in the park. One time I suggested a trip wandering in the mountains, like we used to do before the war. She accepted and we had a wonderful time. I had a camera along and snapped a picture with the self-timer. We did not fool around. We never even considered it. We were raised differently than the young people nowadays.

Chapter 5

Going Back to War

I hadn't used my recovery leave after my first Yellow Jaundice attack. I never went home, but I often saw my parents and my sisters and my grandmother when they visited the hospital. The time came to be discharged from the hospital, so I said goodbye to my family and to Helen, promising to write. Being a soldier, I did not know from one day to the next what would happen to me or where I would go. I had to report to a new unit and none of my old buddies were there. I had to work as a clerk in an office. For a while, I was traveling all over Germany by train, going to different military warehouses and picking up equipment and delivering this equipment to outfits that needed them. Today, a quick entry in a computer and everything is taken care of.

They formed new units and we were again handed tropical uniforms, which meant we were going south again. It was just before Christmas 1942. We were formed into companies again and I was reunited with some of my old buddies. All leaves were canceled and we were loaded on a train, officers in front in a wagon with seats, and non-commissioned officers and men in box cars. The priority of this train was zero, which meant that any other train had priority over us and we had to wait on a side track or even dead track.

Our train slowly crept along, going south. It was now early morning, Christmas Eve, 1942. I noticed the train was actually heading toward my hometown of Bielitz. I figured out that in order to go south, the train had to turn west into Czechoslovakia at the railroad junction in Dziedzic, just half an hour by train from Bielitz. I wanted to make a phone call to my parents and sisters to wish them Merry Christmas. As the train was nearing Dziedzic, I was trying to figure out how I could make a phone call if the train stops on a side track.

The next time we stopped, there were switching buildings near the track. I took my chance. I hopped over the tracks and ran into a building. There was one man in there whom I asked if I could make a phone call to Bielitz to wish my parents a Merry Christmas. "Sure," he said and helped me to make the call.

My mother answered. As soon as she heard my voice she was jubilant. "Where are you?" she asked. I told her, on a train somewhere on a side track. She said, "You've got to come home. You've got to come home." I told her all leaves were canceled and nobody can come home. She said again, "You've got to come home. You've got to come home." I told her again that it was not possible for me to come home. She asked, "Where are you?" I said that we were heading for Dziedzic and probably turn west to Mahrish-Ostrau.

She said, "I'll find you! I'll find you!" and hung up.

The train slowly kept on heading toward Dziedzic. By the time the train had arrived in Dziedzic, my mother would have had time to take the next rain from Bielitz, but I did not believe she would do it. I did not believe it!

As we stood on the farthest track of this big railroad junction, it had eight or more tracks somebody said, "Look at that woman crossing the railroad tracks. It looks like she is coming to our train." I looked out and saw a woman crossing the tracks in a heavy winter coat, heading toward our train. She went from one box-car to the next, asking for something or someone. As she kept coming closer, somebody pointed her to our car.

I heard her call my name and I shouted, "Here I am." She stopped in front of our boxcar and we had to lift her up and pull her in. There were no steps.

After kissing and embracing, we sat down on the floor of the boxcar and talked. I asked her why she had come all the way here. There was no chance I would get a leave. She said I had to come home and that she did not believe that there was no chance to get a leave. She said, "Let me talk to your company commander." I told her he was in the front of the train with the other officers. She wanted to know his name and who his superiors were. She wanted to know everything.

Suddenly the train started rolling. We waited for the next stop. As the train came to a stop, we lifted her out of the car and she headed toward the officer's wagon. Our eyes followed her as she talked to someone and got into their wagon. Soon the train started rolling again. Every time the train stopped, everyone in our car had their eyes on the officer's car to see if or when my mother came out.

After many train stops, already deep in Czechoslovakia, the train again stopped on a side track. No houses could be seen around us. We looked out again. My mother was coming out of the officer's wagon holding something in her hand and waving it. She was waving it the whole time she passed one boxcar after the other. I thought there as no way she could have gotten the leave. By the time she came close to the car, I heard her shout, "Sigi, I have your leave. I have your leave." She had actually gotten a leave for me.

She stood in front of our car and said, "I got it. I got it. Let's go home." The look on my buddies' faces showed they were envious that I had gotten a leave. It was only for 24 hours. I had to be back right afterwards and report to my unit in Rome. I got my stuff together, said goodbye to my buddies, and got out of the car. As the train pulled away, we stood there alone on the tracks, somewhere in Czechoslovakia. We asked a farmer where the nearest railroad station was, and luckily, we were not far away from one. We got on a train to Dziedzic and from there to Bielitz.

All this time, my mother had not said why it was so important for me to come home. Now she told me that my sister, Erika, was getting engaged and my father wanted to see me. That seemed to me not urgent, but I did not disagree with my mother. We arrived at our apartment in Bielitz and greeted my sisters, my father, and Erika's boyfriend, a sergeant in a tank company. Everything looked festive and happy. My father looked very thin and haggard and I told him so.

As soon as he had a chance, he took me aside and told me that some time ago he had been arrested by the Gestapo. He had just been released by them for insufficient evidence, but he had been tortured. Despite being released for insufficient evidence, he had lost his job. The Gestapo blocked all his efforts to get a new job. Even his friends were afraid to help him for fear of the Gestapo. He mentioned that the head of the Gestapo was a man I knew. He said, "You remember the socialist union leader you had in your factory. He is heading the Gestapo."

Yes, I knew this man. He was rough and violent. I was afraid of him.

I had to see Helen again. I bought a bouquet of flowers and went to Alexanderfeld, hoping to invite her to our house for dinner on Christmas Day. She had never met my family. Christmas, being such a big family holiday, I did not think she would be able to come. When I came to her house, I met her brothers and sisters and mother, and happily, she agreed to come for dinner.

When she saw how we celebrated Christmas, she told me that they celebrated it exactly the same way. Erika and her boyfriend got engaged. Right after the celebration, it was time to go to the depot. I said goodbye to my parents and wondered if I would see them again soon. My sisters, Erika's fiancé, and Helen had come to the depot. I was too shy to give Helen a kiss; but my sister, Brunhild, urged me on. I tried, but the shield of my hat hit her on the forehead. I told her I was sorry and took my hat off, gave her a kiss, and we said goodbye. I was on my way to Rome, Italy.

Chapter 6

Africa

In Rome, I had to go to military information. They told me where my unit was, but they had just arrived and had no orders. In this waiting period, we all got passes almost every day. I looked at all the sights in town. I went to the Vatican and saw the Sistine Chapel and prayed for a safe return and a safe life for Helen and my family. Suddenly orders came and we were again on a troop transport, crossing the Strait of Messina into Sicily. We came to Palermo, where we got off.

Now that we were in Palermo we knew we would be sent to Africa. Rommel had been pretty much written off by Germany. He had one defeat after the other. Resupplying North Africa was very hard, almost impossible, with the American submarines and airplanes controlling the sea. Every German U-52 plane made out of corrugated steel with no armor and machine guns was shot down like a clay pigeon. It must have been like a turkey shoot for the American pilots. Anybody made to go on these U-52 troop transports got the equivalent of a death sentence. If you made it over alive, you were usually killed landing on the airfield in Tunis, which was completely covered with bomb craters. It did not make any sense to resupply.

What we did not know at that time was that the Italian Navy had refused to go out on any missions. They were anchored in the harbour of Palermo. For the Italians, it was like committing suicide to leave the harbour.

In March the Germans, concocted the plan to storm all the Italian ships and force them to go out. We were loaded into the ships very quietly at night and left the harbour huddled together inside the ships. Everybody was quiet, not a sound, not a word was heard from us. We were told submarines could hear you if you talk. That would give our presence away.

In the morning hours we all had to go on deck, waiting to disembark. We were told ferries will come and hurriedly take us off the ships because the harbour got bombed frequently. We saw that our ships changed from convoy formation to a straight line to go into the narrow harbour entrance of La Golette in Tunis. We were the third ship.

As soon as we entered the harbour, we heard planes coming. They were very high but we could see them. The first bomb missed the first ship by quite a bit. The second bomb grazed the side of the second ship. We, the third ship, got hit. I don't remember much anymore of how I got off. I just remember scenes of people crying, people flying. I saw the ferries coming with some guys eager to jump on the ferry, missing the ferry, and falling in between the ferry and the ship and being crushed. I still don't know how I got off the ship. We were brought to shore. They chased us off the ferries which had to go for the next load.

We were wandering around in the harbour till we were gathered at a wall somewhere. I had lost my rifle, my camera—a Kodak Retina, a gift from my father—gas mask and all that stuff you normally have hanging on you. I still had my back pack. We were looking at the burning ships. After the head count the next day, we knew that some platoons were completely wiped out. One unit had only three men left. We were laying around in the harbour for days. They were going to court martial us because we lost our rifles. You are supposed to lose your life rather than lose your rifle, but nothing happened. We were a sorry bunch. Out in the harbour, some ships were still burning. A lot of what I saw did not register in my mind. I had no feelings, neither good or bad, no emotion.

Afterwards we were handed new rifles and new equipment. We formed into new units and marched toward the front line. I was not used to marching anymore. A lot of guys were not used to marching. We were marching now at night. In marching there is a point when you don't feel your blisters or the blood in your shoes anymore. You are almost unconscious. Your feet are marching but you have no mind, no brain. You march like a machine.

We came to a village. It was close to what we thought was the front line. It was pitch dark. We saw and heard in the distance the flash of guns. We stopped to rest. Most of us laid down where we stood and fell asleep. I saw a wall from a bombed out house nearby and laid down. It was nice, soft and comfortable. Soon, I was asleep. I did not know anything till I heard my name being called. When I woke up, the unit was standing in formation. They were searching for me. They saw me behind the ruins. "What in the heck are you doing down there? We are looking for you." When I got up, I smelled the stench. The place I slept was used as a latrine before and I was covered in excrement. That's why I was sleeping so well.

We did not march any further, nor were we put into combat at that time. Something had happened at the front and they did not need us. We came to an old Foreign Legion fort that was completely abandoned, and we took quarters in there. Some horses were left in the stables, but we had no water. We needed feed for the horses, too. We got the water going and got feed for the horses, relaxed, and tried to get our mental state in order.

We had very meager rations. We never had fresh eggs. Some of the native Arabs told us to go into the desert to some Arab village and bargain for eggs with some of our canned food. We saddled some horses, and with our commanding officer's blessing, one lieutenant and four men went out on a patrol. Of course, the lieutenant got himself a racy-looking horse and others got some good looking horses, too. There was only one big, old horse left. I had to take it. Everybody was laughing at me. The shortest guy on the biggest horse. Luckily, I could adjust the stirrup to the highest point so that my feet just barely made it. So we rode out into the desert.

We were following a "wadi", an old dried out riverbed, to an Arab village. We were not used to riding horses and the horses had just recovered from starvation. It took us a long time to reach that Arab village and another long time bargaining for eggs. We got our eggs, but it was getting dark as we were heading home.

The lieutenant told us not to worry. He had a compass. We could not find the "wadi" anymore, which would have led us back home. My horse did not want to go where the lieutenant told us to go. After a while we were heading toward a light and as we came closer, a dog suddenly barked and spooked the horses. My horse was not spooked at all. We were back at the Arab village. After getting instructions from the Arabs on how to go back, we were lost again because we had come back to our own tracks. This time my horse fought violently to go in the direction we were heading. It was pulling me constantly left. I could not control it. I told the lieutenant that my horse refuses to go where you want us to go.

After a while the lieutenant gave in, and we followed the horse. As long as I let my reigns loose, I was okay. Everybody said the horse was crazy and nobody believed the direction my horse was taking us. Soon we found the "wadi" and then my horse started to go faster and gallop. The other horses followed the fast pace. They smelled the stable and there was nothing we could do to hold them back. My horse was the first one to gallop, and I was holding on for my life. There was a ditch before the entrance to the fort and a wooden bridge in the middle. My horse took the straight line over the ditch, jumped, and I flew off. My horse was safely home, but I had bruises all over my body. The other horses galloped over the bridge. I was thankful to my big, old horse. It brought us home.

Our unit was transferred to the area near Bizerta. In the new reorganized unit, I met an old friend of mine. I had known him since we were in Greece. It was Father Jungst, who was again our priest and medic. At that time I was the mailman for our unit. I had to pick up the mail every day. In the beginning there was no problem, the road was good. Then our unit got transferred farther south of Bizerta, where the American forces had launched an offensive. Our unit was in daily heavy combat while I was picking up mail.

Our unit had heavy casualties and we got new replacements. One of these replacements was our former sergeant from Berlin, the one we all were waiting to shoot in the back—the guy who made our lives miserable and bitter, the one who got demoted to Private. He was still a Private, a meek and mediocre person, full of embarrassed apology and mortified to have his old victims around. Being our subordinate had crumbled him to a shaking and helpless person, but he was still a person to us. None of us from the old outfit, the ones still in this unit, had any notion to kill him. We had grown up, too. A lot of us saw our friends and buddies die, and we had no desire for revenge.

Every morning a driver and a military Volkswagen from the motor pool was waiting for me to pick up the mail. While our unit was in combat, I saw a lot of action myself. Going to pick up the mail, I had to go over and around a lot of sand dunes. The road to Tunis was under constant shelling. When I came out from behind some sand dunes with my Volkswagen we, the driver and I, had to cross an open stretch of road and drive across the stretch as fast as we could before they got their guns adjusted to the distance. After awhile they had me figured out and left the guns adjusted and kept on firing. That's when we lost a lot of drivers and cars and a lot of mail.

I got shot at by the dune-hopping planes. The pilot had his finger on the trigger button and as soon as he saw us, he fired. We did not see the plane, we hardly heard it. By the time you heard it, the plane was shooting at you. We learned a lot there. We learned to jump out from a rolling vehicle. The pilot's sight is on the vehicle. As long as it moves, the pilot shoots at it till it blows up and burns. If you can jump off the rolling vehicle, you escaped death. If you hesitate to jump, you would have been blown up. As soon as we heard a plane, we jumped and let the car roll. Of course, the mail got lost but we escaped. We were good at this. We lost a lot of mail and cars, but hardly any drivers or passengers like me.

Our unit was now constantly in combat. I remember on one occasion our unit was fighting in a desperate try to stop a breakthrough by the Americans. Our company had lost a lot of men, many very good friends of mine. The firepower of the Americans was tremendous. The battlefield was covered by dead and wounded, which the medics could not help because of the intense shooting and shelling. The wounded were crying for help. Our medic and priest, Father Jungst, arranged for a temporary cease fire. Under a white flag he marched to the American side. Then, feverishly fighting time, he and his fellow medics, with the American medics help, picked up the wounded and the dead and brought them out. Father Jungst received the Iron Cross First Class.

I spoke with one of my friends in the field hospital. He said Father Jungst saved his life. His leg was shattered and he would have bled to death. Father Jungst put a splint on his leg, lifted him on his back, and carried him out. Right away he went out again to pick up somebody else. All this was going on at night. He and his medics worked till the cease fire was over.

We lost a lot of people there, many my friends. It was for me a very shattering experience. Not long afterwards we knew that everything was over. The front lines had collapsed. Right and left of us collapsed. It seemed that nobody could stop the advancing American and British troops. What next? What am I going to do now? We knew now that we would become prisoners.

For us, becoming a Prisoner of War meant going to Canada and cutting trees down and working in the woods. The British brought their Prisoners of War to Canada. Jokingly we would say, "Let's go chopping wood in Canada." We had no idea what Americans would do with their prisoners. We first had to bust up all our equipment, rifles, and pistols. We were told not to leave the enemy any usable rifle and pistol. They ordered some details to blow up warehouses and storage facilities. Finally, our officers came to us and said, "Goodbye, everybody is on his own."

A group of us went to the only remaining high hill to see what we ought to do. The Mediterranean Sea was in viewing distance. We could see small fishing boats tied to a dock. We could see many trucks of troop supplies all around us, like ants in an anthill, busily moving back and forth. We felt like an island on top of the hill. Everything around us was peaceful. We were still wondering what to do. We knew we had to give ourselves up.

Two men looked at the fishing boats and said they were going to get a boat and row it to Sicily. First I thought they were joking. I saw them leave us and walk toward the shore. Before they crossed the street, they laid down in the ditch and waited till there was a lull in the traffic and ran to the other side. For a time they were gone. Suddenly we saw a fishing boat taking off from shore. These guys didn't want to become a prisoner. But rowing weeks and weeks without food or water and maybe drifting off and drowning?

Suddenly machine gun fire came from shore and hit the boat. We saw the boat break up in pieces. Their flight was over. Maybe for their own good. This was the last straw for most of us. We broke up in groups of two or three guys and walked in different direction toward the street with all the traffic.

We approached the busy street with our hands raised high. We did not want to get shot at. There we were, on the side of the road with our hands high, and nobody stopped. We go tired of holding our hands high. We were dressed in the Africa Corps uniform and thinking, "Don't they know we are the enemy?" We dropped our hands and I shouted in English, "We give ourselves up."

Nothing happened. They ignored us. We stood there maybe half an hour. Finally a truck stopped in front of us and the GI said, "Hop in." We stood there. I had studied English in school, but "hop in" was not in my vocabulary. The truck driver shouted again, "Come on, hop in" and with a waving hand pointed to the rear of the truck. We got the message and jumped in.

Part IV

Years in Prison

Chapter 1

Prisoner of War

The truck was loaded with ammunition and hand grenades. We crawled toward the opening behind the driver. I could speak English but had not spoken it since school. The driver understood my broken English, which made me feel good. The driver said he was from Milwaukee and his name was Miller, which his parents had changed from Mueller. He asked me where I learned my English. I told him in Turkey and he just nodded. He said he had to drop us off at the POW drop-off point. There must have been thousands standing with their hands up. I guess nobody wanted to be bothered with having to drive us to the POW drop-off point.

We waved goodbye to the GI named Miller and were told to walk a little way to the POW camp. Nobody followed us or searched us. We went over to a large square meadow, at whose corner points were four tanks. No barbed wire. Nothing. There we met some of the guys from our unit. We were all happy to be alive. Slowly, more and more men from our unit came in until all of us from the group on the hilltop, except the two who fled with the boat, were accounted for.

We found the guys who were ordered to blow up the officers' warehouses and storerooms. They told us that before they blew it up, they went in to see what in the heck they were blowing up. The found cans and cans of Danish butter and sausages. We never had butter in our rations in the German Army, always margarine. The officers had butter. Our men stuffed their backpacks with cans of butter and sausages, and now they shared it with us. From the Americans, we got boxes and boxes of canned rations. What an irony! Our first day as Prisoners of War, and we were stuffing ourselves with food. Just the pure joy of eating was something we were dreaming of, not just butter and sausages again.

We were on this meadow only one night. The next day we were picked up by trucks and brought to Mateur, a huge POW gathering area. If you can visualize this—as far as you could see, an area as big as an airfield and surrounded all around by barbed wire, and surrounded by a desert. In this barbed wire area, a sea of humanity—all German soldiers. The Americans had stretched out all this barbed wire in a short time. They unwound rolls of rolls of barbed wire. They did not stake it. They just rolled it out, made some entrances, and divided it inside into smaller areas with the name and number of German units.

There we were, in the desert, under the African sun, with no shade except our hats or tropical helmets. They dropped boxes and boxes of food in for us, C or K rations, but no water. The American tank trucks drove day and night to where they picked up the water and brought it to the huge POW camp. They stayed outside the barbed wire fence, opened the large faucet of this water truck, and the water rushed out like from a fire hydrant. If you stood in front of it, the force blew you over. We stood our ground, filling our canteens or cups with water and getting a shower at the same time. As soon as one truck was empty, it took off for refilling while another truck arrived with fresh water. These trucks were going all day and night. I assume that 90% or more of the water was wasted, but we had enough cool water to drink.

I don't remember how long we stayed there, maybe two days and two nights. We were put on military trucks with benches on each side and told not to stand up, but nobody told us where we were going. We must have been barely 15 minutes on the way when I stood up. I had to see where we were going. I was the only one standing and I noticed we were in a long column of trucks loaded with German POWs.

We were going uphill when I saw a column of American tanks coming downhill in the other lane. As I looked, I saw the track of one of the tanks coming off and head toward our truck. I knew the tank had no way of stopping or turning. As the tank was coming toward the left side of our truck, I shouted to our guys, "Get away from this side. We will be hit!" Just a few heard what I was saying and left their seats. The others were hit by the tank as it ripped open the left side of the truck. Some of the ones who did not get away fast enough were badly hurt. These were sent to a hospital. As we were getting on another truck, I was thinking, "Even as a Prisoner of War, your life can end abruptly."

Soon our trucks were heading into the Atlas Mountains. We went higher and higher on a narrow road with a speed like that of a race car. We heard the squealing brakes and inhaled the dusty clouds of road dirt. The Atlas Mountains have steep drop offs, and there was oncoming traffic all the time. The truck drivers were predominantly blacks who spoke English in a dialect I did not understand. Now I knew it as Southern slang.

We begged them to drive slower; but either they could not understand us, or they did not care. After what we had gone through, staying alive during the war, we did not want to die now. Slipping down a hill from the road would have meant certain death for us. These drivers cheated death all the time. Once in a while we stopped and got something to drink and more boxes of rations. Soon we were back on the road again with these drivers, the steep drop offs, and the small dusty roads. Now, thinking back, the drivers were good drivers. At that time I thought these maniacs were going to kill us. We made it to Bone and stopped in front of a British POW camp and were handed over to the British.

Chapter 2

The Monkey Rock of Bone

Bone is a town in Algeria. I never heard of it before, but it left an imprint on my mind as the worst day of my life. It is unbelievable that with British and German officers standing by, a massacre almost happened.

When they opened the rear gates of the trucks, native Algerian or Moroccan troops, under the command of British soldiers, chased us out. We knew we had been handed over to the British. They chased us into the prison compound, hitting us with their rifle butts and shouting, "Empty your pockets. Throw everything on this pile. Everything. Everything." I did not think they would take everything away from us. Not the pictures of my parents. Not the picture of my girl friend. Not my blanket or canteen. Not the personal stuff. They did. If you were too slow to part with your mementos, you got hit in the back with their rifle butts. They took everything away—my watch, my pocket knife, and my tropical helmet. I had to throw it on a pile, which was already two feet high.

They chased us up to the highest point of this POW compound. We looked around at our new quarters on top of a hill. We noticed it was a bare rock. No grass or anything was growing on it. It had no shade at all. The toilets were three or four oil barrels which you were supposed to use by climbing on top of them. They were overflowing and full of flies from all the stench. We did not receive any food nor water. We remembered the canteens of water we had to put on the pile and the food we had left behind in the trucks. The ones who had their tropical helmets taken away had nothing else to cover heir heads. At night, in a tropical area, you need a winter coat or blanket, and they took all our blankets away.

There we were, on this rock in the heat of the African sun without any means to create shade, with nothing to eat and nothing to drink. When we looked down into the camp, there were many compounds which had grass and shade trees; but up in our place, we were crowded together, hundreds of us, with only rock under our feet.

As we looked down, we could not believe our eyes. In a compound for German officers they were showering outdoors, their orderlies pouring water over them. The day went by and we did not get any water. We begged for water but nobody listened. We shouted at the native guards patrolling the fence to give us water or something to eat. Nothing. The night brought utter misery. Huddled together to keep warm and still shivering, we rotated so the outside guys could slowly get to the middle of the huddle. We tried to make the best of it.

The second day was the same thing again. Soon the men in our compound were in a rage. With the sun mercilessly beating down on us, people soon didn't know what they were doing. I was at the fence shouting, "Water, water, water…" with the rest of the guys and looking down at the officers bathing and showering. Soon, more and more men came to the fence and were shouting and pushing, and I knew I had to get away from the fence. I crawled out between the feet of the men behind me. The pushing became so hard that the fence was bending outward.

The British, afraid of a breakout, set up a machine gun in front of that bending fence. If the fence broke, the machine gun would have fired into the crowd coming through the fence. About 90% of us now were at the fence, pushing and shouting. I was huddled in the middle of the compound, getting some shade from another person and anticipating the breakthrough.

Suddenly somebody in the center of the push climbed on the fence. I said to myself, "Oh my God, here they go." It was a staff sergeant. As he got on top of the fence, he stopped. In his Austrian dialect he said, "All of us are starving and thirsty. If we go through this fence, we all will die. Did you try to stay alive all this time to die for this? You are smarter than that. The British don't care if you die! But somebody at home will care. Let's get the British officials to come and try to get our officers to come." He was desperately holding on to the barbed wire with his hands and trying for a long time to talk some sense into the crowd. Finally, they agreed to do it his way.

He came down from the fence and got together with the hotheads. They decided on a different approach. First, we shouted for our officers to come but they did not hear us. There was no reaction from them. Finally, one of our officers came up with a British officer and they were standing behind the barbed wire, not daring to come into our compound. The German officer only came up to investigate what the noise was we were making.

Now he heard a lot of our stored up frustration. The German officer did not believe us. When he confronted the British officer, the officer had all kinds of excuses for it. He agreed to let us go down to the pile, only two men at a time, and get our stuff. Regarding the water, the British officer's excuse was that we bombed them and it was our own fault that we had no water. As to the question of the German officers taking a shower, he said it was swamp water. But he would allow us to get water. To the question of why we had no food, the British officer's answer was that they did not receive any food either, at least not for our compound.

The reality looked different. When we went to the pile of stuff, the pile was four or five feet high. Everyone going through the pile mixed things up. You were allowed only five minutes to go through it. A lot of men never found their stuff. I was lucky. To this day, I thank God that I found some of my pictures. They kept my spirits and my hope up for the next three and a half years. That was all that we were actually looking for—pictures of our loved ones.

We were allowed only one five gallon canister of water for all of us. One group of two or three men with the canister went with a guard for water. They must have been gone for hours. When they finally arrived, they had that five gallon canister of water and one cup for all of us to use. They had to get it from a swamp by slowly skimming off from the top. Our problem now was to figure out how much water each of us would get. We had only one eight-ounce cup. Each man in the compound would get only a little bit of water, maybe only one eighth of a cup per person. We divided it this way and we hardly had any complaints. But we still had nothing to eat. To our surprise, we were ordered to leave this rock and march through the city of Bone.

We all felt a hatred for the British. It was clear to all of us that the British wanted us to suffer. They never made an attempt to talk to us. I will never forget how they treated us in this POW camp. The British treated their officers differently than their men. We saw how the British put officers on a pedestal, even enemy officers, and how low the men were judged by them.

We were soldiers, brought together by fate, on this rock. We were Germans and Austrians, but first, we were human beings. Treated by the British so inhumanely instilled a defiance in us. Everything that separated Germans and Austrians was gone. The hate for the British was greater than the animosity between Germans and Austrians. How different we were treated by the Americans. The attitude of the Americans was so unlike the British. The Americans said, "For you, the war is over. Let's forget our differences." That was the message we got. They did their utmost to feed, give water and shelter, and treated you like a human being.

The march through the town showed our frustration and hatred for the British. We were not allowed to sing during the march, another of the rules the British were forcing on us. We not only sang with all our strength, but we sang all the anti-British songs we could think of. We were hoarse when we came into the harbour, but it felt good.

We were ordered to go through a de-licing and put on a freighter crowded together in the cargo bays. I can only compare it to a slave ship bringing slaves over from Africa. On deck were these oil drums as toilets again. When they were full, we had to dump the contents overboard, clean them, and put them up on deck again. We still did not get anything to eat. We were just laying around, crowded together. Some were sleeping.

In the Oran harbour, we were handed over to the Americans again. We had to go through the de-licing procedure again. We stripped down naked and put our personal belongings on a table. Our uniforms and undergarments were discarded. We were deloused with a powder and given new undergarments and new uniforms. We got all our personal belongings back.

We then walked to a huge oceanliner, the "Rotterdam", where we embarked. This was a monstrous ship—clean, neat and huge. We were split into smaller groups of 10 or 12 men on bunk beds in each cabin. I had a porthole over my bed and could see the water right below splashing against the porthole. We would be cruising the Atlantic. I knew that my adopted brother, Alfred, was in the Atlantic in his U-boat, trying to sink as many ships as he could. A big oceanliner would be a trophy for him. It was a refurbished oceanliner, now used as a troop transport to bring GIs to the war area and return with Prisoners of War to the United States.

When we boarded the ship, our eyes popped wide open. Despite being converted to a troop transport, it was still, in every way, an oceanliner. Luxury was still everywhere, as long as it did not interfere with the huge number of sleeping quarters necessary for the troops.

They were looking for volunteers to work in the kitchen and the huge freezer room, or scrubbing the floors. I remember the freezer room. To me it looked like an airplane hangar, with rows and rows of beef halves and boxes of hamburgers, hot dogs, and other meat and chicken. The meals we ate on the ship were unbelievable. I never dreamed I would ever eat like that. We had meat, vegetables, potatoes, puddings, cake and ice cream—the normal food any GI would get.

We could not get over it. After what we had just experienced in the British POW camp, it was like going from hell to heaven. A lot of us were wondering why the United States did that. Why do they stuff you with all this good food? I remembered the story of Hansel and Gretel, where the witch stuffed the two kids with food to eat them herself. Other people in our cabin had the same thought. We were full of questions but no answers.

As we steamed out of the harbour of Oran, I noticed we were in a convoy formation with many other ships. We heard honking noises, saw signaling, and so on from the porthole. In the beginning, we were not allowed to go on deck; but later on we were allowed to go on deck at least twice a day for fresh air and exercise. When we went through the Strait of Gibraltar, we stood on deck. At that time, the Strait of Gibraltar and the famous rock did not mean much to me. The first time we were on deck, I met the most memorable person ever in my life.

Chapter 3

The Chaplain on the Rotterdam

People talk about the "ugly American". He was what would be the complete opposite. An American who was a shining example of what America stands for or what America is supposed to stand for. An American who was honest, who was not tainted by propaganda, who talked the way his heart felt. He was a chaplain. I think he was a Lutheran chaplain because he talked about his wife. He met us as we came on deck. He was always there. I don't know if he was supposed to be there or if was doing it voluntarily.

He first asked if anyone could speak English. I was the only one in our group who spoke English. He asked me if I would be willing to translate for him and I said I would. He asked us how we felt, how we were doing, how we liked everything? Of course, we were fine and we liked everything. Then we asked him questions. The men in the group were very hesitant at first to ask questions, thinking they would be punished for questioning an American officer. Soon they saw there were no trick questions from him and only honest questions from us.

When they saw they were not punished or persecuted for asking them, they got bolder and bolder in their questions. We were going to America, that was clear, but what to we did not know. What we would find there was scary to us. Most of us did not know what America was like. We had one guy in our group who said he remembered being in America as a kid, but he had forgotten all the details. The rest of them had never seen America. They only knew what they had read in books or from German propaganda.

The knowledge I had came from reading the Karl May books about Indians, about the trapper Old Shatterhand and his Indian friend Winnetou, who were trying to make people understand the Christian and nonviolent way of living together. These were books where the nonviolent way always won out. Old Shatterhand always won without shooting people.

We asked the chaplain all kinds of questions and he answered them all straight-out. Sometimes I refused to translate a question from the group because the question was typical Nazi propaganda, or the question attacked the character of the chaplain. He asked me what was going on and why I would not translate certain things. I told him what the reasons were. He said that it would not matter to him and I should go ahead and translate it. His answers were frank and honest.

What kind of questions did we ask? Why America entered the war against Germany? How come the Negroes and the Indians are still enslaved? At that time, black people were only know as Negroes. Some asked me to translate—What is America doing in Europe? They have no business to be in Europe. Why are they fighting us, the Germans? His answers were to the point and sounded logical to me.

He did not pretend to know all the answers but he told us things that startled us. I do not know the exact words he used, but I got the feeling this is what he said.

When you come to America, many time you will be confused and mixed up by what people do. We have a freedom in America that lets people do whatever they want to do. We don't have all the personal restrictions you have in your country. The freedom our people have creates a wide variety of opinions and a variety of deeds. You might not understand it. Freedom means different things for different people. You might object to some things people do. Some things may seem strange to you and you might not agree with the amount of freedom people have. We give people all this freedom to express themselves but we have the law, too. The law is the part where freedom stops and responsibility begins. You are still responsible for what you do in the United States. The law curtails your freedom enough so that you do not step on somebody else's freedom. That is what makes us Americans.

I had already formed a different opinion about America just by listening to him, and I communicated it to the other guys. Many times after the group had to go back to their cabin, he noticed I had more questions for him; so he asked me to stay on deck. We did not have a question and answer time, we had long conversations. This chaplain became the most interesting person I ever encountered. He answered, in a short and simple way, what would happen to us. He said, "I don't know where you are going, but wherever you go, you will be treated under the laws of the Geneva Convention. You have to have your ears and eyes wide open and have to think, to understand America and the Americans." He seemed to me, now that I am looking back after all this time, as a real good American. He knew what America was, what it was supposed to stand for, and he also knew what America had not yet accomplished by 1943.

He frankly admitted that discrimination is still widespread and how the blacks were treated or really mistreated. He knew there were a lot of things wrong in American that eventually will be righted. He was not afraid to say that. He mentioned that America would get over all these problems without a revolution, without a dictatorship. Through Congress, people pass laws that can be enforced to change things. He said there are many injustices around and only in a society like a democracy, can injustices be ironed out permanently. Not right away. It takes time in a democracy for one injustice to be removed without creating more injustices. These discussions went on all through the weeks.

When we were on deck asking the questions, we could see we were in a big convoy. We could see there were tankers, freighters, troop transports, cruisers, and smaller military ships; and they all had to adjust to the slowest ship in the convoy. Once in a while, there were signal lights flashing and ships started to scramble. It looked to us like the ships were criss-crossing all around us. It seemed they would hit each other, but they never did. It was all planned.

Then you heard the depth charges. We knew they were dropping them on submerged U-boats. I thought of my adopted brother. He may be out there. Maybe he was in this pack of U-boats attacking us? Maybe he was aiming a torpedo at us right now, not knowing that the troop transport was full of German POWs and I was on it. When we were in our bunk beds in our cabins and we heard the scrambling and the noises of another U-boat attack going on, I thought of the possibility of a torpedo sinking us. What an irony this would have been. Life is sometimes full of ironies.

We had fantastic food. Everyday we were eating meat. We had beef, chicken, potatoes, vegetables, cake, ice cream—all the things we hardly ever saw in our military life. Nobody could remember ever eating that good in the German Army. The kitchen on this ship was incredible. The cooks must have been very proud of their place of work. Everything was always spic and span. They must have been professional cooks. I didn't see any POWs serving or helping the cooks. Our group was working bringing the meat out of the freezer into the kitchen. Our work on the ship was pleasant and fun.

Chapter 4

I Am In America

We had been at sea about three weeks when we arrived in the harbour of Boston. When we went on deck to disembark, we noticed the harbour full of blimps. They were tied with steel cables to the ground as a protection against possible air attacks. It was a very busy harbour from all the crazy traffic around us. All the boats and ships in the harbour and the many cars on land made it look like a beehive. We were again deliced; and after we got new clothes and all our personal belongings back, we waited.

We saw something startling. On the tracks by the harbour were railroad wagons of glass. They looked to us like luxury class railroad cars. We did not know that these were regular cars. Suddenly, we were led to these cars and we got in. We would not believe it. Plush seats, soft and comfortable, and big glass windows. We were still thinking, where is the catch to it? All the years in the German Army we were transported in boxcars or cattle wagons. We would lay on straw with many people crowded together. Officers would sit in cars with wooden benches or wooden seats. There is no first class or second class in America. We felt we were being treated like royalty.

As we traveled through the United States, we still ate good. There were rules, of course. Guards on each end of the railroad car and only one person was allowed to stand up and ask permission to go to the toilet. But we were relaxed and enjoying the scenery through the huge glass windows. I don't remember the towns anymore, but I think we must have gone through Washington, DC, because we saw a lot of blooming trees like the cherry trees in Washington.

The scenery changed. We saw endless prairies and finally arrived in what we found out later was, Opelika, Alabama. We were led out of these wagons by a row of soldiers who had their rifles down and their fingers on the trigger. It seemed like an endless row of GIs, some very young and shaky, till we finally came to the first gate of the new POW camp. They had erected a brand new stockade with many towers and divided camps inside, with brand new barracks.

In our camp, an American soldier was assigned to us who told us what to do in very broken German. He said he was from Bremen, Germany, and he would talk in German to us. Boy, did we laugh at his accent. A lot of words he did not remember anymore and said them in English. Some of his English I could not understand and translate. Despite that, I established myself right away as a translator. Now, I probably speak German worse than this guy did in Opelika.

In the first days, I was just trying to find old friends who were with me in the same camp. Father Jungst, the priest, was there; and I found friends I had thought were killed and friends I was separated from since boot camp. The first interrogation in camp was mostly name, rank, serial number, and the address to whom you will be allowed to write. I had only two addresses—my parents and Helen's. Later on, in follow-up interrogations, they asked more.

When they asked me my profession I didn't know what to answer. When I explained what I was doing and learning, they wanted to write student; but I told them I was not only a student, I worked in a textile factory. They said that was too long. So they wrote, "Mechanic". This became my profession all the time I was a POW. As a political affiliation: SA, SS, Nazi party. I, of course, said no political affiliation. I told them about the few months I was in the Hitler Youth group, which they wrote down.

Getting cigarettes was a problem. I was not smoking, but people who smoked were in a bind. If anyone threw a cigarette butt away, three or four people stormed to the spot to pick it up. They also were forming discussion groups. Some POWs had a desire for knowledge and others wanted to express their opinion. Political discussion groups were formed and political pressure groups were active. Nazis were the top power group. They were hoping to run the camp. There were religious groups, philosophical groups and many others. Every one of these groups held some kind of discussions. You could go from one group to the other and get a variety of opinions.

There was one group of former doctors and mental health employees who explained the biological clock that is in every person. This group attracted a lot of people. Father Yungst was very interested in it also. He saw where these discussions were leading to. One day he participated in the discussion. He asked the group of doctors and mental health employees if the biological clock controls our lives. Are we, as a person, bound to follow the clock? They said it is the clock that determines your destiny. Father Yungst told them that the destiny of a person is determined by his own choosing, not by a biological clock. A person has his own ability to say "yes" or "no" to what he will do. He will be judged by his own deeds, for which he is responsible. That stopped this discussion group. It was the end of them.

Some were trying to learn more of America. I was one of them. I remembered the words of the chaplain on the Rotterdam. To learn about America you have to learn from everything that's happening around you, the good and the bad, and then form your opinion. I expressed to the American soldier assigned to our camp, my wish to know more about America. Suddenly I was confronted by a lot of guys who asked me, "What are you trying to do, become a traitor?" This was one of the cliques, who for some reason felt they had to tell everyone else what to do. They were trying to force their opinion on the others and in so doing, dominate life in the camp. Of course, there were enough others who were trying to not let that happen.

We were told by the American commander of the camp the rules of the Geneva Convention. Sergeants don't have to work. Everybody below that rank had to go to work. They would be paid for their work—80 cents for a whole day of work. You could buy food and cigarettes in the PX (post exchange). We had a PX but no money to buy anything.

I was a sergeant, so I would not have to work. But how could I learn about America if I never met any people outside? So I decided to go out to work. Rumors were going around that we would be working for farmers. They first asked for volunteers but there were not many who wanted to go. They told me I was not required to go to work, but I told the camp commander I would like to. This group who tried to control everything were telling me not to do it or they would bust my head. They told me I was a traitor. I explained to them, "How are we going to find out how it is on the outside, how people live, what people are like, if we don't go out? Having some money for food and cigarettes seems all right also."

They told me I was supporting the enemy.

I told them, "What do we know of the enemy? Nothing, unless we go out and meet him." That calmed them down.

I will never forget the very first time we went to work. We were a group of 10 or 12 POWs with the POW stamped on every part of our clothes and about 30 guards. I am not lying. There were more than two guards for every prisoner. We went into a field and were harvesting, probably tobacco or corn at that time. For each one of us, there were at least two guys with guns following you, and they all had their fingers on the trigger. Every move you made, they were watching you. We were scared to work. We were Prisoners of War, not having committed a crime, but they would have shot us immediately if they thought we were doing something wrong. Just a stupid move by us would have ended our lives. Lots of us were thinking, we tried so hard to stay alive all through the war. We did not want to get shot now by one trigger-happy guard. No, no way will we go out again.

The American camp commander knew about our attitude. Despite promises of change, there was no change for weeks. After weeks of no incidents, they changed to one guard for each prisoner. Later, in other camps, they had one guard for three or four prisoners. Not till we were in Fort Bennigan and at the Air Force Base at Moody Field in Valdosta, Georgia, did we have one guard for 10 to 15 prisoners.

I remember when I got my first money. It was camp money. I could now buy stuff in the PX. The men who were not working had no money to buy things like cigarettes, chocolate, or ice cream. Later on we could buy shirts, socks, daily newspapers, and magazines. Having money changed a lot of people. In a short time, a lot of sergeants went out to work. They were thinking—to hell with the Geneva Convention rules. As long as you can make money, you can buy stuff for it. Mostly, the money for cigarettes drove them to work.

Chapter 5

The Camp On The Prairie

I remember an event a little time after we arrived in the Opelika camp. One day we were told we would be leaving for a longer stay in a different camp. About 80 to 100 of us prisoners were transported by truck on a very long drive. We were never told where we were going. Suddenly we came to a newly-built camp right in the middle of a prairie-like countryside. It was surrounded by a high barbed wire fence and had a big gate; but there were no towers, as they usually have. It was a tent city—two cots to each tent—with wash, shower and toilet facilities. Everything was brand new. We were told we would help the farmers here with the harvesting. We were never told the name of the city we worked in, but I believe it must have been Swainsboro, Georgia.

Every day we went out to work. We had teams of 10 to 12 men and I was team leader and translator. We already knew how to work in peanut, sweet potato, sugar cane, tobacco, corn and watermelon fields, having harvested in all of them.

What we were doing there was picking peanuts. First the farmer loosens the plants with his machinery. Then we went through the rows, picking the green bushes of peanuts out of the ground, shaking the dirt off, and stacking them around stakes with the peanuts to the inside and the greens outside. We worked hard and we came back to our tent city very tired. We had to fulfill a quota which was not always easy for those of us not used to farm work. Most of us had common professions. We had lawyers, bankers, plumbers, and some were German farmers who never had to harvest peanuts in their lives. Others were used to heavy work, like miners or ship builders. Some never had to do any work with their hands, while others were used to this heavy work.

We had very good food. Since we came into the POW camps, we had the same ration that any American soldier had—the normal GI ration. The Americans, at that time, followed the strict rules of the Geneva Convention. How many times did I compare our treatment as Prisoners of War with the way the Russians treated their German war prisoners? They starved them and worked them to death. A lot of German prisoners in Russian camps died there from sickness and malnutrition. We were thinking, so far we were treated very humanely and by the rules of the Geneva Convention. But in this camp, we had another experience, completely unexpected and incomprehensible waiting for us.

It was a normal day. We were all in our tents when we noticed, outside the barbed wire fence, a lot of military cars and trucks coming to our camp. One American officer got out of the car and came to the gate. He wanted to speak to our German camp leader. Before the camp leader arrived, a bunch of us had gathered around the fence to find out what was going on. The American officer asked our German camp leader if he would give them permission to play some marches. They were the Philip Sousa Military Band.

We at the fence heard all this. The camp leader turned to us and said, "Did you hear this? Do you know what he asked me? He asked for our permission to play for us. The Military Band wants to play for us. Can you believe that?" Of course it was okay. As this band got ready to play outside the barbed wire fence, we all gathered inside the fence. Then the concert started. They played "Stars and Stripes Forever," which is a very familiar march in the German Army. They played a lot of Sousa marches and a lot of German and Austrian marches like "Under the Double Eagle". What a concert! What music! We did not know how starved we were for music. This band played with "Schmiss," a word in German for zip or snap. Germans only credit that to German bands. This band really played "schmissig."

Through the barbed wire, they asked us if we had any favorite march we would like to hear from them. They played our requests without notes, just from memory. This was so nice. We applauded them over and over and again and again. We were really happy, and seeing this made them happy also.

We sang along with some of the marches. We had one professional baritone in our group, and you could hear his voice rising out over our voices. This baritone asked if they knew a certain song very popular at that time in Germany and also popular at that time in the United States. It was about the quietness on a prairie. If course they knew it and they played it without any notes. I still remember the baritone's voice flowing over the vastness of the prairie. He alone created the colors with his voice and with the music of the band in the background. This was an event none of us will ever forget. I talked to one guy through the fence and asked the reason why they wanted to do that. They wanted to know how they stacked up to any good German band. This band won out by a big margin.

After our work was done in Swainsboro, we went back to Opelika again. We had our first Christmas in the United States there. No cold weather. No snow. I had my first Christmas in the warm South. I also remember posing for a painting for a friend of mine. At that time I had a beard. My friend said it made my face interesting. He called this painting "Juengling mit Bart" (youth with beard).

Later on we were shipped to Fort Benning, Georgia, which now became our main camp. We were living in the GI barracks with barbed wire around our camp. We did a lot of work there—heavy work, dirty work, that the GIs stationed there did not want to do. We had good food and plenty of time to relax. One day the huge POW camp in Fort Benning was dissolved. We were divided into smaller groups and I, with a group of 200 to 300 prisoners, was sent to Moody Field, Georgia, a military air base near Valdosta.

Our camp was inside the air base. It was surrounded by barbed wire and towers and had a double gate. This camp became our home now for the next few years.

Chapter 6

Moody Field, Georgia

I was helping the farmers again. I worked on the air base and in the woods cutting pulpwood. Cutting pulpwood now became more of our primary work when we were not needed for harvesting. The first work I did on the air base was at the stables. We were brushing horses and getting rid of the old straw and adding new straw. Soon, all this work on the base stopped because the farmers needed us. The farmers were very eager to have us. They had to pay us only 80 cents a day and an additional 80 cents to the government. That came to only $1.60 a day. If they had to hire other farm workers, mostly black people, they had to pay much higher wages to them. $1.60 a day for prisoner work was cheap. There were many incidents where farmers let black people go and switched over to hiring POWs.

All the money we earned, we got to keep. For 80 cents a day, I could buy a lot in our camp PX. It was only camp money; but in our PX I could buy candies, ice cream, newspapers, and magazines. Any money I did not spend was put in a savings account for me in camp. I could buy good shirts, socks—any kind of clothes. The only problem was, every cloth worn on the outside of your body had to have POW in big capital letters on it, and you had to do it yourself. You got a POW stencil and put it on your clothes and brushed white or black paint on it. Of course, you had to darn your own socks, do your own sewing and wash your own laundry by hand.

The farmer had to pick us up in the morning. His pick-up truck had to have wooden benches. He was waiting outside the double gate. He put 10 to 15 prisoners in his truck and a guard in a jeep was following the truck. We went harvesting or cutting pulpwood, whatever we were told to do. When we came back to the camp, we ate good food and played soccer and saw German movies. We even had a soccer league. Every weekend we played against other teams from other branch POW camps; and sometimes our team traveled to the other branch camps for league play. Our team had good soccer players—some were former professional players.

But POW life was like any other prison. When you are caged in for months and months, it affects you., I remember walking, sometimes half the night, around the fence past the guard towers, like a caged animal. Sometimes you see lions or tigers pacing back and forth, back and forth, in a cage. I saw this happening to every prisoner, some more than others. Something is happening in you. You are in a cage and there is nothing you can do about it. When you go back and forth past an illuminated fence, past the towers, you feel caged in. The fence is a wall between you and the outside world. This wall keeps you inside, but it also protects you from the unknown outside world. In two years only one prisoner from our camp escaped. They found him the next day, stuck somewhere in a swamp, yelling for help.

Long prison life, no matter how good everything is, has a strange effect on some prisoners. I remember one guy and how it started with him. We were playing table tennis and he suddenly stopped and said a fly was watching him. Every time he played he got more irritated by the fly. After weeks and weeks, the fly got bigger and bigger; and one day it attacked him. Of course, there was no fly. He imagined it. He was going crazy. He was transferred and we never heard form him again.

We were a varied group of people in this camp, from different units and different branches of the army. When they assigned you beds, you had no knowledge who your bed neighbor would be. Next to me was a very intelligent man. After a month of talking to him and telling him about my life, I noticed he never talked much about his. It took a few months before he finally opened up to me. He was from a German Concentration Camp. He told me that the only way to get out of a Concentration Camp was to join a "Straf" battalion. "Straf" battalion would be a punishment battalion or a delinquent battalion. You never had a chance to get out of a Concentration Camp till the German Army formed these delinquent battalions. You had to volunteer for it. For him and a lot of the volunteers it was a hope to escape, a chance to be free again.

In the Concentration Camps were murderers and sex offenders. Regular criminals were mixed with political prisoners. These regular criminals were awarded jobs as section leaders. They mistreated and sometimes cruelly tortured the prisoners who were in for political opposition. I learned that political prisoners had to go through hell just to stay alive in their camps.

I was teaching English in camp from the <u>Readers Digest</u> article "7 Crosses", about life in a Concentration Camp. I asked him if this article was true. He said, "Yes, and more." He wanted to convince me that Socialism was the only way for the German people. He was an honest and good man and had incredible ideas and I often thought of my grandfather Hoffmann who was also a Socialist. I do not know what my grandfather's beliefs were, but Socialism is nothing but a welfare program on a large scale to me. I volunteered to take some special courses in American government and Democracy. He was against it. He said, "Nobody can teach me about Democracy, at least not the Americans." That made me wonder about his fanaticism. I remembered what the chaplain on the Rotterdam said to me, "You've got to listen and learn from everybody, but you yourself have to make up your mind as to what is right. Keep your eyes open and learn. You've got to have an open mind." His father was a staunch defender and important Socialist leader, and he was following in his father's footsteps, till the Nazis arrested him. He knew so much. He had a brilliant mind, but in many ways his views were one track views. Only Socialism was the right way.

The Nazis told him that if he wanted to rehabilitate himself, he could volunteer to fight in this Delinquent battalion. He never wanted to shoot anybody. When they were at the front, they were the first to see action; and behind them, they had the SS watching them so that nobody escaped to the rear. Either way they would have been killed. Over the years, I learned a lot from him about life in these camps which I did not know about before.

I took a lot of courses to learn more about America. I subscribed to the New York Times, Life magazine, and Readers Digest; and I took extension courses from the Universities of Michigan and Minnesota. I followed the American, British, and German war reports daily in the New York Times, where the changing front lines were daily marked. You could learn what was going on at the different front lines. My intention was to become a teacher. I was teaching and studying here and I could get more education in teaching as soon as the war was over.

Playing soccer was our biggest enjoyment. When we played in our championship matches against teams from other POW branch camps, they were always big events. Full of excitement, like The World Series. We got packages from the German Red Cross and we also got German movies. One day, we got a package of three loaves of pumpernickel bread. Normally, we had a lottery for small things that could not be divided. That was the suggestion of our camp committee, to let these three loaves go on a lottery. A big storm of protest from almost everyone in our camp stopped that. All of us felt that we didn't care how small a piece of the pumpernickel bread we got, as long as we all could have some. Our kitchen people mathematically divided these three loaves, but every one of us got a tiny piece of it. By the smiling faces of everybody, you could see it was the right solution.

As rationing in the United States became tougher, the United States had to cut here and there. We read in the paper that the government had decided to stop making the white bread. By adding some bran, it would switch to darker bread. This decision brought a big smile to our faces. Finally we will eat dark bread.

As weeks and months passed by, we got impatient. Finally we asked the American Camp commander why we were not getting the darker bread, as the government promised. The Camp Commander laughed and said, "You guys have been eating this dark bread already for months." We were shocked. This bread was hardly any darker than the white bread and tasted the same as the white bread. The added bran did not darken the bread, nor did it change the taste. This was a big disappointment for us.

In the meantime, we were getting more experience in harvesting and in cutting pulpwood. In harvesting peanuts, we were no longer picking up the peanut bush and shaking off the dirt with our hands. Now we were using pitchforks. Every year, for four harvests, our quota had increased from 4 to 24 stakes per person, per day. It was faster with a pitchfork and safe, too, when you consider how often you picked up a snake in the peanut bush.

Luckily, very few POWs were ever bitten by snakes, but snakes were everywhere. In the woods we had to be watchful for rattlesnakes. Near water we had to be watchful for water moccasins or land moccasins. There were also copperheads and other snakes. Many times poisonous snakes were running over my hand, but I was never bitten. We had to live with many types of snakes all during our stay in our POW camp.

After working and sweating in the awful heat on a Georgia farm, we were longing to get back to our camp for a cool shower. The farmer was very nice to us. He had placed containers of water all over the fields for us to drink. We thanked him for that. He asked us if he could do anything else for us. We told him that we appreciated his kindness, but we were looking forward to a cool shower in camp. He said, "Why don't you go to a lake nearby and take a swim?" We asked our guard if we could take a swim in this lake. He said okay.

The farmer brought us to this lake and we stripped down to our underpants and were in the process of jumping in the water when the farmer said, "Watch out for snakes." Most did not hear it. The guard only shouted for us not to swim too far out. The water was cool and refreshing, and we had a great time. Suddenly shots were fired and I saw the guard firing into the air. Everybody scrambled to get back to the shore. I saw the guard pointing behind me. In turning around to see what he was pointing at, I saw the waving outline of a swimming snake heading toward me. Boy, did I take off in a hurry. We were glad to be out of the water. A short time before, we were so eager to jump in. The farmer said it was a water moccasin, the most feared poisonous snake.

I never had heard of a hurricane before and never experienced one. A day or two before, we heard of the impending threat of an approaching hurricane, and we had to prepare our camp. Everything that could fly away had to be moved, stored away, or secured. All the planes form the base were flown out and we had to stay in the barracks. The hurricane hit us and this experience is still etched in my mind. I don't think we got the full force of it. We saw many things flying by our windows and some hitting our barracks wall. After it was over, we went outside and looked at the damage. Our barracks looked like it was hit by sledge hammers. Nothing made me realize the power of a hurricane more than a blade of straw sticking out of the wooden wall of our barrack. The wind was so strong that the blade of straw had penetrated the wood.

Another time, we were called to fight a forest fire not far from the entrance of the base. We got shovels and were fighting the fire along with men from the base. I could only smash the fire out with the shovel and was digging trenches to keep the fire from spreading. I remember fighting very hard not to get encircled by the fire. The fear to die in a fire made me realize how precious your own life is to you.

When we went out to work, each team got two five-gallon cans of hot coffee to drink, and everybody got a lunch bag. By the time we were at our working place, the coffee in the five-gallon cans was already cold. If we had a chance, we put the cans into a flowing brook or creek. It cooled off fast and tasted more refreshing. From that time on, I always preferred to drink my coffee cold.

We were working in the woods in Georgia. Wild animals, especially wild pigs, were abundant around us. Wild hogs were a big nuisance. They ate our lunch if we forgot to leave it high enough in a tree. Some of us had dogs we could bring to work and back into our POW camp.

We always had lots of leftover scraps from our kitchen food. Normally we would have thrown it away. We got permission from our American camp commander to catch these wild pigs, bring them to our camp and feed them our kitchen scraps. Now we had pork chops to eat.

We also got permission to catch alligators to display in a pond we made in camp. These were only small alligators and the most we had were two. We also had permission to catch flying squirrels. We made large long cages with trees in them along our barracks and put the squirrels in them. They were kept and fed and you could watch them for hours, like in a zoo.

We had many discussion groups in our camp. Scientific, religious and world problems were discussed. Our camp was almost like a college. Every evening people went from class to class like a campus of a university. We also had a place where we played table tennis, chess, and other games. Despite this rosy, almost normal life, we still felt in prison.

Chapter 7

Arrested In Prison And My Work On Airplanes

It was a normal working day, like so many days before. We were lined up for work assignment. Our military personnel from the guard unit assigned our work for the day. Like any other day, I was in charge of a working team. I was given my work assignment with the team waiting and listening. I was told that there was a farmer who had his corn crop destroyed by pigs. The person who did the scheduling told me directly, "Sig, do whatever you can to try and save his crop." Of course we would try. We always did. The farmer was waiting to pick us up and everything was routine. The guard, in a jeep, was following the truck.

When we arrived at the farmers field, we saw the mess he had. Almost every cornstalk was down, as far as we could see. The pigs, probably wild hogs, must have roamed around his fields for a long time. It seemed like a tornado had crushed everything. I was in charge of our working group and I asked the farmer how many of his fields looked like this one. He said many more.

Right in the beginning I told the farmer that there was not much we would be able to save, and he agreed. I was worried about our quota and I told the farmer that it would be impossible to make the quota. Quotas were goals of achievement for a normal field. The farmer agreed that he did not look for anything like that. It was important for him to save something from this mess. During all this time, the guard stood next to the farmer and I and listened to what we said.

I got my team together and told them that we would try very hard to save what we can. It was tough. Most of the corn was laying flat on the ground and a lot was chewed off. We had not saved too much, and I told that to the farmer. He said that he saw that and it was fine with him. We had two fifteen-minute cigarette breaks a day. When our time for a cigarette break came, I asked my team if they could work through. There was so much work ahead of us that I felt we could afford to give up the cigarette breaks. They agreed.

We worked real hard. I always did the same work along with the rest of the guys. We had some tall, strong guys who could easily outperform me. In a quota field, they were the first ones done and I and others were always last; but here, we all worked hard to accomplish it. During our lunch break I saw the guard talking to the farmer intensively. The farmer seemed upset and talked back to the guard, but I could not hear what they said.

During the afternoon, I occasionally glanced to the guard and the farmer. I still could not hear what they were saying and the discussion seemed the same, with the guard talking intensively and the farmer shaking his head. It was getting very late and we were still working. Finally I said, "That's it. That's all we can do." We were bushed. We saw the farmer signing a paper that the guard gave him and then the farmer brought us back to our prison camp. During the trip back, nobody was talking. I assume everybody was looking forward to going to sleep. The farmer stopped, as usual, outside the double gate. When the gate opened, we went through and waited till the gate behind us closed. Then the inside gate would open. This time the inside gate did not open. We saw our guard inside the guard building talking to his officer. The officer came out with some other guards and told us that, because of a complaint from the farmer, he had to put us all under arrest. I asked him what the complaint was and he said that we refused to work.

Everyone was put under arrest and placed in a different spot in the building. I think they call this incommunicado. I was the first one to be interrogated. As tired as I was, I had to go through this interrogation. First I was asked what had actually happened. I told them, frankly and honestly, what happened as I remembered. All that I had done and described before, I had to go over and over with them. Finally I was sent, under guard, to a tent they had erected close to a tower and away from all the buildings in camp. I was the first one who entered. There were cots for every man in my team. I sat in the tent thinking how could it be possible, that after a real hard day of work, we were arrested for refusing to work? It was getting dark before the next man arrived in the tent. The first thing I wanted to know was what they asked him. They repeatedly asked him the same questions. Because he saw the guard and the farmer intensively talking, he gave the same answers as me. This kept on all through the night. Some saw more and some saw less. All heard the farmer say, "Don't worry about the quotas, try to salvage as much as you can from these fields." The camp commander thought this must be a conspiracy because we all were saying exactly the same thing. He was thinking we were coached to say the same thing. We were all put on bread and water. We all knew we were unjustly accused and arrested. Getting only bread and water was just another unfair punishment. We did not feel guilty of anything. We felt we had done our best to help a farmer in distress. Now we were wondering how bread and water tastes? After eating such good food in our mess hall, we were anxious about getting bread and water.

Very early in the morning we heard some scratching noises in back of our tent. Somebody from our kitchen, who had heard about us being put on bread and water, crawled on his hands and knees through the open field to our tent to bring us regular food. He slipped this food under the tent flaps. We did not want to eat it. We were waiting for bread and water, and we all had agreed to give it back to him. The guy from our kitchen had to take the food back. He probably was mad at us. In the morning, some of us were called back for interrogation with no change in our status.

During the time we were isolated in the tent, something was going on that we knew nothing about. In the morning was our church service and Father Yungst came to hold mass. He noticed that some of us were not at mass; and when he asked where we were, he was told that we were arrested for refusing to work. Right away he said, "Not Sigi. He would never do that. I've known him too long. He is not that kind of a guy." He asked for permission to speak to the camp commander who told him what the complaint was. Father Yungst said, "That is not possible. Sig would never do that." He told the commander how well he knew me. The commander said that he thought he knew me, too. The commander also said that during interrogation, he found everybody saying the same thing; and at first he thought that we had rehearsed our answers, but now he was not so sure. He said he would speak with the farmer again. When the farmer arrived, he was asked more questions and said he had only agreed to sign this complaint after being constantly badgered by the guard to sign it. The guard told him that the men were not doing their jobs. He was very satisfied that we were doing our best. The camp commander said he still had to talk to the guard again. We knew nothing about all of this. We were eating bread and drinking water, imagining it were steaks and champagne. It tasted great to us.

During the day, the camp commander talked to the guard, but we did not know anything of what was going on in the camp commander's office. We were still in the tent. In the evening, when the camp commander came to our tent, he slowly and with great hesitation apologized and said he had done a great injustice to us. The complaint was unfounded and we were released.

The following details we found out later from talking to other guards. When the guard was interrogated, they found out he was of Polish descent. His brother had just been killed by German troops and he felt hatred toward Germans. He was full of revenge toward Germans and that's why he fabricated this story to force the farmer to sign the complaint, despite the fact he farmer did not want to do it. He wanted to get even with the Germans for the death of his brother. The guard was removed from duty and later on transferred. We were rehabilitated. For some, it created an anger they kept constantly inside. For me, it was different. Surely this incident deeply affected me but for other reasons. It showed me how easily you can be convicted of something you did not do; but at the same time, only a fair and thorough investigation can bring out the truth. It was an experience I will never forget.

My next job was a surprise for me. I was told by our camp commander that I would be working on the air base. All of my former teammates were already working in harvesting and cutting pulpwood. After not working for a while, I was told I would be working with another prisoner in the reclamation yard. That word "reclamation" did not mean anything to me. The reclamation yard was just a place close to our prison camp. We walked daily, without a guard, to this place. A high, solid wood fence was around the reclamation yard to keep people out and from looking in. No military personnel were allowed in this yard. The only time they were allowed in was on official business.

We worked on the base airplane accidents, which were daily brought into this yard on flatbed trucks. We, with the help of Mr. Croy, our boss who was operating the big bulldozer, had to unload the plane and reassemble the pieces of the plane on the ground. We had to assemble the pieces so that the break points would be visible for the air base commission, who was responsible for judging the cause of the accident. Sometimes we had to take parts out of old crashed planes stored in the yard because they were needed on the base. Sometimes we had to get bodies out that were still in the plane. That was our daily chore. Mr. Croy was an American Indian and, I believe, a war veteran.

Across from the reclamation yard entrance was the oil storage area for the base. It was operated by Joe Sims. He was the only employee. He was an older man with gray hair and a World War I veteran. He looked a little bit like Oliver Hardy. He was a jolly person like Ollie. He always came over to the reclamation yard and had his lunch with Mr. Croy.

We prisoners ate our lunch in the adjoining room, but the door was open and we often had very nice conversations. The second prisoner with me did not speak English and he had no intention or willingness to learn or to understand it. So it was a three-way conversation—Mr. Croy, Joe Sims and me. After we got to know each other better, Joe said to me, "I never had a son. Why don't you call me 'Pops'?" So, from that time on, I called him "Pops" and he called me, "My son."

Our work would not have been very bad if it had not been for removing bodies. Airplane crashes occurred every day. If there was no crash one day, there were two crashes the next day. I remember a day when two planes crashed and each plane had instructors and student pilots aboard. Both were landing at the same time and one landed on top of the other. The cockpit of the lower plane had an instructor and seven students in it when it crashed to the ground. The cockpit was totally flat. We had to take the bodies out and Mr. Croy used the welding torch while we pried the metal apart. I will not describe any more. It was tough for us to do because we were thinking of the next of kin and how they would feel. We found all the ID tags.

Chapter 8

The War In Germany Comes To An End

Since I was a Prisoner of War, I could write to my parents and to Helen. Only one letter a month was allowed. I had two addresses—one to my parents in Bielitz, the next month Helen got a letter from me, wherever she was. They answered me back every other month.

It was December 1944 when Helen's letters suddenly stopped coming. I still kept writing her. The last letter I had received from her came from the field hospital in Olmuetz, Czechoslovakia. After writing a few months, I stopped, not knowing what happened. Beginning in 1945, no more letters came from home; and I did not write anymore either. I was hoping my parents would write me from another town if they had managed to be evacuated. I followed the movement of the front line in Europe by following the daily reports in the New York Times. This must have been in January 1945. For weeks, the front line between German and Russian troops went right through Bielitz. Sometimes it was east and sometimes it was west of the town. It had kept on changing back and forth for a month. I expected heavy fighting in that area, but not for that long a time. Then the front line moved west, and that meant to me that the Russians had captured Bielitz.

There was no longer a place to go home to. No longer a place to go to school and get my education. My work in the reclamation yard was all that kept my mind occupied. On May 8, 1945, after coming home from work, I picked up my New York Times from the PX. The headline read, "The war in Europe is ended! Surrender is unconditional; V-E will be proclaimed today!"

The days following the capitulation of the German Army were most quiet and reflective in our camp. Nobody was talking. Most of us were thinking, "What next?" How is life going to be for us?" For me, it seemed foolish to be sent home into a Communist-occupied home town. Friends offered me their home address to get sent to. We were all prepared to go home now, but nothing happened. Our daily work routine continued.

The newspapers and magazines described the discovery of many Concentration Camps, where Jewish people were starved and gassed. They showed pictures of Concentration Camp inmates dead from starvation. This created an uproar in the United States and in our POW camp. We read articles in the U.S. papers where readers were complaining about the coddling of the German Prisoners of War. They compared the treatment of the Concentration Camp inmates by the Nazis to the treatment of the German Prisoners of War by the Americans and some readers demanded that the German POWs not get coddled any more.

Suddenly, the GI rations were reduced and our meat rations were discontinued. For half a year after the War was over, the only meat we had was brain, probably beef brain. For half a year we had only brain, brain, brain. Our cook was very ingenious producing a different dish every day, but there is a limit to what you can do with brain. After eating brain for half a year, they switched over to fish; so for another half a year, we were eating fish. As soon as the war was over, we all noticed the rules of the Geneva Convention were abandoned. We not only had no more meat, but the entire ration became less. We began to see articles in the papers about German POWs starving and collapsing at work because they did not get enough to eat. It happened in our camp also. The farmers were afraid that prisoners would collapse during work at their farms, so they had water containers set up along the working area of the prisoners so you could drink water any time you wanted. They sometimes brought in sandwiches and drinks and stacked them up along the fields for the prisoners to eat and drink. This was welcome help, especially in hot working conditions.

My work was still at the reclamation yard. At our three-way conversations, Mr. Croy and Pops asked if they could see our lunch bags. The lunch was very small and contained no meat, so they split their own lunch and handed it to us. Pops and Mr. Croy agreed that we worked hard in the reclamation yard and we needed good food, not the inadequate lunch we got. From that time on, we always had plenty to eat. We talked about going home soon. Pops knew my hometown was occupied by the Russians and promised to help me in Europe. Mr. Croy also asked me to stay in touch with him.

Soon, our whole camp at Moody Field was closed down and we were shipped to Fort Benning to close that place down. Next, we were sent to the railroad station in Columbus, Georgia. It as one of those strange events. The press was there to interview us and there were thank you speeches to us, so we thought that we were going home. After all, it was 1946. It seemed we were the last POWs to go home.

We took the train to Atlanta where we stopped at Fort McPherson and disembarked. At that time, Fort McPherson was a military distribution center. Trains with troops from Europe, their trucks, and vehicles had to unload their vehicles and the troops got re-assigned. It was the "Grand Central Station" of the military. I worked in the kitchen, first scrubbing floors and then making coffee—lots of coffee—about 40 gallons a day. Everybody had a job, either in the kitchen or unloading the vehicles. Many times we had food ready for a train which did not arrive and every bit of food had to be emptied into the garbage. Imagine 10, 20, or more big roasted pineapple hams, swimming in the garbage; and we were still on the meager rations. We had to prepare for the next train. Every day and night, the trains would come and the food had to be ready.

In this place I met a GI named Donald Olmsted. He worked as a guard in the kitchen. Whenever he needed help, he asked for me. During this time we got acquainted pretty well. He had returned from Europe and was waiting for his new assignment. We had long conversations about each other's life. I told him what kind of work I did in prison and for the farmers. He was impressed about all the farm work I did. He was a student at the University of Minnesota, and his father had a farm in that state. He noticed how much I had worked on farms over the last few years, and he offered to help me if I needed it.

One day I got a letter. It was the first letter in a year and a half. It was mailed form New York City. It was a letter from my parents, telling me they were in Salzburg and I should try to get released to their address. I was overjoyed. How that letter got mailed from New York and how it passed through the American censors I did not know, but I did not care. I had gotten an address of my parents in the nick of time. Now, I had a place to go home to.

Chapter 9

Going Home To Salzburg

It was in the nick of time that I found out where my parents lived. The place I was supposed to go home was already established and approved a year ago, right after the war in Europe had ended. I had chosen a friend's address where I could stay in his parent's house. First, I did not know if I could change that to the new address of my parents, but I was told it was in the nick of time. It was not too late to have my discharge destination changed. The day we would be going home was not known. We still worked in Fort McPherson, and I had many conversations with Don Olmsted. He talked about his parent's farm in Little Falls, Minnesota, and his studies at the University of Minnesota. I talked about my parents and sisters and my fiancé, Helen. Now that I had heard from my parents, I was not worried about them anymore because I knew that they and my sisters had made it through the war. I was still very worried about Helen, knowing she was a nurse stationed at the front line.

Nothing happened for awhile. As usual, when you expect it the least, it happens. One day we were told to gather our things and were put on a train. This time we felt it was for real. We were on a train going north. We did not know where we were going to get off, but by the signs at the railroad stations and the towns we were going through, we knew we were going very far north. The train went through Washington, DC, and the state of New York; but this was all we knew. When the train stopped, we got off and were marched through a military town located on the west side of the Hudson River. We stayed in a camp there and then embarked on a Liberty ship.

We went down the Hudson River, but we did not see any of the sights because we were kept in the men's quarters below deck. Suddenly, we stopped. We stayed at this spot for some time, and this allowed our guards to let us up on deck. We were anchored right in front of the Statue of Liberty in the harbour of New York. We gazed in awe at the Statue of Liberty, and the guards and sailors on board were proud to tell us everything they knew of the history and symbolism of the Statue.

We stayed at this spot a few days. We heard that the Liberty ship had developed some engine problems and they were waiting for parts to repair it. This gave us ample opportunity to gaze and admire the Statue of Liberty. We had an otherwise uneventful trip across the Atlantic. When we sailed into the English Channel, we still did not know where we were heading. Finally the ship turned to LeHavre, France, where we disembarked and were put into the POW camp of Bolbec, close to the harbour.

Bolbec was another huge prison camp. Some prisoners had already been there a very long time. I thought to myself, how long was I going to be in here? Suddenly, they picked out all the mechanics and we were shipped by trucks to the south, west of Paris, to the town of Rambouillet. There, in the courtyard of the big castle of Rambouillet, we were unloaded.

All the stables at the castle had been modified into garages. We put up our tents in the castle's park. We heard that an American multi-millionaire was picking up, with the help of German Prisoners of War, all the abandoned vehicles the Army had left behind in Europe. He brought them to Rambouillet, repaired them with the help of German prisoners, and sold them to countries who needed them. We heard that the multi-millionaire had a contract with the U.S. government, but I don't know if it was a rumor or the truth.

A German sergeant was in charge of us in Rambouillet. Some POWs were sent to pick up the vehicles in Holland, Belgium, and other countries and bring them back by driving through Paris. Sometimes one good truck would pull two disabled trucks through the heavy traffic in Paris. I was working on trucks and jeeps in the garages. The German sergeant told us that if we finished a certain number of trucks and jeeps, they would be the next shipment to Austria, and everybody from Austria would go along and be discharged. That sounded good, but we did not believe it.

The day came, the vehicles were ready, and lo and behold we Austrians were put on the trucks. The guards drove the jeeps and we were on the way home. First we went through Germany and were shocked by all the towns in ruins, especially the town of Ulm. The center of the town was completely in ruins. Most of us were silent during the ride. We were all thinking and trying to explain this disaster to ourselves. Germany was in ruins, completely devastated. My opinion was that it would take generations to restore everything to what it was before.

There were three of us going to Salzburg. On the ride, we talked about what we would do when we arrived home. One guy said to me that we would have to take the streetcar to his place. "The streetcar stops right in front of my parent's house," he said. I told him that I had never been in Salzburg before and I didn't know where in Niederalm my parents lived. He told me that the streetcar goes to Anif, and from there it is only a half an hour walk to Niederalm. The guards were going to officially hand us over to the local government.

It was Sunday when we arrived and all the offices were closed. They handed us over to the Red Cross who gave us all kinds of information for "Heimkehrer", the home comer. That was what the returning soldiers were called. They gave us tickets for the streetcar, and we were on our way to the streetcar stop. When the streetcar arrived, we could not sit down because our duffel bags were too big, especially mine.

When I had left Moody Field, Georgia, I had taken some of my books along. I had taken 12 books which made the bag awfully heavy. All my friends called me stupid. Some were big books like "Collected Short Stories of Somerset Maughan", "Heritage, a Collection of English Literature", "American Social and Political History", "American Democracy and Social Change", "The United States and its Place in World Affairs", and more. Up to now, I never had to carry them, but now I wondered if I would be able to carry this bag for the half hour walk after the end of the streetcar line. I felt I needed these books. I love to read books of English literature.

The first guy did not have far to go home. After a few streetcar stops he left, wishing us "Good Luck". The second guy was counting down every streetcar stop. "Three more stops to go to my house. Two more stops. One more stop." I was anxiously awaiting his house, too, having heard so much about it from him. "This is the stop," he said. The streetcar stopped but we did not see any house. The guy got out of the streetcar and stood before the spot where his house was supposed to be. There was nothing, just a big empty hole. As the streetcar started rolling again, I shouted "Goodbye" and "Good Luck" to him as he stood there looking at the big empty hole. I found out later that a stray bomb fell on this house. They never did rebuilt on the spot, and I never found out what happened to that fellow and his family.

The streetcar followed the road out of Salzburg. My eyes were fixed on the many beautiful old buildings and high mountains in the background. Slowly the crowded buildings gave way to open countryside with its beauty and stillness. Before I knew it, the streetcar came to a stop. The end of the line and the town of Anif. I asked some people at the stop how to get to the next village of Niederalm. They pointed to a small path between the fields and told me to follow this path. This was the short cut to Niederalm. I placed my big duffel bag on my shoulder, tried to get it balanced right and holding the front with my hand, I followed the path.

After walking for fifteen minutes, I could barely hold it anymore. I was dead tired and worried. There was no place in the field to put the bag down; and if I did, how would I get the bag up on my shoulder again. In the distance I could see a church. I thought it must be Niederalm, so I kept on going. I had lost all feeling in my arm and shoulder, and I could barely move as I came closer and closer to the church.

The church was on the outskirts of the village and I was heading straight at the church. I saw a cemetery surrounding the church, and around the cemetery was a high stone wall. It was too high to put my bag on, but coming closer I saw a dip in the wall. Two sections of the wall came together and one section was lower, forming a dip. I headed for this dip, completely exhausted and on the point of collapse. I had not met anybody on the road and there was nobody on the streets of Niederalm. With my last strength, I put my bag on the wall and then relaxed.

It as wonderful to get the circulation going and regain my breath and my strength. I was not yet ready to go, when I saw a young girl coming down the street toward me. She casually looked at me; and as she came closer, she seemed to recognize me. Suddenly she crossed the street and asked me if I was Siegfried Hoffmann.

I said, "Yes."

She said that my parents were waiting for me, grabbed me, and pulled me away from the wall. I was not ready to go and struggling to put my bag on my shoulder, she kept on pulling me away from the wall. I said to her, "Please let me put my bag on my shoulder." I got the bag on my shoulder and we walked through the village to my parent's place. She introduced herself as the Hinterberger girl, a common way to call somebody's name in Austria. She lived only one street away from my parents and showed me how to get to my parent's place. My bag was killing me and if I stopped again, I could never have lifted it back on my shoulder. I walked through the wooden gate to a house where I saw two elderly persons working in a vegetable garden.

Part V

Getting A Fresh Start

Chapter 1

A Mournful Wiedersehen

I almost did not recognize my mother and father. They were bending down and weeding. They slowly got up and looked at me. I must have looked like a stranger to them but just for a short time. Gazing at me, the stranger soon vanished. We embraced and cried. We were so happy that we had survived. We went into the house and sat down. My father said, "You are looking good." My mother looked thin and tired.

I looked at my father and said, "You are looking very thin and worn out." He told me to wait for a while. He was not ready to tell me about his life during the War.

I asked my father where Brunhild was. He said that Brunhild was working downtown in Salzburg and not home yet. Then I asked him where Erika was. My father and mother stopped talking. I saw the pain in my mother's eyes and she started crying.

I asked, "What happened?"

Then my father told me. Just a month ago, as she always did, Erika went to Glasenbach where the Americans were stationed to pick up laundry that she would wash at home. She did that regularly to make money. There was no streetcar or bus going in that direction so she had to thumb her way, trying to get a ride from any truck or car going that direction. GIs were not allowed to give a ride to civilians. This day, a truck stopped and she hopped into the back of the open truck.

Close to Anif, two giggling young schoolgirls were jumping and running along this busy highway. Just before the truck was going to pass them, one girl ran halfway across the street. The truck driver swerved to avoid the schoolgirl, but too late. The swerving threw Erika off the truck and it tipped over on top of her. Both the schoolgirl and Erika were killed.

For a while, I was silent. I tried to sort everything out in my mind. I asked my father where she was buried. He said that she was buried in the cemetery by the church here in Niederalm. He also said that the whole village turned out for her funeral because she was well known and liked by everybody. I asked my father, "Where, approximately, is she buried? I would like to go and see her grave."

He said to me, "Close to where the dip is in the wall. Right behind the lowest point in the wall." I was just standing there with my duffel bag on the wall and my back to the cemetery. He told me that my sister's name was on a wooden cross he had erected for her.

If I had turned around I would have seen my sister's name on the cross. Then I remembered the girl pulling me away. She knew my name. She knew that my sister was buried behind me. She knew that if I had turned around, I would have seen my sister's name and asked questions. She did not want me to find out this way.

We kept on talking. There was so much we did not know. They told me what they had gone through and I told them what I had experienced. When Brunhild came home from work, we were so happy to see each other again. We hugged and kissed. She told me what she had gone through to stay alive. When I asked her if she had heard anything from Helen, she said no. She had not heard from her since Helen was in Olmuetz. She had placed an ad in the Salzburg paper some months before, asking if anyone knew the whereabouts of a Red Cross nurse named Helene Urbanke and to contact Brunhild Hoffmann at this address. After many months, she had not received any answer. Of course, the Salzburg paper at that time had a very small circulation.

I put what my father and mother told me about their life during the war together. I will now continue with their story.

After they had tortured him to get a confession out of him, my father had been released by the Gestapo because of insufficient evidence. He was arrested for helping some of his Jewish friends, whose property had been confiscated, to get papers and money out of the sealed up homes. Insufficient evidence did not deter the Gestapo from treating him as a guilty person. He could not get a job nor any jobless benefits. His many friends did not dare to do anything to help him for fear they would be suspected of supporting an enemy of Germany. They would not have anything to do with him. He said, "At that time, there were no more friends to help him. They were afraid to be called an enemy of Germany, afraid to end somewhere in a Concentration Camp."

The Gestapo finally allowed him to have a job. Germany decided to gather all the bodies of soldiers killed in the War in southern Poland and put them in a new military cemetery outside of Bielitz. He was to inspect all the bodies of unknown German soldiers before re-burial and try to identify them. If he identified any, he had to write a letter to the next of kin. He told me that many mothers, fathers, or wives wrote him letters thanking him for finding their loved ones.

In the beginning of 1945, they drafted him into the "Volksturm", a unit of old men and youngsters. It was a last ditch effort of the German Army to get troops into the battle. His unit was to defend the town of Breslau in Silesia from the Russian "Stalin" tanks. He was ordered to make Molotov cocktails, dig himself a foxhole, and wait till the tanks appeared. When the tanks appeared, they threw the Molotov cocktails at the tanks. It did not have any effect on the tanks. On the contrary, the tanks would make half a turn over the foxhole and the man in the hole would be buried alive. His company commander got killed. He had to take over the company. After the battle they found my father. He was not wounded, but a mentally broken man. They discharged him but kept many old men and youngsters who had lost arms and legs.

In the meantime, my mother and sisters were evacuated from Bielitz. They fled to Vienna, where my uncle lived. This was the place they had agreed to meet in an emergency. My father had himself discharged to Vienna, where they were reunited. Vienna was close to being overrun by the Russians when the War ended, and they had truly to take the last train out.

Somewhere between Czechoslovakia and Germany, on an open field with no houses or towns around, the train stopped. Everyone was left on their own. On the road with hundreds of other refugees they were walking north. In a town, my father said it was Dresden, they were looking at the depot for any train. There the bombs hit the town and the depot which was crowded with refugees. Everyone was running for cover. He fell to the ground, trampled by people who stepped on him. He could not get up. Before him, at arms length, was a billfold stuffed with money. It was probably someone's life savings. He could not get up, people in panic still stepping on him. Finally he could grab it and he could run for cover while everything around him crashed down. Luckily he found my mother and my sisters. They joined thousands and thousands of refugees who were being chased and hounded by the Russians. I remember my mother telling me how my father protected my sisters. The Russians went through the shelter to look for young men who were suspected to be German soldiers. In fact they were looking for girls to rape. My father had my sisters crawl together, put straw over them, and sat on the straw. Before the Russians came, he took his false teeth out. They saw an old man and an old woman and left them alone. They lived with the atrocities, always trying to get to the American Army, who they hoped would treat them humanely. They were forced to eat anything eatable from the fields, including dandelions. They were starving for days and weeks till they finally got to the Americans. Now they were at least safe but still starving. The Americans did not feed them, at least not in the beginning. There was this "no fraternization order" where any American soldier was prohibited to give food to their enemy. Besides, there were too many starving people. Maybe that was what changed the mind of the American authorities, and they began to feed them. Somewhere in Germany, they took shelter in a camp with thousands of others. Money could not buy them anything. Just the pity, mercy, and the humane behavior of the American troops saved them.

It was in this camp where they heard rumors of work was available in the Salzburg area. They decided to leave that camp in Germany and go to Salzburg. When I arrived, they lived in a wooden barrack. They had one room and a kitchen. They shared this with Brunhild and Erika. Another family lived next to them in the same barrack. This type of barracks was called, at that time, a "Behelfsheim", a temporary home. Right next to them, in a big and stately house, lived the Silberhauer's, the owners of the property. They were very friendly and helpful to the many refugees who settled around them. They built the temporary home for my parents.

Brunhild, Erika, and my father had started to work for a construction architect from Bielitz. This architect had established, with the permission of the local authorities, a building site next to the Koenigsee River in Niederalm, where he produced bricks and sewage pipes made of cement and asbestos. The demand for these bricks and pipes was tremendous. He mostly hired people from Bielitz, as many as were willing or able to work. The wages were very low and the work very hard.

Later my sisters started to work in other jobs where they made better money. My father worked for a while making the bricks and sewer pipes, but soon it was too much for him and he had to stop working. Since his discharge from the German Volksturm, his health was failing him more and more. Many times the ambulance brought him to the hospital where he stayed for a few days to weeks. Two World Wars had taken a toll on him.

I asked my parents if they heard anything from Alfred, my adopted brother. In a composed and low voice, my father told me Alfred went down with his U-boat and crew in May 1943. No survivors. They got the official notification when they were still in Bielitz. They could not tell me that in the letters to the prison camp. It would not have gone through the German censors. I told them how we were under U-boat attacks when we crossed the Atlantic on the Rotterdam in May 1943. It could have been that his U-boat was in on these attacks. Maybe he was somewhere else. We will never know.

As sick as my father was, he wanted to do something to help his family, so he started painting. After the War, there were no brushes or paint available to buy. He started to make his own brushes and his own simple paint. He began to paint flowers, like an Edelweiss or Gentian, and he painted on cardboard or wood. People liked what he painted and bought them. When paints became available, his paintings became better and more elaborate. He painted mountains, lakes, and the scenery surrounding the Salzburg area—like the Untersberg and the Salzburg fortress, later made famous in the movie "Sound of Music". There were a lot of GIs who wanted to have a souvenir from Austria. My father painted for a long time just to get something to eat. He never made any money. As long as he felt fine, he painted. He had never painted before. He just had an inherent talent that I did not have. Many painting were brought to the U.S. by GIs going home.

Chapter 2

My Work During The Time In Austria

This chapter comprises the time period when I arrived and when we, as a family, left Austria.

Just a few days after I had come home, I went to the "Arbeitsant", an employment office, to ask for a job for a "Heimkehrer". Everybody told me that the only jobs they have for returning soldiers are in the cement factory. Sure enough, that's what they offered me. The job consisted of blasting rocks off the mountains and crushing the big rocks into little ones. Then the little rocks were crushed further into a powder, made into cement, and filled into bags. Any new employee started on the worst part of the job, the blasting and crushing. I knew that and I didn't want it. It was a dangerous job and your lungs got filled by this damaging dust. This was no job for me.

I wanted a safer and healthier job, so I joined my sister in Salzburg as a sales clerk in the American Gift Shop. My sister spoke very good English. She had learned it in the same school as I in Istanbul. All the GIs called her Bruni, so I began to call her Bruni too. I found out that the Americans stationed in Glasenbach needed an English-speaking handyman, which paid a lot more than the sales clerk job I had. At the military base in Glasenbach, my job consisted of filling the soda fountain with Coke syrup, ice cream cans, fruit toppings, ice cubes, and all the stuff that was needed in a soda fountain. I quickly learned everything there was to learn, and soon I was running the soda fountain with an American GI named Mr. Durkee. I remember him very well. He was an extraordinary character, and he treated his employees like human beings. He was concerned for everyone's life and helped wherever he could. He was a fantastic person. At the end of his tour of duty, he left to go back to the U.S.

In the meantime, I was teaching English at home to anyone who wanted to learn English. My first pupils were the children of the Haug family. They were Austrians. On one of their trips to the U.S. before the War their daughter, Hannelore, was born. The U.S. government reminded them that their daughter had a claim on U.S. citizenship, and they were preparing to take advantage of it. Their daughter and her brother were my first pupils; and later on in the U.S., the Haugs were still our best friends. My pupils were farm children whose parents wanted them to learn English, and the rich and famous people who lived in beautiful estates in this village. I did not ask much for a lesson, but the popularity of knowing English rose tremendously in this little village of Niederalm. Now, of course, Niederalm is a town with many industries having settled there. Even Sony has a plant there and is making CD disks.

Getting back to describing my work in Glasenbach. The name Glasenbach was dropped and the installation was renamed "Camp Truscott", after the first U.S. soldier killed in action in Austria. Later we opened up a snackbar to go with the soda fountain. I first worked as a cook, then as a waiter, and finally as a cashier. Again, I learned everything—every phase of the food and beverage department—until I became manager of the snackbar and fountain.

The PX was building an ice cream factory in Camp Truscott and I became manager of the ice cream factory. We had four machines which each made five gallons of ice cream in 15 minutes; that was 20 gallons in 15 minuets, 80 gallons an hour, and 640 gallons in an 8-hour day, theoretically, of course. The washing of the machines, especially when changing flavors, reduced that amount. The ice cream was delivered to every U.S. installation in the American zone in Austria.

When the U.S. troops in Saalfelden opened up a snackbar and soda fountain, I was called there to get it going. When the American Red Cross opened up a soda fountain in Salzburg in the Mirabell Casino, I opened and managed it. All this time I worked under contract to the U.S. Forces in Austria. I never got paid for overtime. I spent many hours after work making schedules, working on the profit and loss statements, inventories, and constantly checking that nobody stole our inventory from the stockroom or warehouse.

Before I left for the U.S. Helen's brother, Viki, and I were talking about working together. He was a master plumber and worked on a project for the U.S. Forces in Austria installing the plumbing in the sergeants' family buildings. He said I could make at least double the money I was now earning working on these projects as a plumber's helper. So I quit my job with the U.S. Forces in Austria and worked as a plumber's helper. Right he was. Oh, how right he was. I easily made twice what I made as a manager. It was hard and exhaustive work.

I remember the time we ran out of galvanized pipes. All the plumbing parts were furnished by the U.S. Forces if our plumbing company could not get them on the open market in Austria. This was the case most of the time. The U.S. Forces could confiscate products in the American zones in Germany and Austria. Our plumbing company had a stipulation in the contract, where it would be paid a bonus for each day work was done ahead of the scheduled day of completion, and a stiff penalty for each day over the scheduled day of completion. We were racing to be well ahead of schedule.

Suddenly we ran out of galvanized pipes. We asked the U.S. Forces in Austria for help. They looked all over the American zone in Germany and Austria to no avail. We had to meet the deadline. So we left walls open, especially the main access shaft which went up every one of the three-story buildings. We had to work around it, wherever it was possible. The deadline came nearer and nearer. Our company was afraid of the penalty for each day they would go over.

Then, almost too late, the pipes arrived. We worked and worked, 24 hours straight, without interruption. We fell asleep while we were working. Once, I woke up and I was cutting pipes. We kept on working 24 hours more; 48 hours with only two hours of sleep. I can still hear Viki shouting and cussing at me. He was my boss and, like me, he was dead tired too. But our paycheck was sweet and fat.

Chapter 3

The Stahlhouse

To tell this story, I have to go back in time when I had arrived in Salzburg and I was searching for Helen.

In the beginning of 1947, as I came home from work in Glasenbach, Bruni showed me a letter she had just received from Helen. She wrote from Northern Germany and said she had gotten this ad from her aunt, who saw it in a Salzburg paper some time ago and kept it. When her aunt found out where Helen was, she sent her the ad she had cut out. Helen's letter asked Bruni if she had heard anything from Sigi. What a surprise and what a lucky turn of events!

I sat down right away and wrote Helen a letter and soon we were corresponding again. We both had changed during the War and we wanted to find out if we felt the same for each other. We wanted to meet, but the borders were closed and nobody could go across the border to see anybody, relative nor friend. Austria was crowded with refugees from all over Europe and they could not afford to feed any more people.

Everybody knew that there were lodges in the mountains which were half in Austria and half in Germany. The border goes right through the middle of some of these lodges. They were always a big tourist attraction for people who wanted to go up and meet people from the other side. Now a sizable number of border guards were watching over people who would try to cross the border illegally. They watched from many spots on the mountain. I had heard a lot of stories about people who fooled them.

I decided on the Stahlhouse. It was easily accessible from Austria and Germany and was located between two mountain peaks, so I hoped it would be more sheltered. I never knew how tough the climb was from the German side. Nowadays there is a lift going up to this lodge from the German side. First I had to write Helen and ask her if she would meet me in the mountains. Viki, her brother from Linz, Austria would come along with me and my sister, Bruni. Helen's return letter said she would gladly meet me. She did not mention any problems she would have to overcome. She mentioned that her sister, Liesl, and her husband, Robert, would come along.

The day of the climb arrived. It was a nice day, just some clouds high above the mountains. Viki, Bruni and I took the train to the foot of the mountain. We all had heavy mountain climbing shoes on and were equipped with the necessary things for mountain climbing. To our surprise, the climb started easy. The path was clearly marked and not too steep, and it went through mostly wooded areas.

Later on it became steeper but still wound through woods until we hit the tree line and snow fields. Yes, it was summertime, but the snow does not melt up in these elevations.

We could see part of the Stahlhouse between a few hills appearing in the distance. The climb was coming to an end but we did not slow down. In fact, we seemed to increase our pace with the goal in sight. The climb probably took us three or four hours, but we were not exhausted at the end. It was so nice to come to a place of shelter, to relax and have the comfort of home. The Stahlhouse provided us with all the modern conveniences of a home. We brought our own food along just to save us some money.

We looked at the lodge registry, which is like a guest book, but no Helen Urbanke nor Liesl or Robert Grabski was in the book. We went outside to look toward the side they would come from. We saw the border marked with a long steel fence with some barbed wire on the top. The path from the other side led to an opening in the fence on our side. Nobody was coming. Over the next few hours, we looked many times. Viki had his binoculars along. We could see the faces of the people coming up from the German side. We all were worried now. The rooms had to be reserved, but we waited to do that in case they were not coming.

We thought we had planned everything. We could not understand what had gone wrong. It was late in the afternoon when we again went outside. Viki watched the German side with his binoculars and described the people coming up. This late in the day, nobody was coming up anymore. Suddenly, he saw one single person coming up in the distance. He told us, "It's a woman." Then he told us, "It's a local girl. She is wearing a 'Dirndl.'" A Dirndl is a dress worn by girls in Bavaria and Austria. We asked him if she looked like Helen. He said, "No. She has light sandals. She must be a Sennerin." Sennerin is a local girl, who lives up in the mountains in the summer.

I asked Viki to give me the binoculars to see for myself. She did not look like Helen, at least not the Helen I remembered. Besides, she was alone and had sandals on. She must be a native girl, I thought. The way she walked seemed familiar. The closer she came, the more familiar she appeared to me. So, we all went closer to the fence. The closer I came, the more she looked like Helen. When I heard her saying the word "Sigi", which was faint but still loud enough for me to hear, I knew it had to be Helen. I ran towards the fence and Helen was running towards the fence on the German side. We met at the opening of the fence. We kissed and hugged. Tears of joy were running down our faces. It was a wonderful feeling, brother and sister, girlfriend and boyfriend, who had not seen each other for a long time. What a happy reunion! The many years of separation, the years of longing vanished in the fulfillment of a "Wiedersehen".

Helen had a lot to tell us about her climb. Liesl and Robert would come up the next day. By now, there were no more beds available in the lodge. We had to stay in the hayloft, which we did not mind. All night we talked and talked. We had a ball in the hayloft. As the daylight appeared over the mountain peaks, we were still talking, and for Helen and I, making plans to get married. The next day Liesl and Robert came up. Another round of kissing and hugging and telling each other how we survived the War years. During the day, we walked through fields of beautiful clean snow.

I had gotten, with the permission of Mr. Durkee, some ice cream toping. I believe it was cherry and strawberry. We scraped off the top layer from the snow, put the snow underneath in cups, and added some of the toppings. This made beautiful snow cones. We all enjoyed it.

This meeting up at the Stahlhouse was a very joyous moment in our lives, but it also came to an end. Liesl, Robert, and Helen had to leave early because they had to take a train for the northern part of Germany. We only had a short trip to Salzburg once we were back at the foot of the mountain. It was tough to say "goodbye" after just saying "hello", but the prospect of seeing each other soon made it easier to say "goodbye". We parted, each in the hope the "Wiedersehen" would be soon.

Chapter 4

The Purtscheller House

Before I went to the Stahlhouse, I had already inquired with Austrian officials about what paperwork I needed to get married. After the meeting at the Stahlhouse and talking with Helen she said she had all the necessary papers or could get them. Over the next month, the letters from her contained all the necessary papers. Mine were ready, and soon I had all the papers.

When I asked one Austrian official where I could get the permission for the entry permit for Helen, he told me that there are no entry permits given to anyone. I told him that she has to cross the border to come here to get married. He said, "Sorry, nobody is allowed to enter this country." I was angry and I told him that this is stupid.

"How can you give me the permission to marry somebody from Germany and the permission to live here but don't give the permission to let her into this country?"

He said, and I remember his words very well, "Once she is in this country, we can't very well do anything about how she got in. Can we?" This gave me the answer. If she got in secretly, and that could only be done illegally, there's nothing the official can or would do. That was the answer.

We had a friend in Niederalm, actually he was also a friend of my father, who sold all the pictures my father painted. One thing I did not know was that he was a mountain guide and mountain climber. His name was Toni. He was a well trained man, young and strong and good looking. He offered to help me bring Helen across the border. When I promised I would pay him, he said in a quiet voice, "I do not want your money. I do this for you because you are my friend." He wanted us to promise that we would follow his instructions down to the last detail.

The instructions included that Helen and I were not to acknowledge each other when we met. Helen again was coming up with Liesl and Bruni, and I would climb up from the Austrian side. We were never to look at him, only to watch for his signs. We will see him only if it is necessary for him. He told us the mountain police, gendarmes or border patrols, are watching you from the time you start climbing. They have their observation posts high in the mountains where they can observe every trail.

At that distance, they can only recognize you by the color of the clothes you are wearing. If you are coming up, for instance wearing a brown jacket and black trousers, you will have to go back down wearing a brown jacket and black trousers. If you don't or you go down the other side, they got you. We had to follow his rules. All the time we would have to pretend not to know him and not to know Helen and Liesl. We would only communicate with certain signals. He wanted Helen to wear bright colored clothes. Since Helen and Bruni were the same size, he did not see any problem.

As a crossing point, he suggested the Purtscheller House. It was not far from Salzburg, easily accessible from the German and the Austrian side, and harder for the border guards to watch. I informed Helen immediately. In my next letters, I repeated Toni's instructions over and over again for she and I to remember. They were probably strange for Helen. I did not know why he wanted it this way but we followed his orders. I was ready and Helen was ready. The date was set and the day finally arrived.

Bruni and I took the train to the foot of the mountain. Toni was on the same train, but he pretended not to know us. It was again a very nice day. In the case of rain or a storm, we had no alternative plan. We could only postpone it to the next day and we would have to stay the night at the Purtscheller House. This would have caused some problems with our plan. Changing the plan was impossible because we could not communicate it to Helen. As soon as we got off the train, I noticed there were border patrols all over. They were obviously watching us and it looked like they were counting the people that got out of the train. They did not ask for any identification. We were dressed as Austrian tourists and we both spoke German. They looked us over as if they wanted to memorize what we were wearing.

We finally went on our way and the climb started slowly. We made the trip over the Rossfeld; and as we were standing on the road and looking to the German side, Toni appeared out of nowhere. He pointed to the German side with Berchtesgaden in the background and Hitler's hideout in front of us. Farther up, on the top of the mountain, he pointed to a building. He told us, "This is the Teahouse or commonly called the "Eagles Nest". When I asked him where Helen was going to climb up, he pointed to Hitler's hideout and said, "She might come up from there." As fast as he had appeared, he was gone again.

Soon we saw the Purtscheller House in the distance. We could see it clearly because there were no hills or other obstructions in front of it. When we arrived at the Purtscheller House, we were not tired but our nerves were on edge. A lot of people were already up at the lodge. Toni was there, but again, we pretended not to know him. It was hard to find Helen and Liesl. Finally we found them, but we had to pretend we did not know them.

The next hours were very strange. I passed Helen and Liesl, but no move of mine showed that we knew each other. When I got the sign from Toni to exchange the clothes, I gave the sign to Bruni and Helen. Bruni had the papers

Helen needed and they both disappeared, separately, to the bathroom. Shortly afterward, Bruni appeared in Helen's clothing and Helen in Bruni's clothing. They did not come back to me. They stayed away from me and from each other, so as not to cause any suspicions. So far, so good!

Now we needed to leave slowly and without anybody looking scared or panicky. I was waiting for Toni to give me the sign. No sign, nothing. I saw Toni going in and out of the lodge. It did not seem to me that there was any reason not to go. When I looked at the beer counter, there were two border patrolmen in uniform drinking beer and talking to a civilian. I was wondering if they saw or heard anything. Did they notice the clothing switch? This must be, by now, a common trick up here at the lodge.

Time was passing and no signal from Toni. In fact, I did not see Toni, nor did I know where he was. The two border patrolmen had left and everything seemed normal. Suddenly, there was Toni. He gave the sign and I gave the sign to Helen to follow me. Slowly I got up from the chair and headed toward the door. At the door I looked back at Helen, hoping that she understood the sign. She was slowly getting up, too.

Helen now had on Bruni's clothes, so it would have been safe for her to walk with me. Just in case anybody was thinking there was something fishy going on, we went separately to the Austrian side. Bruni now had Helen's clothes on. They would surely suspect her of crossing illegally and watch her.

When I thought I was far enough away on the trail, I stopped and waited for Helen. Now we could talk and we embraced and kissed. Helen was sorry that she could not say goodbye to Liesl. Her sister had to go back down to Germany alone, not knowing if Helen had made it.

Many years afterwards, Liesl told us what happened as she went down the German side. A German border policeman stopped her and she jokingly said, "You got me." After he checked her papers, she continued to joke with him till he laughingly let her go. In her backpack she had Helen's German ID papers, which Liesl took back home again. Who knows what would have happened if he had found Helen's identification papers.

Bruni had gone ahead of us and met Helen later. Suddenly Toni was there. He had been watching us all the time. Toni told us to travel in small groups and join other groups going down. He told us to go with one group for a while and then switch to other groups. He said that before he got to the end of the trail, he would meet us again.

Now we were together. Down the trail we went, slowly joining other groups. When we were together again, we had so many things to talk about. We noticed that we were actually going down a lot faster when we were together and talking. Suddenly, Toni appeared. He was already coming up from the end of the trail. He explained to us the problem we would be facing when we came close to the rail-road station. The trail ends before a bridge. On this bridge were border patrols checking everyone's papers. There would be no way to go around this bridge.

His plan was this—Toni and I would go first across the bridge. Then, some time later, Helen, and very last Bruni. "If anyone can join up with another group on the trail, the better," he said. "At the station," he said, "we still do not know each other. We are still strangers till I see that everything is clear."

I still did not understand the reason for his plan but we followed it. As we came out of the woods, we could see the bridge. Toni and I were in deep conver-sation discussing what we would have to do, when we approached the two border patrolmen. Toni recognized one of them right away; and as they greeted each other and talked of having not seen each other for some time, I showed my pa-pers to the other man. I pointed out to him that I had the papers of my wife also, but she is coming down with another group behind me. I pointed to a group just coming out of the woods and he nodded.

My papers were in order and I waited for Toni to finish his conversation with the other man. Toni told him that he was married and his wife had twins. Toni got his billfold out and showed him the pictures of his twins. They were in a very in-tense and friendly conversation and I was getting impatient because Helen was coming closer. But Toni had a lot of pictures of his twins and he kept talking. I left and walked slowly towards the railroad station.

Toni's plan was to keep the two men from the border patrol distracted to let Helen go through. They were focusing on Bruni anyway, who was wearing Helen's clothes. When Helen arrived with a group of people, they all showed their papers. Helen had some of the papers and she said, "My husband has all the other papers and he went ahead of me." The border patrolman remembered that I had told him that my wife was coming with a group behind me, so he let her through. They were all focusing on Bruni. When they found Bruni's papers in or-der, they had to let her go through.

At the railroad station we were again surrounded by many border guards. Any mistake, such as showing joy or embracing, would have lead to an investiga-tion and an arrest. We remembered Toni's instructions. We all acted like strang-ers. We got on the rain and still played our dangerous game. When the train pulled into Salzburg and we got out, Toni, who was also on the train, came up to us and said we would not have to pretend anymore. It felt like a big stone fell off my heart. We did it! Helen and I embraced and kissed for a long time. It was over.

Everything went smooth. Many thanks to Toni for helping us to find a way. The law should have provided Helen with a safe entry into Austria. Later when our first child, Brigitte, was born he brought Helen's mother and sister across the border illegally and back again. Not over the mountains this time, just through the flat areas near Salzburg. The law still prevented them from coming legally into Austria to visit grandchildren and relatives. Thank you, Toni!

When we came home, Helen was welcomed as if she had always been part of our family. She was used to living in crowded quarters in Gruenenplan. She was likewise now living in very crowded quarters in a room and a kitchen with four other people in Niederalm.

We were now actively preparing for the wedding, as soon as it was possible. Helen had to have a bridal gown. A cousin of Helen's had one she could borrow. I needed a suit. After a year in Austria, I still did not have anything to wear except the POW clothes I came to Austria with. The painted POW I had already scraped off and washed out, but you still could see it. I could not go the wedding like that. From my work in the USA, I had saved 210 Dollars, which I now had to use. I bought some good material on the black market. It was made from worsted yarn, the best I could get. I had to go to a tailor and have my suit tailor-made in a hurry. It cost me all of the 210 Dollars.

First, the civil ceremony was held in the most beautiful place for a civil wedding in Europe, the Mirabell Castle in Salzburg. Its grand room had a palace-like appearance with marble and gold. It used to be the Archbishop's audience room. It looked like a king's palace, like Versailles or Schoenbrunn.

The church ceremony was two weeks later, in our little church in Niederalm. We invited a few friends to the church wedding. It was a beautiful ceremony. A friend of ours played the "Ave Maria" on his cello. He had asked us which one of the "Ave Maria's" we wanted—the Schubert or the Gounot. We did not answer right away, so he said he would play both of them. A friend of ours who had a car drove us to and from the church. After the wedding, he drove with me to a place near Hellbrunn where we picked up the wedding present from Mr. Durkee—a five gallon can of maple nut ice cream.

On the same day and at the same time, Queen Elizabeth II was married in St. Paul's Cathedral in London. We did not plan to coincide our wedding with the Queen's, and we are sure it wasn't her decision either. But it's nice to have the same wedding date.

We had a small wedding party. Traveling in Austria was still very expensive at that time. Helen's relatives from Germany—her mother, sister and brother-in-law were not allowed to come. The borders were still closed for them. One of Helen's brother's, Rudi, had died in Siberia. She had not heard from her brother, Karl, in years. Helen had only her brother, Viki, an uncle and an aunt, and two cousins in Austria at the wedding. Some areas of Austria and Germany still had no buses or trains. It was the 20th of November, 1947.

A cartoonist friend of mine, who was in the wedding party, made caricature drawings of all the people in the wedding party and gave this to us in a book as a wedding gift. We still have it and enjoy and reminisce a lot. Everyone of our relatives was notified, but only some could make it. The crowning touch of the wedding meal was the maple nut ice cream. Nobody had ever eaten anything like it. Smooth, creamy, rich, and so much of it. Afterwards, Helen and I left by train for Zell am See, a resort town in the Alps, where we stayed for two days and enjoyed the mountains and the lake. Afterwards, I had to go back to work again.

Part VI

Our Story

Chapter 1

Our Lives Together

Since I had arrived in Salzburg, my friend Don Olmsted and I had been writing to each other, as was Pop Sims from Valdosta. They were sending me packages, some were CARE packages, which helped our meager rations. Don wanted to know if I still had the intention of coming to the U.S. I wrote him back that I did, if I didn't make headway over here. I could not go to school because I was not considered an Austrian. I was considered a Displaced Person—in short called a DP. The reason the Austrian government gave was that I was not from the original Austria before World War II. My father could not get his veteran's pension despite that he was in the Austrian-Hungarian Army in World War I. He was a staff sergeant and was wounded two times. Of course, he would get nothing from the Austrians for his time in the German Army. He got nothing for being a prisoner of the Gestapo because he was released and not captured while in a camp. The laws were different in Germany.

I had prepared myself to become a teacher. I had taken extension courses in the U.S., but I could not continue my studies at the University. I took some courses in bookkeeping and Russian language at the University of Salzburg, which I had to pay for myself., If I was going to immigrate to the U.S., I had to file my immigration papers; so I did.

The situation in Austria was so terrible and confused that it is hard to describe. Austria was full of refugees from all over Eastern Europe. They were housed all over Austria. In Salzburg, they lived in any kind of housing they could find. Just a bit away from Niederalm in Groedig, for instance, over a hundred people lived in one huge room, families only divided from each other by curtains. They still lived there years after we had immigrated to the U.S.

Most of the refugees in Salzburg, now officially classified as Displaced Persons, lived in all kinds of camps all over Salzburg. Some camps had thousands of people living close together, little towns or villages unto themselves. We were living in a barrack, five people in a room and kitchen. This was almost luxury compared to what others had to cope with.

When our daughter, Brigitte, was born on April 3, 1949, we added a little crying baby to this room and kitchen. It was a happy occasion for us. My parents were happy to have little Brigitte in their midst. My father was especially excited. He seemed to feel better, despite the fact we knew his health was failing. The little crying baby was no problem for him. He said she was like an angel that came to perk him up and make him better. For us it was a time to look for a room to ourselves.

Austria had, at that time, about seven million inhabitants, without counting the many refugees. The Austrian government said it was unable to feed and take care of these refugees. The newly-formed United Nations tried to form a refugee relief organization. The tremendous task of feeding and helping all these desperate people must have been beyond belief. Many organizations failed. But the Austrian government, as soon as the international community started helping, did little to relieve the plight of the refugees. The refugees were on their own to keep themselves alive.

When we started to look for a room for ourselves, we could not get any help—not from the government, the village, or any kind of organization. We were constantly searching and searching for just a room. We were considering living way up in the mountains near Helen's aunt's place. To come to work was an hour long bus trip. That would have been two hours daily on the bus. If you missed the bus, the next one was four hours later.

We finally found a room in a basement in Niederalm and grabbed it right away. It was a small room. The small refrigerator was out in the dark basement hall. No stove, cooking, or room heating was available. The window was very small and faced the back of the house. We looked into a cage of nutras or minks. In fact, they were looking into our window. We never could open the window.

Now to look for a stove. It had to be a wood and coal stove because electric or gas stoves were not available. It was impossible to find one. No new stoves were being built yet and used ones were very hard to get. In desperation, we decided to get a restored antique stove that cost me plenty of money. We would have to use wood and coal for it. That was all anyone ever had in this village. We had a problem bringing it down into our basement room, but now we could cook a meal; and we had heat, and little Brigitte did not have to freeze.

My good friend, Pop Sims, was now living in the Veteran's Hospital in Bath, New York, and collected clothes from his friends there for me and my family. They seemed to be new clothes, but Pop insisted they were used. They sure helped me during the cold winter. I had hoped to see him when I came to the U.S. When I received the notification of his death, I was shocked. He considered me his son, having had no children. This was what he always wanted. He treated me and helped me as if I was his real son.

My father adored his granddaughter, Brigitte. My mother and Bruni also loved that child. She grew up being spoiled by everyone, including us parents.

Brigitte loved her grandpa very much. It was a love affair between them you could hear and see constantly. Every morning, when my father got up and dressed, he went to see if Brigitte was up and dressed also. He could hardly wait till Helen had her dressed. Soon after breakfast the two took off, hand in hand, walking toward the woods and the Königsee River. They were gone for hours—the old grandpa and his little granddaughter. When they came home, Brigitte was always very excited, telling us she saw a deer, or a rabbit, or a fox. Sometimes she had a bouquet of wildflowers for her mother or her grandmother. The next day Brigitte herself could hardly wait to go for a stroll with grandpa. He would explain and name for her every flower and every bush and tree. The days with Brigitte seemed to help my father tremendously. He still was brought by ambulance once in a while to the hospital. It seemed only little Brigitte gave him some of his strength back.

My sister, Bruni, was working in an office in downtown Salzburg but, as a hobby, she was exploring caves in the Salzburg mountains. She was officially called a "spelunker" but was an amateur explorer. In collaboration with these lay people the scientists mapped, made pictures, measured, and explored all the caves in the Tennen and Hagen Mountain Range near Salzburg. These people did all these things in the famous "Eis Riesen Welt", Giant Ice World, a 50 km long cave with the most beautiful natural ice sculptures. Only a small part of this cave was open to the public. Helen and I were invited by Bruni and some of the main scientists to walk and crawl into the other part of the cave and see the natural untouched treasures it contained.

One of the most daring explorations my sister was involved in was the exploration of the Tantal Cave. It was a complete assault on a cave that was done like the scaling of Mount Everest. Along the path in the cave they built camps—1, 2, 3, and so on. Each campsite was stocked with food, water, medication and equipment and was connected to each other by telephone.

Bruni was the only woman ever to go to camp three and cook for the scientists and try an experiment playing a radio deep inside the mountain. She was slender and agile and could carry her own load. It went smoothly. Her experiment was a success. Deep in the mountain, she turned on her battery-operated radio. You could hear dance music as loud and clear as outside. The scientists and Bruni were dancing to music, deep in the heart of the mountain. When they returned to the cave entrance after 85 hours without sunlight and lots of new charts and photographs, and after exploring a new part of the cave no one had ever seen before, the spelunkers, including Bruni, were already planning and preparing for the next exploration.

Bruni's boyfriend, Walter Ramer, was a bicycle racer in Austria. He was the Austrian Champion for quite some years. Bruni, Helen, and I were in many of these races—not as participants, but as the supply team who followed the racers with the truck of spare parts and spare bikes.

Bruni and Walter later on got married. Walter immigrated to Australia and Bruni soon followed him to Sydney, where they were living. Walter suddenly died in 1993.

Chapter 2

Immigrate To The US

I would like to write about our experiences in the immigration effort, from the beginning to the final day of departure, three or four years later. There were many thousands who wanted to immigrate to the U.S. We had to stand in line outside for many blocks. Many days we stood in line at the numerous offices in biting cold in winter and heat and rain in summer. Many times, when our turn came, they closed the offices. We had the birth certificates and the marriage certificate. We also had to get a moral certificate from our local police, in which the police stated that they knew us and attested that we were morally upstanding citizens and had committed no crimes. We had to see doctors and get a check up to get health certificates and many other certificates. All this had to be paid for with our own money. We also had to file with the IRO, the International Refugee Organization. After waiting for months to get our hearing and finding out that more files were required, the IRO suddenly collapsed; and we were told a new organization was taking over and we would have to file again. We wanted our old papers back and were told they were in a room in a certain building. When we went to this room, the files with the papers were scattered about and piled three feet high. People were standing over the pile rummaging for their own files. We had to do the same thing to find our own files, but to no avail. We could not find our papers anymore.

The new organization was called UNRRA, United Nations Relief and Rehabilitation Administration. We had to get new birth certificates and papers, including the papers from the police and the doctors. We also had to stand outside in line again, day after day and month after month. We often took over waiting for each other. I had to take off from work when I relieved Helen in line. That's the way it was. Everybody was doing it. There were no other solutions.

Brigitte had grown up a bit. She was only 2 ½ but was talking up a storm. Her grandpa liked her talk. If grandpa held her by her hand, she would follow him around; but if he was lying down tired and exhausted, she was running around keeping her mother and her grandmother going. She was fun—too much fun sometimes. We were wondering what that would do to my father if we left Salzburg.

During this time I was corresponding with Donald to inform him about our problems. He told me that the way the immigration law is written, he had to be responsible for us in the United States till we became citizens, which could only happen after five years in the U.S. The government had no responsibility for the new immigrants and therefore it was up to the sponsor, like Donald.

In my correspondence with Don, he informed me about the work possibilities for me in the US. He also wrote to me about the beauty of Minnesota. In one letter dated April 21, 1949, he described Minnesota in these words, and I quote:

"You asked me to tell you more about Minnesota. I imagine that with all your reading, you may know more of the real history than I do. But you are probably more interested in present day things. Just now we hope that spring has arrived. The first of April was nice and warm, and we thought that winter was gone; but on the seventh it snowed six inches, then it warmed up again, but on the 14th it snowed again. Everyone is out raking lawns and starting their gardens and all those other little things people do in the spring.

This week in the Minneapolis Auditorium we are having what we call a Sportsman's Show. All companies making goods for outdoor sports are invited to put up a booth and show their products. There are thousands of items to be seen. There is a boat show, a trailer house show, a dog show, and many other smaller booths. I spent five hours looking around and I only got to see about half of it. Minnesota is a tourist state to a large extent, especially in the Northern state. We have a lot of fishing here. St. Paul has a big winter carnival every winter that thousands of people come to see. Minneapolis has a water carnival in the summer, which is just as big. Have you read about our fictitious legendary figure Paul Bunyan? He was a lumberjack who created most of the things in Minnesota. I will send you a folder explaining a little about him that I got at the Sportsman's Show. He is the main theme of our winter sports.

The northern half of Minnesota is mainly covered with pine forest and lakes, while the southern half is farm land. Our farm is just on the border between the two of them.

As far as appearance is concerned, Minneapolis looks a lot like Atlanta. That is, homes and factories and other buildings are much the same. Homes here are constructed better due to the cold. The farms are, on the average, better than in the south. Barns and houses are larger and nicer. The farms have more buildings because more livestock is raised as well as the crops. Our new house has seven rooms, a basement and a bathroom. We have a coal furnace, and an automatic water heater. There is a stove in the kitchen with city gas. We will have a small garden, too. There is also a vacant lot next door that we are going to try to buy. If we get that, we will have a large garden."

This is just part of a letter Don wrote me. He was not bragging. He was just trying to explain to me in a simple way the life in Minnesota. If I immigrated to the US, I had to know what the state looked like and what people do there for a living or for fun. I learned more and more.

We were getting close to the final stages of our effort to come to America when Helen said she was pregnant. On July 12, 1951, our son, Eric, was born. The joy was great. Now we had a girl and a boy. We also had new problem with UNRRA. We had to file additional papers and some of the papers had to be changed. It should have been easy, but not for UNRRA. If there was an easy and a hard way to do it, UNRRA always chose the hard way. More standing in line, more costs for doctors' certificates, more papers to fill out.

Donald in Minnesota was constantly informed by us about our situation. He had to know. He had gotten me a job. Any change in our status affected him and his papers for us and the job. We were supposed to go to Little Falls, Minnesota, where his father had a farm. We were going to work on his farm. In the meantime, his father got injured on the farm and could not do any more farm work. Don was anxiously waiting for me to come.

Fist, we were told by UNRRA that we would be flying to the U.S. because young babies like Eric cannot survive a trip by ship. Now we were on the list of people flying across. We were told by the UNRRA not to worry, they would notify us by phone. We were now waiting for the phone call…and waiting…and waiting…and waiting. Nothing happened. Weeks, even months went by, and nothing happened.

It was winter and 1951 was coming to a close. There was a long line of people standing outside again. I just went ahead of everybody as if I worked there. When somebody tried to stop me from going into the building, I forced my way in. Years of frustration suddenly came out. I knew the room number of the guy who told me not to worry and he would notify me by phone. I walked right in and there he was on the phone. I stood right next to him for about five minutes while he was on the phone. That gave me time to look at his desk. In the "out" section of his files was a list. I could read the names on it and one of them was, "family of Siegfried and Helen Hoffmann". I was startled. When he was done phoning he said to me in an angry voice, "What do you want?"

I shot back, "Can you tell me what this list if right here?"

His voice was now full of anger and he answered, "This is a list of people who have left already."

Angered by his belligerent tone of voice and not being able to comprehend what had happened, my voice now was loud and firm and I asked him, "How come my name is on it?"

For a moment he stopped. Now he came back with all kinds of excuses to explain it like—I did not come, I did not answer the phone. Then he started to investigate it on the phone. Somehow he found out that I was never notified, but he had me on the list as being sent to the U.S. My daring to go into his office finally got us going again. I was told again I would be notified. But this time, I was on their tail all the time. I constantly asked them, by phone and in person, if they received my trip papers or if there was any news about our departure date.

Something comes to my mind that I may have forgotten to mention. I had my papers ready after Eric was born. At UNRRA, they told me to see the U.S. Consul at the Consular Office in Salzburg and get his okay. Helen and I went and the U.S. Consul looked at the files before him and said, "So, you were a Prisoner of War in America?:"

I said, "Yes."

"We will have to check this out. You will hear from me as soon as I get an answer."

There followed another waiting period. During this waiting period, I was wondering—what if they found out about that incident in the prison camp when I and my working group were arrested? They may not let me into the U.S. Not that I felt guilty, but I did not know what was in my files about that incident. After months of waiting, we were called and told to report to the U.S. Consul. Helen and I waited outside his office. I expected him to say, we are sorry, we cannot let you go to the U.S. Finally we were called in. The Consul got up and came over to me like he had something important to tell me. His face lit up. He smiled broadly and said, "We got all your files from your time in the prison camps. I only can tell you we will be happy and honored to have you become new citizens of the United States." He shook my hand and Helen's. I was still surprised. I did not know what to say.

Finally I got the list of items I was allowed to take along to the U.S. We were going by ship. Eric was big enough now to travel on a ship. On the list were so many things we did not have. I wanted to take as much along as possible so as not to have to buy them over there. My father had a lot of experience in packing. He had worked for a while as a shipping clerk when he was a student.

He gave me a lot of good suggestions. One of them was to take some of our Christmas decorations along. I would feel more at home having familiar decorations on the Christmas tree. My father had some old pots with holes in them. He plugged the holes with rivets and solder, as he had done on the farm, so that I could use the pots in the beginning. My father made four crates for me. We had to make a lit of each item that went into these crates. I took along all the books from the prison camp. These were my treasures.

Don had written me that they had to sell the farm in Little Falls, Minnesota, a town where Lindbergh had lived. Don had promised me a job and now he may have been worried about it. Don asked me what kind of work I would like to do. There was lots of work available in the U.S. I wrote him back that I would do any type or work, whatever he got me. Supporting a family with two children, I had to do everything possible. This satisfied Don, and I had the intention to do it.

Our Story

We were instructed to go to Camp Grohn near Bremen, Germany, before going on the ship. We had to sign an official declaration that, with our trip to the U.S., we abdicate and forfeit any rights and duties of the Austrian government. That may not be the right wording, but in essence, it got the Austrian government off the hook. After years of telling us we were not Austrians, the Austrian government had no duty to help or feed us. Now they used this occasion to document that they had no obligation toward us anymore.

We could not take any money along either. The last Austrian Schillings I had I spent to get Helen a birthday present. We expected to be on the High Seas on that day, so I bought some nice Austrian jewelry for her and kept it hidden so she had no idea about it. Made from Austrian crystal, it looked very nice.

The hardest thing to cope with now lay ahead of us—saying goodbye to my parents and Bruni at the railroad station in Salzburg. I did not know that it would be the last time I would see my father alive. My father probably knew how I felt. What we didn't know was how hard the departure of Brigitte would affect my father. He had left Bielitz and moved to Turkey with my mother and three small kids, and he was very optimistic and not worried about me. My mother was more worried about how our kids would survive in America. I knew they would have a great future in the U.S. but I could no convince my mother about it. She was still worried. My sister, Bruni, was very happy about my trip. I think she was probably also toying with the idea to emigrate. Only when our train left Salzburg did it dawn on me what a monumental step our family was undertaking.

In Camp Grohn, outside Bremen, we had to wait again. There were thousands like us waiting. Helen's three sisters Trude, Mimi, and Liesl, came to visit her in the camp. We had already figured out that Brigitte was going to be a problem child on this trip because she was always running away so fast. We could not keep up with her and never knew where she was. We had to put her on a leash. We could buy them in camp. Helen's sisters bought one for us. It was actually a dog leash, and we put it around her chest and kept her on a long leash. That was the best thing we could do. On the ship we had control of her. She could not run away from us and get lost. Eric was nine months old.

The final day in Germany came for us. We were embarking on a liberty ship named "General Taylor". A new chapter begins. A new chapter in the book and a new chapter of our lives.

Chapter 3

The Hard Beginning Of A New Life

It was May 13th, 1952—a day we will always have in our memory. We walked up the long ramp to the "General Taylor" and wondered what was in store for us, onboard ship and in the U.S. Our four crates already were supposed to be on the ship. We had Eric and Brigitte and some carry-on bags with us. Right away, I was separated from Helen and the children. The captain had strict rules for this trip. Every man had to work. Every woman without children had to work, and women with young children had cabins.

Helen was put with the children in a two-bed cabin with a crib under the port-hole. Helen slept on the upper bunk, Brigitte on the lower bunk, and Eric in the crib. I slept with all the other men in the big, main quarters of the Liberty ship, which was normally used for troop transport. My job was to work in the ship's laundry, which was back in the rear of the ship, right above the ship's propeller.

It was very nice in the beginning. The food was very good and plentiful. I was working on the huge dryers, some people were ironing, and some were at the washers in the laundry. My job required me to load the washed laundry into the dryers. When I closed the huge dryer doors, they slammed shut, really tight! It was hard for me to open them afterward. We all worked eight hours before we were relieved by the next shift. It was not too hard, all in all, not too bad.

I met a guy from the ship's crew and got well acquainted with him. His name was Sam Chernoff. We got along very well. We had long talks and he gave me his address in New York and told me to let him know once in a while how we were doing. Some of the other sailors said hat he was a relative of the "RCA" Sarnoff. I did not know what they were talking about and they laughed when they said it, so I think he was not. There were a lot of German emigrants on the ship. They were mostly workers or owners from German vineyards. They told me they brought the grape seeds from their vineyards and were going to the U.S. where they already had jobs lined up.

So far the trip was okay. We had our own ship newspaper and our own police force, all run by our own people. The first few days we traveled through the English Channel. Passing Dover on one side and Dunkirk on the other side, my mind wandered off to the time I spent in East Dunkirk as a German soldier. Passing LeHavre, my mind was on my arrival back as a POW. Then we came into the Atlantic. After a few days, the sea became rougher and rougher.

I hardly had time to see Helen. Her birthday was spent on board. It was the 15th of May. Early in the morning before work, I went to see her. I knocked on the cabin door and Helen opened up. We embraced, I wished her a happy birthday and handed her the bracelet. She seemed not too happy. I only heard her say, "I am so sick." She was already seasick. I also was getting a little bit seasick, but not too bad. I was not vomiting yet. During work I felt it and soon I was getting worse. Our ship newspaper had informed us of a storm in the Atlantic that we were heading into.

The next few days were chaotic. The ship paper said that the captain had decided to try to avoid the storm and go around it. Every day the sea got rougher and more and more people got seasick. If you got seasick, you were first brought to sick bay; but soon there were so many that neither the ship's crew nor our own police could manage to bring all the sick to the doctor. People were laying all over the ship. Even the ship's crew and our own ship police were seasick. They were laying wherever they got sick. It was really a big mess.

The waves were high and almost everyone on board was seasick, but I was forced to go to work. We were forced to eat to get something into our stomachs. It was important. You can not vomit if you don't have anything in your stomach. It becomes a danger for you. Eat, even if it comes out the next moment.

Helen had a big problem with our kids. It was not that the kids were sick. We learned that kids don't get seasick. They were hungry. Helen, as sick as she was, had to go to the mess hall with the kids. What a great idea it was to have Brigitte on a leash. With the ship going up and down and sideways and Brigitte not being seasick but hungry, it would have been impossible to control her. With Brigitte on a leash in one hand and in the other arm, Eric and the bag to vomit in, Helen went to the mess hall with the ship rolling up and down. In the mess hall Helen forced herself to eat something but vomited it our right away. Brigitte was hungry and ate everything she had on the plate. She also had to hold on to the sliding plates and cups on the table. In the meantime, Helen was busy feeding Eric. After eating, she went back the same way to the cabin.

I was very sick myself. At work, the roaring of the ship's propeller was deafening in the laundry room. The ship's propeller was right underneath the laundry room. Every time the propeller came out of the water, the lack of resistance from the water made it turn faster and the roar could be heard all over the ship. My challenge was not to fall into the dryer when the ship lifted suddenly out of the water and came down again. I could easily fit in any of the dryers with all the laundry in it. At that moment the heavy doors could slam shut and nobody would know I was in the dryer.

Going back to my quarters down the long hall, I was literally walking on the side walls, right or left, depending on the way the ship was rolling. The way the ship was shaking and creaking when it hit the water worried me. I remembered what my father said to me about when the ship he was on in the Black Sea went down. He had said the creaking of the ship when it hits the water causes most of the leaks. At that time, I had no knowledge of how many Liberty ships broke apart during storms.

Helen and I were often separated from each other. It was the captain's strict order. We were not supposed to see each other, but we tried. On one of these visits, she told me she had left the porthole open during the night because it was so stuffy in the cabin. Suddenly during the night, she heard Eric crying. She came down from the upper bunk to see him gulping for air and swallowing water which had come through the porthole. He could barely cry. She closed the porthole but the crib was all wet. The waves were so high that they washed in through the porthole. This was Eric's first experience with sea water.

We all on board remembered the terrible sound of the fog horn. During the storm, the fog horn was always on. Constantly sounding in a deep and mysterious tone, to me it was more of a scary sound than a warning sound. During the first few months in the U.S., we always heard this sound in our ears. It took us some time to realize the sound was not in our ears but was an imprint on our mind.

Finally, four days late, we arrived in the harbour of New York.

Chapter 4

We Are In The U.S.

It was May 23, 1952. We were disembarking and lining up for customs inspection. Inside a long building, we put our belongings on a table for the customs inspectors. For some reason custom's inspectors have good senses. When he looked through my stuff, right away he went into my suitcase and found the jewelry I had bought for Helen. He looked at it and noticed it had no diamonds, so he laughed at me and put it back again. I was going to explain but he was gone to the next person.

When we were finished with the customs people, we heard over the loudspeaker: "Siegfried and Helen Hoffmann, please come to the office." So we went to this office and there we saw the Haugs. I had written my friends, the Haugs, who were from Niederalm. They were the ones whose children I taught English and who had emigrated to the U.S. long before us. They lived in Bound Brook, New Jersey. We did not know they had been waiting for us. They had come every day, for four days, to the New York harbour. They wanted us to come and see them in Bound Brook. They had talked to the people who were in charge of our transportation. We had all our train tickets and Donald was informed of our late arrival and everything was set for us to go to continue the trip. But the Haugs were very persistent. We would only stay one day in Bound Brook and Mr. Haug promised to bring us back to the train depot one day later. Finally, the people in charge of our transportation gave in. We got the tickets for the next train. We were told what railroad station in New York to go to and in what railroad station in Chicago to transfer. I could not remember everything, but Mr. Haug promised he would put us on the right train and give us the right instructions.

We went with the Haugs through New York. The high skyscrapers, the traffic, the many people—so many things to see. We rode through the Holland Tunnel to New Jersey and arrived in Bound Brook. Everything we saw was new to us, even for me, who had lived three and a half years in the U.S. I knew the U.S. only through books and the American movies I saw as a Prisoner of War. By the time we arrived at their place in Bound Brook, we were very tired. We were surprised to see many people waiting for us. They were all Mr. And Mrs. Haug's friends to welcome us to the U.S.

One of Mr. Haug's friends said to us that he would give us a "pilgrim welcome". I did not know what he meant. We were invited to his house as honored guests. They had a typical American Thanksgiving dinner prepared for us with all the trimmings. The huge turkey, the dressing, cranberry sauce, everything. It was a feast to remember. We had never seen so much food in our lives. We were told about the tradition of how the pilgrims landed on Plymouth Rock and how the Indians and the pilgrims sat together at a turkey dinner like ours. My family had never eaten turkey before. It tasted delicious. Now we knew what a "pilgrim dinner" was. Something else was introduced to us. We saw television for the first time. In 1952, television was not as developed as it is today, but it was new to us.

We all slept like logs the first night in the U.S. Coming from an area devastated by the War to a country that had everything in abundance—this glaring difference intrigued us. From one minute to the next we were in awe and thrilled by what we saw.

The next day the Haugs were going to bring us to the train depot in New York and we were getting ready. It was hard to say goodbye to the many good friends we had just acquired. The Haugs brought us to Grand Central Station. They gave us the information we needed and we said "Auf Wiedersehen" to them. We were now heading for Chicago.

One of the instructions given us was "If you have a problem, see anyone in Traveler's Aid, and they will surely help you." In Chicago we went straight to the Traveler's Aid people. I never will forget this woman. I still have a picture of her face in my mind. A very good looking, friendly young woman who saw us right away, guessed what we needed, and told us exactly how to get there. She told us where to pick up the taxi and not to pay more to the taxi driver than a certain amount, and then go to a certain track in the other station. She gave us snacks and reminded us of the other Traveler's Aid people who would help us get to the right train. We followed her instruction and were picked up at the other station by a Traveler's Aid woman who was also helpful. We were so happy that we had come to America.

I had no idea what lay ahead for us. We were on a train heading for Minneapolis. I remember one experience. On the train was an older man and we told him we were new immigrants going to Minnesota. He said, "Minnesota? Not Minnesota! That is a lousy state. Cold and snow like in Siberia." That shocked us. That was not what Donald had described in his letters to us.

When we arrived at Union Station in St. Paul, we were going to get off when the train attendant said to wait till we were in Minneapolis. We waited in Union Station in St. Paul for quite some time. I guess we were very anxious to get to Minneapolis. It was very late at night when our train pulled into Union Station in Minneapolis.

Our children were asleep and we had to wake them up. We got our things together and left the train. We did not know for sure if anyone had notified Don that we would be arriving one day late. If not, we would have to get help from the Traveler's Aid. As we walked toward the station building, I saw Donald waiting with a little tiny woman standing next to him. He introduced me to his mother and I, in turn, introduced Helen and Brigitte and little Eric to Don and his mother. Helen did not speak English.

Inside the station we talked about many things. Don asked me if it was all right with us if we stayed, in the beginning, with his parents in southeast Minneapolis where his parents had bought a house. Of course it was okay. Helen asked me how we should address Donald's mother. Don asked his mother, "What shall they call you?"

She said with a smile, "Just call me Grandma." It was such a beautiful sound. I never will forget these words spoken by Don's mother. It gave us the feeling we were home. We had somebody who liked us enough to be our mother and grandmother. I translated it to Helen and Helen had tears in her eyes. She embraced Grandma Olmsted and said thank you to her. What a welcome we had! We had no family here and a person we never met before said, "Just call me Grandma." That's how we were greeted by the Olmsteds.

We rode through Minneapolis at night in Don's car. All the lights from Hennepin Avenue and the many high buildings were impressive. A big city with a lot of grand buildings and a lot of grand people. That thought always stuck in my mind. We drove down to southeast Minneapolis where Don's parents lived. Of course, Don lived there, too. We met Don's father, a tall slender man who worked hard all his life on his farm. We got a room close to the attic. That was our living quarters for a while.

The day after we arrived, Don asked me what I would like to do. I said, "Don, I don't care what I do as long as I get a job to support my family." He told me his father worked as a janitor at the University of Minnesota and if I would like to have a job like that, he would go with me to the University and help me apply for a job. I said, "I would be glad to do that." So I went with Don to apply for a job.

At the University of Minnesota they said they had an opening at the farm campus in St. Paul as a janitor. I would have to live there on the campus and work. The campus was closed down now they said, and I would be working in an empty dormitory and could sleep there. When they asked me what day I wanted to start, I told them any day.

"How about tomorrow?" they asked. It was okay with me.

The next day I started working as a janitor at the University of Minnesota. The starting wage was $1.99 an hour. No overtime was allowed. I came home on weekends. It was a good start. I worked there cleaning and waxing floors, cleaning windows and toilets. The whole building was my job.

Helen had it tough in the beginning. Because she did not speak English, she did not dare to talk to Grandma Olmsted. It was sometimes very hot in our room but Helen did not dare to go down. Grandma Olmsted came up and with a little sign language, she and Helen talked to each other. It was great for Helen to have the help of a Grandma.

We were anxious to find our own place. Don's sister, Nancy, also lived in an apartment building in southeast Minneapolis. There was an opening there. It was on Fourth Street Southeast, close to the main campus of the University of Minnesota. We went to see the place and liked it. It was one room on the third floor, and on the other side of the long floor was a closet that would be part of the deal. It had space for a hot plate. I would build some shelves in this closet and we could cook and have a small kitchen. The room had a very high ceiling, as did all the rooms in this old apartment house. We did not like being on the third floor but that was all we could afford.

We moved into this place and had some very nice times there. The kids were growing up. It was our own place. We had no big expenses—no car—and the streetcar went by our house. To the surprise of our grandchildren, we could travel all over the city on a streetcar. In the meantime, I had transferred to the main campus and was working at the Coffmann Memorial Union building as a janitor. As soon as we could, we paid Don back for his expenses. For instance, he had to pay the train tickets for us. Even with all these payments, we had money left over to save. Just imagine, on $1.99 an hour we saved.

My mother wrote us many times that my father's health was getting worse now that Brigitte had left Salzburg. They were happy to hear that all went smoothly with our lives. Brigitte missed her grandpa very much. We promised we would make a phonograph recording of the voices of our children and send it to them, which we did.

We came from a place that cherished food as God-given nourishment. We felt we could not waste food. When we or the children dropped food on the floor, we picked it up, cleaned it if it needed it and ate it. That was our strict rule for a long time. Soon, we behaved like so many Americans—food is not important, we can waste it. There is more where that came from. At that time we became regular normal Americans who waste more than they eat. We bought all our furniture from Salvation Army stores or Disabled Veterans stores. We could afford their prices and their stuff was clean.

At this time I also got acquainted with Mr. Noodleman. He was a Metropolitan Life Insurance salesman. He was a very good friend. Not only did he advise us on life insurance, but he also gave us hints about how to live in the U.S. He was already an older fellow, having immigrated to the U.S. from Russia many years ago. Many days he came to our house for a visit.

Helen quickly got a job at this apartment. She was babysiting for a couple on the first floor. He was a law student at the University and his wife was working.

Their baby, Cynthia, was a very well behaved child. Helen could take care of our children and Cynthia without any problem.

I knew that my janitor job was only a starting point for me. I had to learn a trade to be able to support my family. Television was a coming thing. Everybody advised me to became a television technician. I could not use my experience in textile machinery as a starting point. There was no demand in Minneapolis for that. I would have to switch to some other trade completely.

Television interested me but the technology more than the media. A correspondence course would give me the freedom to work and study. There were many correspondence courses available at that time. I gave all of them a thorough check. One course in particular interested me. It offered radio and television training plus industrial electronics; and after the end of the course, I would be able to apply for an FCC license. It would be more expensive than some of the other courses, but it would give me parts to build test equipment, a radio, a signal generator, and a television set. I chose this course offered by RTTA—Radio and Television Training Association.

Studying and working in a room that was bedroom, nursery, living room, and dining room all in one was tough. We were used to smaller and more confined places and we found a way. In the beginning, I studied the fundamentals of electricity, soldering, and the formulas for electronics. Then I began building test equipment. It began with a simple Ohm and Volt meter. At certain intervals, I had to fill out test forms and submit them to RTTA. They sent it back, graded. I found out what I did wrong and sometimes would have to submit the same test form again. I had to know my stuff before RTTA sent me more parts to build test equipment or whatever was going to be built. If I did not pay the next payment, they would hold back my next lessons. There was always an incentive to go ahead. The parts I received were not pre-assembled parts. They had to be assembled, soldered, and tested with equipment I had previously built. The reading of actual circuits was entered in the test forms and sent in for grading. I had no knowledge of electronics before, but now it became fun and I was always looking forward to the next lesson.

Our kids were always looking down at the street from the windows. The windows could be opened, but the screen was so tight that we never could open them up. We read in the paper that a house was for rent at the main campus. It was a house that we could afford. It had many rooms for us and more rooms to rent out to students. From the income you got from the students, you could live free in your house, the ad said.

We went and looked at the house. It was a two-story house on the corner of Union Street and Washington Ave. We would live on the lower floor and rent out the rooms on the upper floor. The house was big and we liked it. We had a big kitchen, a bedroom, and another room for the children. The upper floor rooms we rented out to students. It was right across from Memorial Stadium. It does not exist anymore. On its site and other houses stands the big new dentistry skyscraper. A that time, our house was in the middle of the campus. We signed the lease and gave the landlady at the Fourth Street apartment our notice. We had to move right into the house and asked the landlady if we could come on the weekend to clean up our old apartment. She said she had people who wanted to see the room, but it was okay.

Chapter 5

Union Street and Experiencing Minnesota

We now had so much space that the kids had a chance to run around. Eric, who was two years old now, was running around full of joy. He fell and hit his head on the radiator, and he had a big gash on his forehead.

The weekend came and Helen, I, and the kids left for our old apartment to clean it as we had promised. Helen was vacuuming in the room and I was on the other end of the floor tearing down some shelves I had put up in the closet. Suddenly, Helen came running and screaming that Eric fell out the window. She was running down the stairs before I realized what she said. I ran after her because the telephone was downstairs on the first floor. Right away, I called the hospital for the ambulance to come. I was pleading for help to come immediately. Helen brought Eric in from the outside. He was lying limply in her arms and quietly crying. She put him down on the bed of the apartment where she used to babysit. Helen was sobbing and trying to check Eric out very carefully for broken bones and injuries. I was still on the phone begging the ambulance to come and the operator kept asking for the address of the accident. Then I realized I had not mentioned that. I was still giving the address and describing how to get here when I heard the siren of the ambulance. At the same time the ambulance and police arrived, reporters and TV crews arrived and tried to take pictures. Soon a big crowd had gathered outside and some tried to get in our house. Police kept them out. I was in a daze. The paramedics checked Eric out and could not find any broken bones, but he was bleeding profusely from a wound on his forehead. The paramedics said they would have to bring him to the hospital. They wanted to know which of us would come along. We agreed that Helen would go. A policeman carried him outside while the reporters snapped pictures. The paramedics took Eric from the policeman, laid him in the ambulance, and with Helen, drove to General Hospital. For me, the world suddenly came crashing down on me. For Helen, who was crying all the time, it must have been the same. The life of her child was all she cared about at that moment.

My thoughts were with Helen and Eric alone in the hospital. I could not stand it any longer. My place had to be at Helen's side in the hospital. Our dreams seemed suddenly shattered. I did not know if Eric would survive or how much the hospital would cost us. Now that we had a start on a new life, this tragic event had to happen!

Eric was two years old and we had no health insurance. Just a small life insurance policy for the children. Somebody offered to bring me to the hospital. I left Brigitte with the landlady and left for the emergency room at General Hospital.

Helen was waiting outside the emergency room. She told me that the doctors found no broken bones but sent Eric for head x-rays because of the bleeding wound on his forehead. The x-rays showed no head injuries. The doctors said they wanted him in the hospital for observation overnight, and there was nothing we could do. We should go home. We were somewhat relieved but reluctantly had to go home. All evening and all night Eric, his future, and our future was on our minds.

The next day we came to see Eric in the hospital. He was in a crib in the hall and we saw him smile broadly. He said half in English, half in German, "Mommy, I fell out the fenster." "Fenster" is German for "window". His smile, his alertness, and his actual remembering made us feel better. The doctor said his right side was paralyzed. We asked him if there was a chance it could get better. He said there was always a chance. He also mentioned that children of Eric's age don't fall in fear. They fall relaxed. Their body is not tense. They are not expecting to get hurt. That's why there are usually light injuries in cases like that. His bones were still soft, not as hard as children a little bit older.

The doctor was wondering how he got the wound on his forehead. I explained to him that he had hit his head, before his fall, on a cast iron radiator in the new house. It was exactly on the same spot where he was bleeding now. The doctor was glad to hear that. He said, "That explains it now. It must have popped wide open from the fall." The doctor assured us Eric had no broken bones.

The next day we went to the hospital to see Eric again. He could move his right arm and the shoulder. The doctor said we could take him home, but we had to come every other day for the next month as an outpatient. The doctor said in a fall like that we had to be prepared that something may suddenly show up. It could be in the next few days, it could be in a few years.

Eric was glad to come home. So were we. How can anyone explain this? We were thanking God for His shield and protection.

We were still at a loss as to what actually happened at the Fourth Street house where Eric fell out of the window. The landlady admitted on the weekend before, she had shown our room to some new people. She had opened the screen—the one that we could never open ourselves—and left it unlocked. Eric climbed on the radiator to look out the window, as he did before, when the screen gave way. He fell three stories down between a garden hose faucet and a big stone flower pot on to the grass. The hospital asked me to pay the bill. I had to get a lawyer. I found one at the University. At the court hearing, the landlady's insurance company had to pay the hospital bills and Eric got $300, which was only to be paid to him at age 18. The amount he got a age 18 was only $500.

For the next month we faithfully went every other day to the hospital. Everything was okay. We were well aware that any day something could come up but what, we did not know. Soon we went every third day, then every week, and finally every month to the hospital for his routine check up. So far nothing had happened. This stretched out over two years. One day we came for our check up for Eric. The doctor knew Eric very well. "Hi, Eric. Come over to me," she asked. He went over to her. Suddenly, we noticed a very strong limp. The doctor was startled, and so were we. The doctor said, "Eric, turn around and go back to your parents." So he turned around and limped back to us. We knew that he did not do that before. "What happened?" the doctor asked. "Did he do that before?"

We said, "No."

For a while there was a strange silence in the doctor's office. Then we saw the doctor dip her hand into a box and come out with a lollipop. She said, "Eric, would you like this?"

Eric started to run to the doctor saying, "Oh, yes." And his limp was gone. A stone fell from our heart.

Our doctor smiled and said, "What an actor, what an actor, scaring us to death." There wasn't anything wrong with him. He had no limp. He was acting. This must have been the first acting performance in his life in front of other people.

Our house at the University was right across from the football stadium. Any time there was a football game, people were looking for a place to park their cars. There was a house exactly like ours next to us which belonged to the Berglund family. We had met them and they were very nice people. The son, Ed Berglund, was a young student. Our two houses had one huge parking lot at the back of our houses. We could have divided them, but Ed suggested we use both lots together and we could hold more cars for renting. He knew how to drive every car and I did not know how to drive a car at all. He said, "You do the talking. I'll bring the cars in." That's what we did. We put signs up that read "Parking One Dollar." I collected the dollar, gave them a ticket, and Ed drove the cars into the parking lot and lined them up to get in as many cars as possible. When the football game was over, the people gave us the ticket for the car, and Ed brought their car out from the parking lot. People were happy. We split the money, despite the fact that Ed had done most of the work. The next football season we did it again. The two families were the best of friends.

We rented out the upper floor to students. There was a lot of turnover in students. Some stayed for only one semester, some longer. We met a lot of nice students and sometimes their parents.

On Sundays we took the streetcar to the many lakes inside the city limits of Minneapolis—especially Lake Hiawatha or Lake Nokomis. These were some of the lakes we frequently visited. We took the streetcar from University Avenue and had to transfer. Because of the weekend schedule, especially on Sunday, we sometimes had to wait for an hour before we got another streetcar. It was tough with two kids and all the stuff you take along for a picnic. We had our hands full but we loved it. It was our greatest relaxation to be on the lakes in Minneapolis.

On Lake Nokomis one day, we met a fascinating lady. We had a very nice day at the lake. As sometimes happens, a sudden rainstorm came up. We packed up our picnic stuff in a hurry and ran to our streetcar stop. It had no shelter but was closer than running across to the other side of the lake. Everybody else ran to their cars, but we had no car. We were at the stop getting soaking wet and the kids started to cry. A car stopped in front of us, a lady got out, and asked us if she could drive us home. She had her two children in the car. We agreed. As we were sitting in the car, she saw how soaking wet we were. She asked us if she could drive us to her house, which was not far away, so that we could dry off. Of course, we agreed. That's how we met Mrs. Goulding.

At her beautiful house she gave us towels and made a warm meal for us. We told her we were from Austria, had come to the U.S. in 1952, and we loved everything in America. She was excited to hear where we came from. She was working at the University, I believe, in the Extension Service. Then she asked, very hesitantly, if we would like to have some clothes that her daughter had grown out of. Helen said we would not mind and would be happy to have them. Brigitte was now getting bigger and we needed clothes for her. Mrs. Goulding came out with a box of clothes. They were beautiful and looked brand new to us. We tried them on Brigitte and they fit her perfectly. She brought out some of her son's clothes that fit Eric, too. Mrs. Goulding said we could have more clothes and should let her know if we needed some more. We could not believe that our children suddenly had brand new looking clothes. She then brought us home. That is how we met and started a marvelous relationship with Mrs. Goulding. We were invited many times to her house. Later on, when we moved to Edina, a rich suburb of Minneapolis, our children—especially Brigitte—were among the best dressed children in school, thanks to Mrs. Goulding and her steady stream of clothes for our children.

Helen was babysitting a lot to earn extra money. I was working at the University as a janitor, at night as a dishwasher at the Loop pharmacy in downtown Minneapolis, and studying my correspondence course at night. The instruments I had built by now were ranging from Morse code devices to radios and signal generators. Now came the most interesting part. I was building my own TV. It was so interesting for me that I could forget everything around me.

The power supply was the first thing, then the I F stages, and the tuner. I had to check the voltages in the circuitry and write them on the test sheets and send them in to RTTA for grading. The test sheets came back showing the readings were right. The day of the final assembly arrived. I was waiting for the arrival of the picture tube. One day, there it was. It came in the mail like the rest of my parts. It was a small picture tube, only 10 or 12 inches. Slowly and carefully I unwrapped it, fully aware of the implosion power of the tube in the event I dropped it. Then I carefully put it through the yoke to the connector and connected the high voltage. Now, all I had to do was plug it in and switch it on. All the years of training was hanging on the line. I plugged it in and switched it on. After waiting for a few seconds to let it warm up, the sound came on and then a picture appeared on the tube. By golly, it worked! My own home-built TV worked. It worked fine. I never thought I could do it. Now I had my own TV, my own home-built TV. I also got my certificate as a television technician, which was the most important accomplishment.

During our years in the US, we always stayed in contact with my parents in Austria and Helen's mother in Germany. In 1957 I got a surprise letter from my parents in Salzburg which indicated that my former teacher and the principal of St. George College in Istanbul, Pater Dworczak, was retired and living in Salzburg. My parents visited him and he was his old self. He still remembered my parents and me and my sister. On their second visit to him, he took a photograph out of his side pocket., It was my First Communion picture at St. George and he told them they could keep it. My parents had lost all our photographs during the war, so it was with great joy they accepted this gift. Soon, too soon after that, he died and I never had a chance to see him and thank him.

Gradually it got tougher for us to go to the lakes on weekends. We had more items to take along, and waiting for a transfer at the street car stop in all kinds of weather, was hard on the children and us. I had to learn to drive. Our mailman agreed to give me driving lessons with his car. We used seldom-driven streets around the University.

In 1956 we got our first car. It was a 1952 Chevy and we called it, very lovingly, "Mariechen", (little Mary). Now a whole new world seemed to open up for us. We began with little trips in the neighborhood to get my driving confidence up and to show off that we had a car. Every weekend before we went on a picnic, we took a map of Minneapolis and St. Paul and discussed where we would go. There are so many lakes and parks in the metropolitan area that we had no problem finding new and exciting places to go and see. The more I drove, the more confidence I got to drive longer distances and see more of the cities and land of Minnesota.

One day, we had our Minnesota map in front of us and were planning the next weekend's trip. Helen said, "Here is a town called Hoffman. Let's go to that town." Just a few second later Helen said, "Hey, there is one town that has my name. It's called Urbank." Her maiden name is Urbanke.

I said, "Gee, that's not too far away from Hoffman on the map." So we decided to go to Hoffman and Urbank. We had a small tent, our kids liked camping, and we drove to Hoffman. When we came to the town, we were not impressed by it. Sorry to say, we did not bother to inquire how this town got its name. We kept on driving some miles north to the town of Urbank.

We could see the steeple of the church some distance away. It was a small, neat town. Helen and I always go to see the church first. When we entered the vestibule, on the right side was a wooden cross about five feet high with a German inscription on top, "Rette Deine Seele", "Save Your Soul". That surprised us. As we entered, the church altar seemed very familiar to us. Helen cried. Tears were rolling down her face, she was so shook up. She recognized the altar as being a carbon copy of the altar in the church in Alt Bielitz, a church which was now 820 years old. That's why it was so familiar to us.

When we went outside to the cemetery next to the church, we were again astonished. The names on the old grave stones were familiar names that we had at home in Bielitz and the inscriptions were in German. There were names like Suchy, Krol, Klimek and Woida, names not normally found in German-speaking towns but exclusively found in Bielitz. We were flabbergasted! We could not believe it. We traveled across an ocean to come over to a country we hardly knew and found familiar names of people who created the church the way they remembered it from home.

We were wondering how something like that could happen. Then we went to the creamery in Urbank to get some good old-fashioned ice cream. In talking with the man in the creamery, we heard an astonishing fact. The town was founded by a Catholic priest named Urbanke, who came with his parish to this area. Everybody settled there and built the church and the town. The parishioners named the town after Father Urbanke. From that time on, Helen and I searched for the history of these people, their priest Father Urbanke, and the settlement and founding of the town of Urbank.

Not far from Urbank is Inspiration Peak, the highest peak in Minnesota, excluding some higher ones on the Minnesota-Canadian border. We decided to climb this peak. We were somewhat disappointed. It was only a hill, but the view from the peak was fantastic. We had very nice sunny weather and could see for miles many beautiful lakes and neat little towns and in between small farmhouses with many fields clad in the colorful coats of their crops. Sometimes, nestled between in different shades of green, the woods and forest. There are approximately one hundred lakes around there—a grand place to live or just to vacation.

We asked some people with us at the peak if there was a place we could put up a tent and if they knew anybody who would allow us to do that. They said, "Sure, go down to Spitzer Lake. In Barnack's Camp they will allow you to put up a tent." It was not far from Inspiration Peak. The Barnack's—Cyril and Lily—are an elderly childless couple who owned the resort and had their farm on Spitzer Lake. They gave us permission to put up our tent. They told us to go to the meadow. When we asked Mr. Barnack where on the meadow we were allowed to put up our tent he said, "Anywhere you want." We chose a spot close to the lake. We put up the tent, walked around the shore of Spitzer Lake, and went back to our tent. We ate and went to sleep early. We slept very well. In the morning I woke up to a very strange sound outside the tent. It sounded like somebody was walking outside. I opened the tent flap and looked straight into the face of a cow. We were camped on Barnack's cow pasture which he had called meadow. Now we knew why we saw so many cow chips on the meadow.

We rented a fishing boat from Cyril and all went out on the lake, enjoying what every Minnesotan likes best—being on one of the ten thousand lakes. We had no fishing gear and no outboard motor; I was rowing. Being on a lake was a fascinating experience for us. That was our first trip to Urbank, Inspiration Peak, Spitzer lake, and Barnack's Camp. Many more followed. We were hooked on this area.

We found more and more places to go and see. About 25 miles east of Urbank is the large town of Alexandria. There, in a museum, is the famous Kensington Runestone. This stone is the reason for the belief of Minnesotans that the Vikings were here first. The museum is full of artifacts of the early settlers. We made longer two and three day trips. Don and his family and friends told us of so many beautiful areas to see. We went to Brainerd and saw the fabulous vacationland that Don had written me about.

Wherever we camped or hiked, we always had our children along. Our children were part of our lives. They helped in the house or in the garden or the lawn. They helped with the chores and had the same fun as us. In a car filled to the top with camping gear, with toys and games, with warm jackets and swimsuits, with food and drinks, we went with our kids on weekend outings or a long vacation. Sometimes we planned vacations by touring from one state park to the other. We went from Lindbergh State Park in Little Falls to Itasca State Park, to Bemidji State Park, to Cass Lake and Norway Beach. It took us 10 days. Our children came home with many stories to tell and even wrote about it in school. The trips always included swimming, fishing, wildlife watching, going to museums, or seeing conservation displays. The children had so many things to remember.

We always had tents which were strong and sturdy. The more I got used to driving, the more we expanded our distance of travel. The beauty of the land was fascinating. The blue of the sky and the blue of the lakes, the luscious green of the land, the quiet scene on a farm, the stillness of the forest, a relaxing trip rowing a boat across the lake—all these we experienced and we inhaled the fresh air of the countryside. We saw what a rich state Minnesota is and we saw it in the many farms and fields.

One day some of our friends suggested the towns of Duluth and Superior and a trip along the North Shore of Lake Superior to the Gunflint Trail. The first time we went on this trip, our eyes were glued on the constantly varying scenes we saw. The huge Lake Superior looked like an ocean to us. It seemed we were driving along the shore forever. From harbour towns, waterfalls, lighthouse, wild rivers, and trails and parks, the signs were constantly different. We drove along the most beautiful scenery in the world till we came to the Gunflint Trail. I was lucky I owned an 8 mm movie camera and filmed a lot. There the scenery was even more exciting and rugged. The Gunflint Trail is fifty six miles long, passable in cars with many resorts, campsites, and side trails to nature trails. In the sixties, only rough dusty winding roads went to the End Of The Trail campsite, our favorite camping spot. Living on the campsite made a deep and lasting impression on us. We were close to nature, close to the earth, and close to God. When you walk down a wild river bed in the dry season and see the big boulders and uprooted trees in the river bed, you see the power of nature. When you see fields of corn, grain growing, and herds of cattle grazing, you see the power of the earth. When you see the beauty and color of sunsets, Northern Lights and sunrises, you experience the presence of the Creator. It is so appealing and stimulating, you become reverent and thoughtful. With our own eyes and hearts we saw and felt what God had made for people. This is God's country and you can see His magic and splendor. He made it for all mankind. It is His creation.

In summer, Minnesota is crowded with people from many surrounding states to see and feel God's beauty in the state. All these people come here and enjoy fishing, swimming, boating, camping, hiking, laying in the sun or watching wild life. So many things you can enjoy. You leave Minnesota a better person. In the beginning, we were sleeping in tents. Later we slept in pop up tents, rented campers, and had a pick up truck and rented a topper. We went into Minnesota's wonderland like so many people did and lived in cabins in the many resorts; and always, we had our children along.

We also found God's beauty in the many other states we visited. With our children, we many times visited South Dakota's Badlands and Black Hills, Wyoming's Yellowstone and Grand Teton's, and many more places.

When winter arrives, Minnesotans don't sit next to the fireplace. They go out into the winter wonderland of snow and ice. Former Scandinavians have their outdoor saunas, or ski and skate. Everybody likes snowmobiling. It seems that almost everybody has a snowmobile or two. Snow is very abundant. So is ice cold weather. You can dress up against the cold and when you are having fun, you don't feel the cold. Ski events, ice hockey events, and snowmobiling contests, are abundant also. The laziest Minnesotan, the one who does not want to miss the comforts of home, can go ice fishing. A fish house with bunk beds, TV, warm oven, a table to play cards on—every comfort of home, plus fishing. What a life!

Chapter 6

Ontario Street

We were studying for our citizenship test. We learned many things about the U.S. government that we were not aware of. In 1958, we were called for our citizenship test. We passed that test, but I had to drop one of my middle names. Helen was told she had to drop the "e" in her first name, Helene to Helen. We could never understand why.

The big day finally came. We were all in the court room. People of many nationalities standing to recite the Pledge of Allegiance to the United States of America. Our children were standing next to us when we said it. It was moving and ceremonial. I remember what the judge said that we only have one pledge to honor, no matter how many pledges in foreign countries we had to give. I was thinking of the oath to defend Poland or the oath to the Fuhrer. All were oaths or pledges not of our own free will. The pledge to defend the Constitution of the United States we gave of our own free will. We will do our darndest to be good citizens.

Helen learned to drive a car. Again, I failed to teach it to her. She learned it in a driving school and passed the test with flying colors.

The University of Minnesota needed the space near our house for expansion, so they bought all the properties on Union Street from the owners. We had to move. A house on Ontario Street, close to the university, was our next residence. We rented the whole house. The upper floor was a separate apartment which we rented out. The people we rented to were three women who worked at the university. To our great surprise, one of the women was from Bielitz. Her sponsor was a doctor from Minneapolis. The other women were very interesting also. The older one, a Four-H representative from Montana, had sponsored the younger one, a victim of the bombing attack on Dresden, Germany.

They stayed in our house and we became good friends. Brigitte started first grade in the school nearby. We also remember a young priest in our church, Father Burry. He was in charge of youth education at St. Francis Cabrini. Our two young kids loved him and he visited us often as his time allowed. We always knew when he was coming. Our kids ran toward him, and he always picked one child up on his shoulders and the other one in his arms. Our kids loved to play with him. He would play cowboy with them. He could draw a play pistol like Roy Rogers. He was their hero.

Helen was pregnant and still babysitting a lot. I was still working at the University as a janitor and studying my correspondence course at night. Helen was under strict care by a University obstetrician, Doctor Janda, who had discovered the Rh factor in her blood. It was never discovered in her before in Europe. The doctor mentioned that it may not be dangerous after the first or second baby but is more dangerous after the third baby. He said he would take care of it by giving the baby a complete blood transfusion after its birth, if necessary.

I worked just a house away from the obstetric ward. When Helen called me with labor pains I rushed home, running all the way. When I came home, Helen was reading stories to our children in between her labor pains. Frances, the woman from Montana who lived in our house, brought Helen to the hospital. I had to go back to work right away. Helen said she felt very lonely during that time in the hospital, despite my being just one house away. I was working but waiting for a phone call from the hospital. As soon as the baby arrived, they called me. They told me, "It's a boy!" I left immediately. The doctor had told me before that everything would be ready before the birth of the baby. Right after its birth they would rush the baby's blood test to the waiting lab, and if needed, technicians would give the baby a complete blood transfusion.

As I got into the elevator, Doctor Janda, came out of the elevator. He smiled at me and said laughingly, "Congratulations to the first president of the United States in your family," referring to our first child born in the United States. He said everything went all right and no blood transfusion was necessary. The baby was Rh negative. So, our little Werner was born. He was a very cute boy, who was very sensitive and loving. We had no problems getting babysitters. All three women upstairs helped out in that. When they were working, our neighbor, Miss Filipek, could always be counted on to babysit for us.

Our neighbors across the street were the Maier's—Henry and Jeanne—and their three sons— Mark, Peter, and Scott. First Eric, and later Werner, had playmates. The kids grew up liking each other. Their kids and ours had loving parents. It formed the attitudes of the kids. The Maier's were Quakers, we were Catholic, but this did not make any difference. Our kids were brought up with the same care of love and understanding. Henry was a professor at the University of Minnesota. Later he moved to the University of Washington in Seattle, where he was well liked and became well known as a professor and writer and now as a lecturer. Over the years, we have forged a deep bond between our families that still endures.

Helen took evening courses in English and watched television programs like "Ma Perkins" to learn English. Three fourths of the words she did not understand. She wrote them down and when I came home from work, she asked me what they meant. That's the way she learned English.

My father was now in the hospital for the third year. We heard from my mother that my father often said he wished Brigitte would be there to help him. Suddenly we received the news we were dreading so much. My father had died.

After three years confined to the hospital, he died just one month before his 60th birthday. In his years in Bielitz, he had a tough life to endure. His whole life, in World War I and World War II, he fought for his family, for Austria, and for his beloved Bielitz. The last years, he fought the only way he knew, the injustice to other human beings the Nazis were committing. When we left for the U.S. he was so lonesome for us, especially for his grandchildren. We could not go to the funeral.

Veterans from many suburbs of Salzburg were at his funeral, many with their bands. They all honored him as their comrade. The Austrian government had refused to consider him a veteran but the Veteran's groups accepted him as one of their own.

We finally heard from my Aunt Deli and my Grandmother Hoffmann. They were all transported out of Bielitz sand resettled in Greiz, East Germany. My grandmother, in her old age, was thrown out of her house in Bielitz and transported to East Germany, where the living conditions were very poor.

All of our children were brought up in scouting. First Brigitte became a Brownie in Edina and later became a Girl Scout. She learned so much from the experiences she had with the many den mothers. It gave her a good start in life. Eric wanted to become a Cub Scout, so we also let him join a troop in Edina. I remember it was a very well-to-do community, and the sponsors and the troop had many outings. Later, when we moved to Brooklyn Park, Eric joined Troop 454 which was sponsored by the St. Alphonsus Church. Werner started in scouting also and I became Assistant Scoutmaster.

At that time, the Viking Council used or owned Many Point Scout Camp. Four years in a row, Helen and I spent our vacation time in the scout camp with the boys. One time my mother from Salzburg was with us in camp and enjoyed seeing her grandsons tipping canoes, swimming, hiking, and all the many fun activities scouts have. Both boys were in the Order of the Arrow and both were in the Brotherhood. After very hard work, Eric became an Eagle Scout. In a festive ceremony, Eric received the Boy Scout's highest award, and Helen was honored with a bouquet of roses.

Two events are still in my memory. Both are so typically American. One evening at a campfire with all the boys and their fathers around, one father asked me, "You were in World War II, were you not?"

I said to him, thinking he did not know it, "Yes, I was, but I was on the other side. I was a German soldier."

He said, "I know, but where was your unit stationed?"

I told him that we were close to Biserta in Tunisia. He said that he was there also. We found out we were at the same place. Trying not to offend him, in case he was facing our unit, I said, "I was a mailman."

He answered, "Don't worry, I was a medic." He shook my hand. We were always good friends.

The other event was at an ice fishing contest for Boy Scouts in Glenwood, Minnesota, on Lake Minnewaska. Our scout troop was invited to participate. The auger team had opened up many fishing holes on the lake and all the boys had to do was start fishing. The lake was teeming with scouts. It was a cold but sunny day. Our son, Werner, caught a small fish. By the end of the contest, his fish was still the biggest caught in his class. He won a trip to the Philmont Boy Scout Ranch in New Mexico. This trip was a fantastic experience for him.

A new person became part of our family. Helen later on explains it thoroughly. Let me explain how we met Helmut Kieselbach. Helen, as a nurse at the U of M Hospital, was often called on to be an interpreter for patients who spoke only German or Polish. One day a young man was brought to the hospital by helicopter from North Dakota. He was in an accident and spoke only German. It was too late to save his leg. The doctors had to amputate it. They needed someone to tell him what would happen to him. They asked for Helen.

When Helen talked to him, he was so glad to hear German again. He understood what was going to happen to him. After surgery, he gave up on his life and the hope of a recovery. Helen helped him and convinced him not to give up. We took him under our wing into our family. We treated him like our own son. He got his artificial limb and life looked better for him. He learned English and got a job. He learned to play football with our children and could do everything a normal person could do. We were so happy ourselves.

Chapter 7

Our First Visit to Europe And Experiencing Europe

Our life seemed to get better. I worked for a TV repair shop in Edina and had to drive daily from southeast Minneapolis to Edina. I was looking for a home to buy close to my place of work. An opportunity arose. A 40-year old house had been moved across the street to a new lot on a new basement. We could buy it for $9,000 and we took the chance and bought it. We had happy times ahead because it was the first house we owned. It was a two-story house with a large living room, one bedroom downstairs, and three small bedrooms upstairs. There was a full basement and a large garden.

We had Helmut Kieselbach living with us in one of the upstairs bedrooms. He was happy with us. He loved being the oldest boy in our family. I remember how Alfred came into our family and how he loved having a brother and sisters. Most of all, Alfred loved to have a father and mother again. In this way my father's life was so similar to mine. After Helmut left to be on his own, it felt like we lost our son.

Our family was getting closer together. The children grew bigger and had many friends. Brigitte went to Edina Highlands School and soon our boys started school.

Next to our house was the Edina Mortuary. The owner tried to persuade us to give him the first right of sale if we ever wanted to sell our place. The mortuary wanted to eventually remove the house and expand their parking space. They offered us $15,000. We were calculating. This was a lot of money. We could fly to Europe. In fact, our whole family could fly to Europe. If we sold the house now, we could put money down on a new house, fly to Europe with the family, and stay there for three weeks. Bruni and Walter, my sister and brother-in-law, had emigrated to Australia and were going to come back to Salzburg for the first time and stay there for a whole year. I didn't understand how they could do it, but it would be a great Wiedersehen if we could also be there.

It was 1963. We sold the house and paid some money down on a new house in Brooklyn Park, a northern suburb of Minneapolis. We planned to fly to Europe, stop in London for a few days, in Paris for a few days, and planned to also fly to Cologne. Outside Cologne, in Merzenich, all our relatives from Germany, Austria, and Australia would gather for a great reunion. Helen and the children would stay 2 ½ months in Germany and Austria, and I would go back to work in the good old U.S.A. after four weeks.

During the preparation for the trip, we had to move to the new house and also pack for the trip. Our children worried about what toys they were going to take along and what games they were going to play during the 2 ½ months in Europe. They boys wanted to take along their baseball bats and mitts and plenty of baseballs. Brigitte had her own toys and games she wanted to take along. We had also to take sleeping bags along. When we looked at what the children wanted to take, their wishes had spiraled into a big pile of stuff and they insisted they needed everything. We made an 8mm silent movie of one of our camping trips to the Gunflint Trail to show our relatives the beauty of our new homeland. We bought two canvas bags from the Army Surplus store which were at least 3 x 2 feet and 2 feet high and crammed all the stuff in. Our own suitcases with clothes were additional.

The last few weeks before departure were hectic. The passports did not arrive—a frantic call to Senator Humphrey and in a day the passport were delivered. The day of departure came. We had asked the Brooklyn Park police to check on our house while we were gone. They said they would come over but they made us wait. We were on the way to the airport with a lot of baggage and our three children. The children dreamt of playing for 2 ½ months in a country that now was foreign to them. We missed the plane.

After waiting for a long time at the airport, the five of us were finally rerouted on a different airline and flew to New York where we caught a plane to London. We left most of our baggage at the airport. We stayed in the famous Regency Hotel and did some sightseeing around Piccadilly Circus and Trafalgar Square. We saw Hyde Park and Kensington Palace and Park. It was for all of us a very exciting experience. Everything was more expensive, as we feared, and we were soon running out of money. After two days, we left for Paris.

Because of our money shortage, we had to cut our stay in Paris down considerably. In Paris, there was no baggage storage at the airport so we were told we had to bring it to the railroad station in downtown Paris and store it there. We piled all our baggage on a cart and were in the process of wheeling it to the taxi stand. As we passed through the big hall at the airport, a porter suddenly put his hand on our baggage and said we would have to pay him. I told him to leave us alone. We had put the baggage on the cart and we would also unload it. We argued in English. He insisted he would have to be paid, no matter what we did. Suddenly, frustrated by having to pay somebody for no work, my long hidden French came out and I started to cuss in the meanest French I had. It was loud and everybody stopped and looked at us. Even the security guards up in the balcony looked down and asked in French what was going on. I shouted to them, in French, that this porter wanted me to pay him money and he didn't do a thing. The answer from the balcony was that I would have to pay him. That was the law. I argued with the guards on the balcony, but to no avail; we had to pay the porter. The porter left and didn't help us unload at the taxi stand.

Our Story

The French taxis are small and only two people could sit cramped in the back
seat and one person next to the driver. No taxi driver would take the five of us.
For half an hour we waited. Finally a taxi driver, who came back after delivering
a fair and saw us still waiting, had pity on us. After putting the big canvas bags in
the back seat, there was no more room left. We put the rest of the suitcases in the
small trunk but still had to load us five people. He stuffed Eric and Brigitte right
and left in the packed back seat and slammed the doors on them. Helen and I sat
next to the driver and Werner on Helen's lap. That's the way we rode through
Paris to the railroad station where we left our baggage and took another taxi to
the Hotel Le Centre.

We walked to the Champs Elisee and stood in front of the Arc de Triomphe.
We went to the top of the Eifel Tower, inhaled the French atmosphere, the lifestyle, and ate French food. Our money was again running out. The next day we
flew to Bonn, Germany, which was the airport for Cologne.

When we arrived at the airport in Bonn, they had a unit of German troops
standing for inspection. A band was playing and the rolled out a red carpet. I
said, "You have to be kidding. What is all this?" We asked the stewardess. She
said, "They are rehearsing for tomorrow's arrival of President Kennedy here in
Bonn."

I had previously reserved a car from a car rental company at the airport and
we drove out to Merzenich to our waiting relatives. Helen rang the ball of her
mother's apartment. Her sister, Trude, came out and then it began—the em-
braces, the kisses, the hugging, the tears of joy.

Our mothers were there and my sister, Bruni, and her husband, Walter, were
there from Australia. All of Helen's sisters—Trude, Mimi, Liesl, and her brothers
Karl and Viki—were there. Helen had not seen Karl for 21 years. Mimi's husband, Poldi, and their adopted son, Ernst, and also Karl's wife, Lizzi's two children, Anne and Gunther, were there. Helen's brother Karl, who had been a
prisoner of the French, was released and had married Lizzi, his brother Rudi's
widow, and they had a son, Michael, together. My uncle Theo and his wife,
Paula, who lives east of Cologne had also come. Our children needed only one
day to converse in German.

This visit was a "Wiedersehen" in many ways. For some, there were many
years of war and suffering since the time they last saw each other. Missing brothers and missing sisters finally got together. They filled the gap of knowledge between them. Everybody wanted to know what had happened to the other person
during the long separation. In the meantime, our hosts came out with food and
drinks, and later, more food and drinks. All we did was talk and eat and drink,
and talk and eat and drink again. Days passed by like hours. Our children did not
know that they had so many cousins and aunts and uncles.

On a soccer field we played baseball with our relatives. We really introduced baseball to the people in Merzenich. Almost every evening we played. We marked the bases with sticks and played till it was too dark to see the ball. Our kids were the coaches. People looked on as we played and constantly asked us questions regarding the rules.

Too soon we had to say goodbye. Walter had a Volkswagen bus and our family, with all our baggage, and my mother and Bruni, left for Salzburg, Austria. There we had another great reunion with more friends and relatives. Our family stayed at Mendroks for $1.00 a night. The old Mr. Mendrok was an army buddy of my father from World War I. Our kids learned to play soccer. My mother, the children's grandmother, was the goalie and also a kicker. Our kids could not get over it. Their grandmother defending the goal and doing a pretty good job of it!

Walter had taken a whole year's vacation from the business he had in Australia. He had a plan to make a trip into the Dolomites, a mountain chain in the Alps of northern Italy. Both his father and mine were soldiers in World War I and fought at different places in that region. Walter and Bruni wanted to see this area and our family joined them. They had a tent and camping equipment and enough space in the Volkswagen bus for all of us.

It was a beautiful trip. We drove higher and higher to the former Olympic site, Corinto d' Ampezzo and into the area of Marmolada and Col di Lana, where the Italians had blown off the top of a mountain and killed thousands of Austrian soldiers in World War I. The Italians had dug a shaft deep into the mountain and mined it. In the explosion, they annihilated the Austrians who were defending the top. On a painted map on a hill, one could see the mountain before and after the explosion. We saw many military cemeteries from World War I where Christian and Muslim soldiers were buried. All died for Austria and the Emperor. We saw monstrous pillboxes from that time, still standing. It was 1963, only 45 years after the "war to end all wars".

We came back from Italy over the Brenner Pass into Innsbruck, Tyrol. It was a fantastic trip for us and for our children.

Outside the town of Reutte, Tyrol, we visited my Aunt Mitzi and my three cousins, who also had lived in Turkey. The cousins were all married. Kathie had lost her husband in the war. Hertha had married a Frenchman and her sons spoke only French. Grete had married an Austrian Olympic skier. It was another fabulous and incredible "Wiedersehen". For our children it was an experience meeting relatives who spoke a different language. They always found ways to communicate with each other. We refreshed our memories and added more stories of what happened to our relatives after World War II.

The time quickly came for me to fly home. My four weeks vacation was over. What an incredible four weeks I had. We crowded all the things together in such a short time. Helen and the children still had all summer to enjoy Germany and Austria and visit our relatives again and again. It did not cost them a penny. The relatives paid for everything. They drove them around, they fed them, and gave them shelter. The sleeping bags we took along were very helpful. Sometimes they slept on the floor in their bags.

I came home alone to a new house and a lot of work. Everything was in boxes or bags and left all over the house. Dishes, cooking utensils, canned groceries—all had to be located first and then unpacked and put in the right place. These were tough times for me. I had no money, but I had a job and was working.

When Helen and the children came back, they told me what a great time they had. Every one of the children had to write a story, as long as the memories were fresh, about what they experienced. The things they wrote made us happy. We did not regret a bit that we spent all our money to take our children along and give them a look at our great tight-knit family.

It took us some years to recover financially before we could plan another trip to Europe. After a while, it became necessary for Helen and I to travel separately. We visited each other's relatives, and three or four weeks was not enough time to do all that we planned to do. In 1967 we finally got my mother to come over here.

Many times during our visit to Europe, we had asked our mothers if they would like to come and stay with us in the U.S. and be with their grandchildren for good. Helen's mother was around many of her other grandchildren and was happy with their situation. My mother, who had her only grandchildren in the U.S., had many fears and reservations. We told her that we would take care of her medically and she should stay with us for a try, to find out if she like it here. She did not agree to come.

On Helen's next visit to Europe, Helen again brought this subject up. This time she said yes. She arrived here with Helen. She must have been apprehensive to come along; but traveling with Helen, she was without fear. The flight was a great experience for her and she fitted in our family life very well. She went with our family camping in the Jay Cook State Park and had a great time living in a tent. We went with her to our yearly scout camp at Many Point Lake in Minnesota, where we rented a cabin on Round Lake. We introduced her to fishing. My father was an avid fisherman but very seldom took my mother along. She was so happy fishing with us and catching fish, big walleyes and northerns and crappies,. Our Christmas with her was, for our whole family a happy time, a closeness with our children we never really felt before. She enjoyed it fully.

She was supposed to stay for a year to find out if she liked it or not. After nine months she suddenly wanted to go home. It seemed she was lonely for her friends and relatives she had left in Austria. She could not understand English, no matter how hard she tried. She always had problems with languages. When we were at work and the children in school, she was alone in the house. She could not enjoy any TV program because she did not understand it. If the phone rang, she could not understand who it was and what the person wanted. We think that this must have been the reason that she insisted suddenly to go home. It was for us a very sad day when we said goodbye to her at the airport.

In May 1969, Helen's mother died peacefully in Merzenich. Trude, Mimi, and Liesl were with her. Helen could not be with her. Helen saw her two years before. She was already confused. Once in a while she could recognize Helen. When Helen said goodbye to her that time, she told her, "You won't see my alive again."

We always had hope that Brigitte and her family will visit her relatives in Europe. It finally came to pass in 1980. Helen and I, with Brigitte and her husband, Dennis, and their two children, Robbie and Deedee, made the trip. Eric, who lived in New York, joined us in Merzenich. Besides visiting our relatives, we made a journey on the Rhine River.

Helen's brother, Karl, was vacationing in Switzerland and was recuperating from a heart attack. Our family wanted to see him and we decided to travel to Interlaken, where he lived nearby in the town of Wilderswil. Karl had made a reservation for us to stay in a farm house. It was nice to see him and his wife, Lizzi. We surely did not expect to see the fantastic scenery in front of us. As we looked up, we saw three snow covered mountains—the Eiger, Moench and the Jungfrau. Karl told us we could take a train up to the mountain top. Up there is the highest railway station in Europe, at 11,332 feet. We could reach it with the train from Wilderswil.

We took the train. In Lauterbrunnen, the train switched over to cog wheel and we really started climbing. First along beautiful alpine houses, then higher through tunnels and along sharp drop-offs, higher and higher. We saw the mountains come nearer and nearer. We passed a few resort towns. The air got thinner and thinner, and we got to the tree line. Soon, we had only snow and ice around us, and we were at the foot of the mountains, still climbing. Robbie, Deedee, Brigitte, Dennis, Eric, Helen and I, and Karl and Lizzi—all were going higher and higher and closer and closer to the mountains. At the foot of the Eiger, at the Klein Scheidegg Station, 6,762 feet up, the train stopped and we got out. This is the station where the train takes its last climb through the Eiger and the Moench mountains to come out at the Jungfraujoch. There the meteorological observatory is located and also the end station of the train, at 11,332 feet.

It was summertime and very warm. The air was very thin, but we still could breath. A lot of people, including us, took off their shirts and were sunning. We climbed around Klein Scheidegg, had a snowball fight or two, were rolling around in the snow, made pictures, and enjoyed ourselves.

We sat in a restaurant at the foot of the Eiger north wall, looking at the steep massive mountain where all the famous mountain climbers started their climb.

Our Story

The tunnel entrance for the train was clearly visible. Some of us, the younger generation, walked as close as they could to the tunnel entrance.

We lost the courage to take the train to the end. With the air getting even thinner, it would be too dangerous for us old folks, and too expensive for all the young ones. We decided it was time to return. The train ride downhill was as fascinating as the climb. One more experience we had was a trip on Thuner Lake. We went across on a ship, from Interlaken to a cave which we visited.

We said goodbye to Karl and Lizzi and parted ways. Brigitte and Dennis made a side trip to Rome. Eric made a trip to see the Matterhorn and other spots in Switzerland; and we were on our way to Niederalm, Austria, with Robbie and Deedee. We were all planning to meet in Niederalm.

In Niederalm, we visited my mother, which was a big joy to her, seeing her grandchildren again and especially her great grandchildren for the first time. After Brigitte, Dennis, and Eric arrived, we had our great reunion. Our relatives had organized it. They rented a huge room in a restaurant in Niederalm and this became the meeting place for all the relatives. Our cousins' children had now grown up and had children of their own. They all came together to see their cousins from America. Some of our relatives, mostly uncles and aunts, had passed away. Everybody had work, everybody had vacations, some vacationed all over Europe. No war, no suffering. The new generation was finally a happy generation. We invited them to come and see us in the good old U.S.A. Some wanted to come and some did come.

Brigitte, Dennis, Robbie and Deedee had to leave for home. Eric had more time left to travel through Europe. Helen and I still had one more week which we used to see Salzburg and Berchtesgaden again. Passing the border in the car of a friend, we had our passports ready. The border police didn't even look at us and waved us through. The borders were wide open. They were eager to have many tourists some and spend their money. What a difference from the time of 1947, when crossing the border was a crime.

We visited our relatives some more times. Again we traveled separately, so that at least some of us had contact with my mother or Helen's brothers and sisters. We had sent our mother a tape recorder to have her make tapes and let us know what she was doing and what she needed. We had sent her recordings of our children and later, of our grandchildren and great grandchildren. Now we hoped she would send us her tape recordings. It was too complicated for her. Even when we sent her a cassette tape recorder she did not send any tapes back. It was still too complicated. When my mother went into the nursing home, we knew that we were the ones who would have to interview her and take the tapes home. We were astonished. Her mind was as sharp as that of a young person. We recorded as much as we could. Her memoirs were the foundation of this book.

Part VII

Our Work In The US

Chapter 1

Helen's Work As A Nurse

About four months after Werner was born, Helen applied for a job as a nurse's aid at the University Hospital. Following are Helen's own words regarding her work.

The famous cardiologist, Dr. Lilehei, was my boss; and his father was also a cardiologist. My first patient was Dr. Lilehei's father. I met a lot of people at this station and later on at different stations. I remember one woman, I don't wish to identify, was dying. She told me she was possessed by the devil. The way she died was horrible. She was screaming and thrashing, like she was fighting with somebody. She was making horrible, roaring, blaring, crazy sounds, like she was possessed.

I also remember I had Dr. Piccard as a patient. Sig remembered reading about the Piccard brothers when he was in Turkey in 1931. August was the one who did the balloon experiments and Jean Felix was the deep sea diver.

They knew in the hospital that I spoke Polish and German. Sometimes older people from rural areas of Minnesota could not speak English. They spoke their native tongues, sometimes Polish or German. I always had to be the interpreter.

One day, as I worked the afternoon shift again, the nurses at the front desk asked me for help. They said that the helicopter brought in a young man from North Dakota. He spoke only German, not a word of English. He was in an accident and they had to amputate his leg; but they could not explain to him what was going to happen. They told me the condition he was in and I should go and explain to him what they had to do. He was a very young man. When I started talking German to him, his eyes just lit up. Later on, he told me that it was like an angel had come to him. I explained to him what had happened and what was going to happen to him. Because he had me there, he was relaxed. I had to promise him that I would look after him and be with him. That's how we met him. His name was Helmut Kieselbach.

After the amputation, Helmut was in a lot of pain despite his pain pills. I was not assigned to his care but I visited him as often as I could. He told me how he came to the United States. He and his sister were orphans in Germany after

World War II. A Lutheran Church in North Dakota sponsored him to come to the United States and work in the oil fields as a welder, a job he knew well. He had left his sister in Germany and started as a welder in North Dakota. One cold and icy night, coming home from work, he skidded on the road and crashed into the ditch. It was some time before they found him. To save his leg, they brought him to the University Hospital in Minneapolis—obviously, to no avail.

When he got better, they intended to release him but he did not know where to go. He could not go back to North Dakota again because he could not do the job he was doing there anymore. He had nobody there either. After talking with Sigi, we decided to take him into our house. We decided to try to find a job for him here and let him have a new start. He thought his life was over because he believed he could not do any job anymore.

They had amputated his leg below the knee. I tried to explain to him that they have artificial limbs now and they would fit one for him so that he could walk again normally. He could be able to do any job he would like to. It would take a while. It would take rehabilitation, but there is the possibility he could take any job later on. He did not believe me. He just gave up rebuilding his shattered life. It took me some time to convince him that life goes on. First he had to learn to speak English. He took evening courses and learned pretty fast. We tried to find a job for him. I don't remember anymore what his first job was. He stayed with us and, over time, he got his artificial limb and eventually played football with our kids.

Sig was driving through Minneapolis to Edina, to his job as a radio and television technician. It took a long time to drive and always in heavy traffic. We decided to find a place in Edina. There we found a house, an older house, that we bought. We wanted to have something of our own. It was a two-story house with three small bedrooms upstairs, one for the boys, one for Brigitte, and one for Helmut. Downstairs was a nice size bedroom for us, right off the big kitchen and a living room. The house had a brand new basement and a new foundation. It was actually 40 years old and it had been moved from across the street where they built a new shopping center.

The inside of the house was a terrible mess. We had a lot of cleaning to do and Helmut helped us a lot. He was the oldest of the kids and also the strongest. We considered and treated Helmut as our son, our adopted son. He called me Mutti (mommy) as my other kids called me. I was not that old but still considerably older than he was.

After a while he found an apartment and a better job and could afford more, so he moved out. We kept in constant contact with him. He still had his sister in Germany and brought her over to the United States. I believe the church in North Dakota who had sponsored him, later on sponsored his sister also. He had gotten a big sum of money from the insurance company or the oil company. He lived with his sister for a while. After he got married, we slowly and unintentionally lost complete contact with each other.

When we moved to Edina, I quit the job at the University Hospital and applied for a job in a Minneapolis nursing home. Before I did this, I had taken evening courses in nursing and took some tests to be accepted as an LPN. I think it was 1958 when I started working at Homestead Nursing Home. First, I started as a charge nurse at a station, then I was night supervisor for the whole building. I did this for about four or five years. Then they transferred the people from the nursing home because they handed this Homestead building to Abbott Hospital.

They opened up a new building a few blocks from Homestead called Fair Oaks and I started there as night supervisor. I had to drive back and forth to Edina and this was quite a distance. In the meantime, the children got older. Sig worked as an electronic technician in Edina, and I was a night supervisor in Fair Oaks. I could be with the children during the day. It happened many times that I was so tired I fell asleep at the wheel driving home. I caught myself a few times in the other lane. Luckily, I had no accidents.

It was really tough. The kids, at that age, needed constant supervision. Sig worked during the day, so I had to be awake during the day. Brigitte and Eric were already in school but Werner was still too young. Sometimes I took him to the day care center so I could get some sleep. He was such a good little guy. He let me sleep. When I dozed off and fell asleep, he quietly played by himself. He never went out of the house or did anything wrong.

Sometimes I fell asleep and would wake up because the telephone rang. One morning, I came home and was so tired I could not keep myself awake. I thought I would just lay down for a little while but I fell asleep. When I woke up, it was 12 noon. I thought, oh God! What did Werner do all by himself? I came in the kitchen and he was sitting on the floor and playing with his toys. He said he made himself a peanut butter sandwich because he was hungry. Then he asked me, "Mommy, did you hear the phone?" I said, "No." He took me by my hand and brought me over to the phone. He had put pillows and blankets and coats, anything he could get a hold of, and piled them up on the telephone so I would not hear it. That's how considerate, how sweet, that little guy always was.

I worked at Fair Oaks until we sold the house in Edina. We then bought a house in Brooklyn Park. It was too far to go through traffic for me, to a night job. Besides that, it was too dangerous to drive; so I quit that job and found a job in New Hope at the Ambassador Nursing Home.

I was a charge nurse there also, giving out medication and treatment. Eric and Brigitte worked there also. Eric worked as an orderly and Brigitte was a nurse's aid. I remember, one time a bad storm hit the nursing home. We had to take all our patients into the hall. The patients we could not bring out we shielded with mattresses. After the storm was over, all the windows on the west side were completely broken out. All in all, there were only a few cuts. The patients in the hall or the basement were unhurt. It was a very bad storm. I worked at the Ambassador for three and a half years. Eric started college, so he quit that job.

One day I had an accident on the way to work. It was 6:30 in the morning on a rainy day when I drove to work. On a hilly section of old County Road 18, I saw a semi coming down the hill in the other lane. I was at the foot of the hill, when suddenly I saw a small car coming out from behind the semi into my lane. He was trying to pass the semi. All I could think of was, "He is going to hit me." I swung my car onto the soft shoulder. The small car passed me; but because of the soft shoulder, I skidded across the road into the other lane and hit another car. My car came to a stop in the ditch.

I must have been out for a while. They had to pry the door open to get me out. I had a big gash on my head, but no broken bones. They brought me by ambulance to the hospital. When I was on the stretcher, I asked a man who was standing near me to call my husband and let him know that I will be okay. The man called Sig saying, "Your wife was in an accident. She is on the way to the hospital." Our boys were not in school yet. It was early in the morning, so Sig came with the boys to the hospital. After they fixed me up, they let me go home. Sig took me home because my car was totaled.

At home, I could not go upstairs to the bedroom because I was so bruised. Sig made a bed for me on the couch in the living room. When Eric and Werner, the two jokers, saw how tough it was for me to get up and go to the bathroom, they decided to make it easier for me. They went into the basement and came up with furnace pipes and all kinds of other pipes and made a drain from my couch to the bathroom. They were always so full of the Dickens.

It was too strenuous to drive to the Ambassador, so I was again looking for another job. I applied for a job at the St. Therese Nursing Home, a Catholic nursing home run by Dominican nuns. They had only opened up a year before. They wanted me right away. I started on the first floor. Eric and Brigitte applied for job there also, and they worked under my control on the same station. This was a big mistake. As I said before Eric, Werner, and Brigitte were full of the Dickens. I have to admit, they accused me of giving them more work than the other employees on the station. Brigitte and Eric paid me back with jokes and biting humor, but both did a good job. Eric had to quit St. Therese when he moved to St. Cloud College. Brigitte was pregnant with Deedee and she quit St. Therese also.

First, I worked on the first floor, which was for heavy care patients. Sometimes they switched me around to the other wing on the first floor where they had the confused patients. They added a third floor and this floor was for ambulatory patients and people who could take care of themselves. When they opened up the third floor, they put me in charge of that floor. After a while, when it filled up, they created two stations—the west wing and the east wing. In the middle was a new beautiful dining room. Each wing had 35 patients. I was in charge of both wings for awhile.

After it got to be too much work for me, they got another charge nurse for the other wing. Naturally, we had nurses' aids for both wings.

At St. Therese there was a program where every month they picked an Employee of the Month. One time they picked me. It was for the month of July. On a big poster, they had a history of my life and a photo of me. They displayed it at the entrance of the nursing home.

Our activities director knew a professor at St. John's University. This professor had a brother who was a director of the Vienna Boys Choir in Vienna, Austria. He had invited the Choir to come to Minneapolis. They were at St. John's University first and our activities director had asked them if they would come to St. Therese. They agreed. One day a group from the choir came to St. Therese. Our nursing home wanted to welcome them, but nobody spoke German. They asked me if I would introduce and welcome them and say a few words about them. That's what I did. It was quite an honor for me. After singing, the boys got a dinner served by our staff. I went from one table to the other and talked with them. They were very happy and appreciative to have somebody they could talk to.

I worked at St. Therese for 9 ½ years. These were sometimes tough years. More and more work was piled up on us. We had more and more paperwork to do and less actual nursing. There came a time that we had so much charting to do that we had absolutely no time to talk to patients. I had been a nurse since the War and nursing a patient was what I loved; but there was no time for that. You had to keep track of everything that was done for a patient. There was so much pressure put on the charge nurses not to forget anything that the stress was getting to me. My blood pressure got very high from all the tension. Many patients asked to talk to me but I had so little time to spend with them.

It was a beautiful nursing home. They really took good care of their patients. They always had a lot of activities and went on a lot of trips with their patients. It was one of the best nursing homes in the metropolitan area. You hear so many bad things about nursing homes nowadays, but this was a really fine home. It was not very cheap, but you have to consider the excellent care.

Besides my high blood pressure, I had a lot of other medical problems. I had worked constantly, full time or more than full time, the 9 ½ years in St. Therese. I could not work that hectic pace anymore. I decided to go into private duty nursing by joining the Medical Personnel Pool in Minneapolis. I did private duty nursing from 1977 to 1984. During these years I did all kinds of things as a visiting nurse, hospice nursing, and taking care of people who needed a private nurse. I enjoyed it. I was taking care of quite a few well-known and famous people. For instance, I worked for a university professor who had Alzheimer's disease. That was a very difficult case. He was very difficult to take care of. In Alzheimer's disease, the patient goes through four different stages and I went through all four stages with him till he passed away.

I took care of a Norwegian lady who had a stroke and could not speak anymore. She could only speak Norwegian before she had the stroke. Her son and daughter took care of her. They did not want to put her in a nursing home. They had other nurses for her, but they never lasted long. She was very belligerent and sometimes physical. I had a hard time trying to feed her. When I fed her and she had her mouth full, she would spit at me. When I gave her a tub bath, she intentionally splashed the water around with her legs so that I got more wet than she was. When I tried to dress her and put on her blouse, by the time I had the second sleeve on she already had slipped out of the first one. Things like that are very frustrating to any nurse.

Her son and daughter took care of her in the evening when they came home from work. They only had nurses during the day while they were working. I lasted with her for 18 months. Then I went on vacation. In the meantime, she got pneumonia and was admitted to the hospital. I got a phone call from her son who asked if I would consider going to the hospital and take care of his mother. The nurses there had such a difficult time with her. She did not even react to her children. When I arrived at her bedside in the hospital, her son said, "Ma, Helen is here." Her eyes opened and she had a big smile across her face. Her son stood there and had tears in his eyes. He said, "She has never done this to us." He again asked me to stay with her. I stayed with her for two weeks till she passed away. These were some of the many interesting occurrences I had with my patients.

The last patient I had was Mrs. Pillsbury. She is the wife of the founder of Pillsbury Flour Mill that turned into the giant Pillsbury Company, the matriarch of the large Pillsbury family. She had broken her hip; and after she came home from the hospital, she needed nursing care around the clock. A group of nurses were employed by her just to take care of her. I was one of them. I took care of her for over a year until she decided that she did not need nurses anymore. She let all of them go.

She had a villa in Palm Beach, Florida and she asked me to come with her. At that time I was going to retire and I said, "No, I can't do that." One day in March, I was going to retire in June, I got a call from her in Florida. She said she was coming back to Minneapolis and asked if I would come to take care of her. I told her it would not make any sense to do that because I was retiring in three months. I didn't want her to hire me and in a few months she would have to look for somebody again. She said, "Let me think about it. I'll call you back." She called me back and said, "Even if you will be with me only for a short time, I want you to come and take care of me." I agreed to do it. I stayed with her until I retired. At that time she was already 99 years old. She was a strong-willed person with a tremendous knowledge of the world and world events. She had even visited the Russian Czar a few times. She gave me a book she wrote about her family and her life. It is full of the most interesting experiences any person could have. When she was 99 years old, she put on a Christmas party for 44 people and organized everything herself.

After I retired, I had little chance to stay in contact with her. At her 100th birthday, I wrote her. She wrote me back and asked me to come and see her in Florida. I never found the time. She passed away when she was 104 years old, an almost unbelievable age for any person. She lived an active life in the middle of all the historical events of our nation and the world.

Chapter 2

My 26 Years With Magnetic Controls And ADC Telecommunication

I would like to begin with an interview I had just before retiring after 26 years with Magnetic Controls Company and ADC Telecommunication. I had to describe our whole life to the interviewer. This interview was published in our company paper after I retired. It seems that the interviewer had mixed up the sequence of events in our lives. We don't blame the interviewer. Most of our friends who knew us well could not remember the sequence of events correctly. This book will clear it up. For our children and grandchildren and for anyone who follows them, it will give them a view of what happened in our lives.

With the written permission of ADC Telecommunication, here is the interview:

Sig Hoffman retires after 26 years

Sig Hoffman, 26-year veteran of ADC, retired on June 27 and headed north to his lake home, where he plans to set up permanent residence. Before retiring, Sig worked with the Electronic Test Group at 4200, but his long career with ADC began at Magnetic Controls (a company with which ADC later merged) where Sig was one of the first employees.

During the Magnetic Controls years, Sig worked on a variety of military programs—many related to space research. Along with other people, Sig's work in instrumentation, temperature controls and current sensing was used in well-known national projects such as Skylab, Mercury, Gemini, Apollo and the Space Shuttle. After the Magnetics division was sold, Sig put his electronic knowledge to use in the Automatic Test Department, where he has worked since 1981.

Now that he is retired, Sig and his wife are looking forward to moving out of the city and hunting for a warmer place to spend the winters. Other plans include writing his memoirs—which are very rich in historical detail.

Austrian by birth, Sig was born in what is now Poland and raised in Turkey, where his father had a business in textile machinery. When the Germans launched WW II, he was drafted into the Germany Army and later captured by American troops and placed in a POW camp in Valdosta, Georgia. His wife, who is from Sig's hometown, served as a German Army nurse on the Russian Front, and spent nearly a year in a Russian concentration camp.,

At the conclusion of the war, Sig was released and returned to the home of his parents in Salzburg, where he attended the university. Although his original goal was a career in teaching, the war interrupted his education and eventually received education in engineering so that he could take over his father's business. This was not to be, but the education served him well later in his career.

In the aftermath of the war, as countries were being divided and people displaced from their native countries, Sig decided to take his family to the United States. One of the people he had met in the POW camp became his sponsor; and in 1952, the family arrived. Although Sig admits that it was rough going at first, he eventually got established in Minnesota, a state that he now says he could never leave completely.

Despite his many years in the U.S., Sig still knows more languages than most of us could hope to learn in a lifetime. Among his repertoire are French, German, Turkish, Spanish, Latin and Russian. And he cooks in several different "languages" as well. In fact, on a recent trip to Austria to visit his elderly mother, he spent much of his three weeks there cooking her favorite traditional Polish and Turkish dishes.

Thanks to Sig for his many contributions to ADC. We will miss you.

Now, going back in time to the decision to go into industrial electronics.

I decided that the best thing for me was to change to industrial electronics. I applied for a job close to my home in Edina. It actually was only a five-minute drive from my house to work in Saint Louis Park. Both are suburbs of Minneapolis. I didn't have to drive too far, but I would have to learn a lot. The fun was out of working in radio and television. The fundamentals are the same, but doing antenna work is like working on a house or a construction job. That was what I was doing lately.

I never knew how interesting industrial electronics actually was. I did not know what kind of work Magnetic Controls was doing. For convenience, from now on I will mention Magnetic Controls only as MC, as we ourselves called it. As I had mentioned before, I started on February 29, 1960. The first job I worked on was a temperature control for missiles. My constant aim was to build it right the first time, even if it took longer than the guy next to me.

Right from the start, I was told that the stuff I was doing was secret and I could not talk about it with anybody. This stuff I was doing was military work. I kept this in mind all these years. Even my family and closest friends never knew what I was actually doing. Not only could I not talk about it, but my work was not even mentioned in any published company literature. I did not mind. In order to be able to write about it, I will quote only from published materials from newspapers and Magnetic Controls Company and ADC Communication.

I am quoting now from a brochure from Magnetic Controls Company titled "Products, Production Facilities, Personnel". No date is printed anywhere on this brochure.

> Missile Guidance Temperature Control — Most of the "Big Birds" have guidance or autopilots temperature controlled by Magnetic Controls Company equipment. These controls are designed and produced for the Atlas, Polaris, Snark, Regulus, Thor, and Matador missiles and also for atomic submarines. Some controls are the size of an overnight case — others smaller than a pack of "regular" cigarettes.

On the inside end page is another article:

> Magnetic Controls Company has made 6,147 gyro temperature controls for these missiles. Missiles manufacturers demand light, accurate, reliable gyro temperature controls — delivered on time. Magnetic Controls Company pioneered this field in 1952. Since then we have reduced the weight and size of these controls by 90% while increasing accuracy and reliability. This is why so many missile makers rely on Magnetic Controls Company.

I worked on some of them. The devices Magnetic Controls Company built are based on the principle of magnetic amplification. The magnetic amplifier, the way they were designed by Magnetic Controls Company, were the most stable and sturdiest amplifier. Perfect for space exploration and perfect also for the Navy.

The Minneapolis newspaper, The Minneapolis Star printed an article dated February 7, 1961, which is titled "Third City Firm in Polaris Program". It was written by Ralph Mason, Minneapolis Star Staff Writer.

> When the nuclear submarines Patrick Henry and George Washington went to sea for active duty, they were carrying equipment manufactured by three Minneapolis companies.
>
> Reports already have told of the gyroscopes and accelerometers made by Minneapolis - Honeywell Regulator Co. to guide the Polaris missile carried by the nuclear subs, and the submarine-based computer made by Control Data Corp., used in fixing the missile direction.
>
> Now it has been revealed that a third Twin Cities firm, Magnetic Controls Co., manufactures a temperature control system which not only maintains the guidance system at a precise temperature but also warns by means of bells and lights when the temperature is out of the prescribed limits due to circumstances beyond control of the system.

Each submarine carries one of the Magnetic Controls warning system for each of 16 missile "silos", plus several for spare equipment.

Actually the Polaris guidance system is under the care of Magnetic Controls Co. temperature systems from the time it is first assembled until it is fired from the submarine.

This is accomplished not by one system but by several, each one tailored to the conditions existing at various items between manufacture, storage and firing. Connection is made to an electric heater and a temperature sensing device enclosed in the casing with the guidance assembly.

The Magnetic Controls system is attached to the casing and is set to sound a buzzer and blink a light if the temperature rises or falls a few degrees from the operating temperature. The buzzer can be turned off by a human operator, but the light continues to blink until the temperature returns to normal.

There is even an indication if a fuse blows.

Although every temperature control system was designed by Magnetic Controls for a specific set of conditions prescribed by the Navy, all designs made use of the basic concepts developed by Magnetic Controls over the last eight years.

Without even a guidance system on which to test the temperature control systems, the company moved from preliminary design to finished hardware in 90 days.

"The way it was put up to us," said E. E. Lewis, president of Magnetic Controls, "we had to deliver the goods or the submarines would leave the dock without our equipment."

Lewis reported that, in addition to the Polaris guidance temperature alarm systems, his company manufactures nearly 30 other units for each nuclear submarine including equipment for the submarine's own navigational system.

With 15 nuclear submarines already built or under construction and a possible total of 40 to 45 submarines being discussed, he figures his company will have plenty to do in the next several years.

"It isn't the easiest work in the world," Lewis said, "because the Navy's standards are extremely high and they want everything yesterday, but we're proud to be a part of the program."

Lewis indicated that his company is receiving new contracts on the Polaris program regularly, the latest having been received only a few days ago.

I worked on the devices mentioned in the article.

My jobs got more interesting. It did not have to be a military job to be exciting. We worked on a computerized cement mixer. I guess it was not a big success, that means we did not get many orders in. We worked on "Autostart", a device that starts your parked car automatically in cold winter weather to keep the engine and the car warm. This device is very important for cold Minnesota winters. It is still in use today under the name "Autostart" but manufactured by another company. Another job we worked on was the electronic device in an electric car that works the same as a transmission in a gasoline powered car. This project was constantly improved and submitted to the electric car manufacturers. It was usually rejected. One day, one manufacturer who used it on their electric car, wrote us that it worked perfectly for their car and meets and exceeds all their specifications. We were hoping for a big order but it never came. I assume the car was still too expensive for people to go out and get an electric car. Our product, the electronic transmission, would have been the cheapest part of the car.

Another job seemed exciting enough in the beginning. MC was working on remote electric meter reading. It took a few years to finish it. From a central area the electric meters could get read automatically, without any meter reader going from house to house. I started on the project but was transferred later to another job.

On a military job, I had to weld small gold plated leads of little diodes into a certain configuration. We had a large military order and for at least one year, I was welding and working to assemble other parts in connection with this job. On this miniature welding job, a welding spark hit my left eye, despite my eye protection. I had to have eye surgery and had the lens in my left eye removed. At that time, a lens implant was not used by doctors. I wore a contact lens on my left eye which gave me 20/20 vision in both eyes. It was a work injury, but I did not get any worker's compensation.

My knowledge of languages was well known in the company. Once in a while I was asked to translate certain German letters and literature. I was also asked to be a German translator in a court case filed against our company, a patent case. In all my translations, I was never paid for the time I actually worked on them. The time I used at work was paid by the company as regular wages. Sometimes I had to take my work home because I needed a dictionary. Sometimes they wanted me to translate French letters. Most of them I could translate without a problem, but sometimes I again needed a dictionary. Knowing a foreign language is like knowing how to lift weights or knowing how to run. If you do it often, use the foreign language, you will be good at it. If you slowly stop doing it, either weight lifting or running or using a foreign language, you lose the capability. Like your muscles, you mind needs exercise and stimulation as often as possible.

For a while I was thinking that my Turkish would never be used here in the United States. How wrong I was. At the Festival of Nations in St. Paul, where the culinary products of a multi-national community were shown and eaten, I had many chats at the Turkish booth, to the surprise of the vendors. They claimed my Turkish was excellent just to make me feel good. The only time I felt my Turkish was appreciated was at work. We had a Turkish employee, the wife of a GI who was once stationed in Turkey. She was so helpless, working in our place and hardly understanding the English language. I tried my Turkish on her and she was transformed into the happiest woman. I could explain our production procedures in her own language so now she knew what she was supposed to do. She constantly thanked me for helping her, which is the custom of the people in Turkey.

One of the vice presidents, who had been to an electronic fair in Germany, dropped a handful of German brochures on my desk and asked me if I would please translate them as soon as possible. They were the newest brochures on computer electronics. When I was trying to translate them, I found no help in my dictionaries. Electronics had advanced tremendously since the time of World War II, especially since the start of the computer age and the space race. Even the libraries could not keep up with the newest words used in electronics. To my surprise, the Germans accepted most of the English words in their electronics. The technical dictionaries describe some of the words with a long winded German word, but the people mostly use the shorter English word.

Later on I took courses in Spanish and refresher courses in French.

Some military jobs we got required they be done in "Clean Room Facilities". The Clean Room is an area that is temperature controlled and germ free, a complete environmentally-controlled surrounding like an operating room. I started working in the Clean Room. Everyone working there had to wear a white coat and hat. Before you entered the Clean Room, you had your shoes brushed by a machine and put on white boots over your shoes. In the beginning, we also had to wear gloves and a mask over the mouth. After the first few Apollo moon landings there was no more fear of contamination from and to the moon and a few of the Clean Room requirements were dropped. We still had to sterilize everything we worked with. We had ovens and freezers in which the devices had to be calibrated, which simulated the space environment temperatures. You would have the device in the oven hooked up to your calibration and test equipment unit and you calibrated it for the high temperature. Then you took the device out of the oven, still hooked up to your calibration and test equipment, put it in the freezer, and calibrated it for the low temperature. The device, when it was ready for shipping, had to meet or exceed the required specs.

Our company had acquired another company, ADC, which was at that time a transformer company. ADC stands for Audio Development Company. Both companies produced their products under their own label but were somehow under MC administrative cover.

Chapter 3

Out Of The Ashes

I normally came to work early in the morning. One day, I and the other employees were stopped by the police and not allowed to go into Cambridge Avenue where our plant was located. The police said the plant had burned down overnight. We could see from a distance the still smoldering company building. There we were, all these guys crowding together on this intersection and looking at the smoldering plant where our production building used to be. Somebody from the company came and told us that they can not keep us and we would have to go on unemployment. Out of a clear blue sky, I was suddenly unemployed. I never had that happen to me before. It seemed tough times were ahead. I had to file for unemployment. I had never filed before.

Before I was supposed to get my first money, the company called me back. They told me that if I was willing to work to get all the test equipment out of the ashes, I would have work. I would rather work for the company than get an unemployment check. Some of us returned to work. Sure, I did not get much, only starting wage, but it did not matter. It was important to help the burned down company.

I looked at the mess closely. The steel beams were bent from the heat and the roof had collapsed and burned. I worked in the ashes and tried to recover what I could. I was mostly interested in salvaging our test equipment. Some were totally burned, some were badly burned but still salvageable, and some had only burned spots on the outside. I searched and saved a lot of it from the still smoldering ashes. Everything saved smelled like it came from a smokehouse.

Right across from the fire, the company leased a high garage which was like a little airplane hangar. I had to do everything in there. Clean the junk out from the garage, wash everything out, and create new facilities for us to work in. I painted walls, made cubicles for different departments, and then worked to get the salvaged equipment in working condition. We could not afford new equipment. Most of our equipment was self made. We always had to design our own test equipment. There was nothing with our specifications available on the market. We restored almost all the equipment or built better, more accurate ones. We were back in business in a short time.

These were the times when all of us acquired a certain independence. We designed and built our test equipment ourselves. We had to search for parts out of electronic parts catalogues and sometimes had to go and buy the parts ourselves from the electronic parts dealers in Minneapolis. We not only built the test equipment, but also built the devices to be tested. We did a lot of engineering ourselves.

We had a pilot line that developed certain prototypes. A pilot line would nowadays be called the R and D department—Research and Development department. I worked in this department also for a time. Here your own ideas counted. It made a difference to you if you were valued as a contributor to the project. I give full credit to Ed Lewis, president and CEO or our company at that time. He was an excellent engineer. I can only describe him as an explorer. Before he even got an order from the military for some device, he had already researched it and usually had a device ready. That's the way his mind worked. He was constantly searching for solutions and always gave credit to the ones who contributed to solving the problem.

ADC Telecommunication was planning to have a history of MC and ADC published some time ago. That would have made it easier for me to write in sequence. But this was never published.

ADC was founded by Walter Lehnert and had already existed at that time for 30 or 40 years. Walter Lehnert was a professor and a Dean at the University of Minnesota. He worked in his basement and developed a lot of new items there. All kinds of inventions were credited to him. Over the years, Walter and I got very well acquainted. Every time he visited our company, he stopped by and saw me. He was trying to trace his ancestors in Germany and we often talked about this.

Transformers are also based on the magnetic field principle. We at MC used a lot of transformers in our work. The combining of these two companies would be beneficial to both of them. Now ADC flourished and MC flourished.

I worked for a while in the inspection department of ADC. There was so much work there, it was unbelievable. They had opened up new production lines and the orders were coming in. I was inspecting small transformers, maybe one inch in size, as well as big transformers weighing half a ton and more, and everything in between.

With our workload getting larger and larger and the room to produce it getting smaller and smaller, our company was looking for a larger place to expand. They could not expand in the place they were in now. They bought a building from Rosemount Engineering on Hwy. 494 and Hwy. 100. We were soon in new facilities. The building was so huge, it gave us the possibility to constantly expand without worries.

Ed Lewis had left the company for California, where he opened up another company. Greg Bezat was now running the show and he had a very different idea about the expansion of the company. He bought out many little companies which were supposed to be advantageous to the further development of MC. Some added to the potential of our company and some were so in debt that it required a constant flow of money to keep the company afloat. Some were folding companies and were bought just for the equipment and instruments we needed. I only remember two names of the companies. One was Secode and the other Radiation. I don't know how wise these decisions were because we lost more and more money. Our company, which was expanding so tremendously, was suddenly seemingly broke. From Honeywell came a new man who took over the company. His name was Charles (Chuck) Denny.

He went to each department and talked with each person to get a feel for what the company was doing. He had a neutral commission study the company to see what the outlook was for a company like ours. They came to the conclusion that we were producing more products for communication than for the military. Our future would be in telecommunication, a field slowly becoming more in demand.

A new company was formed with the name "ADC Telecommunication". It started with everybody having to take a pay cut. I think the cut was one third of the wage you had been getting. The ones who did not like that were welcome to leave. The ones who accepted the pay cut would have to get retrained for different jobs. For me, at that time, I had no intention of leaving a company that had given me so many interesting jobs. I would not know what to do if I left the company. And if I left, where would I be able to use my knowledge and skills? In any case, I probably would have to be retrained again. Some people left MC at that time. I did not.

After the reorganization, I was suddenly appointed to run the whole RG department, the Returned Goods department. I had, over the years, worked on almost every facet of Magnetic Controls. I knew each revision of everything ever built. At that time there were no photocopies or records of the revisions available. Our drafting department never made photocopies of revisions. When it came time to work on Returned Goods, nobody knew what the revision numbers meant or which part was changed and where the part was located. I had everything still in my mind. Every returned device that the company ever built came back to me. I had to do the repair, and for one third less wages. There were tough times ahead, but I was glad I had a job.

When we got the big NASA contract, I went back to work on the NASA project. All the people who worked for NASA had to take special training, not only for the procedures; but we had to learn to solder "the NASA way". We all knew how to solder. When I started my radio and television training, I had to learn how to solder; and suddenly, all the soldering I had done in my life was inadequate. NASA had completely different rules.

In short, they were this: "The minimum amount of solder should be used for your part." You don't add any solder because you think it needs it. You only use the amount of solder that is specified. Unnecessary solder increases the fuel load you have to carry to shoot that part into space. You had to solder only one way, the way NASA had approved. That was also the most solid connection. We all made it through the tough soldering training and then we started on our projects, under constant supervision of NASA inspectors. NASA inspected everything. From the time you started building it, to every time you handled it, to the time you were delivering it, you had to sign your name to the files.

NASA's procedures required constant strict inspection. Your name and the NASA inspector's name were on the files. If you moved one part or one device from one shelf to another shelf, you had to sign. Every part we used for assembly came with a big file. Even when the part was only an element in the ground, the person who dug it up had to put his or her name on a file and that started the record. Everyone who added something or moved it had to sign. The tiny parts we got were x-rayed from three sides. These x-rays came with the files. We x-rayed everything during the different stages of our production and all were added to the files. When the final shipment came, the device was the smallest thing. For the files, you needed a truck.

We already worked on the Mercury project which was followed by the Gemini project and ended at that time with the Apollo project. The Apollo project was itself three projects—the command module, the service module, and the lunar module. These projects had an allowed rejection rate of 10%, that is, they allowed 10% more of the order to be built for devices that failed. Our failure rate was 13%, which meant that we had to re-order parts and start new assembly and sometimes were late with the delivery of the missing 3%. That cost our company money.

They put me in charge of production. Slowly I got the rejection rate down to 10% and less. By the time we were working on the Apollo projects, the extra devices built were not needed because there were no rejections. NASA still bought the extra 10% we had for spares.

We did all these projects in the new Clean Room facility. This was a much larger Clean Room than we had before. The inside wall, facing the main assembly hall, was mostly glass, with two huge picture windows. Each of us could be observed working. Our company was proud to show any guests what we were doing. It looked more like a big operating room in a hospital, with all the white coats we were wearing. Of course, if you looked into the Clean Room, you still could not identify exactly what we were doing. Our company was proud of having this facility for NASA. We often had Japanese groups going by and looking through the windows; and, of course, school children were always a happy bunch.

In the beginning we felt like we were in a cage in a zoo. We felt that people were constantly staring at us. When we would see people staring at us, suddenly some of us began to act like monkeys. We were making fun of them, more jokingly than serious. Eventually we got used to being watched. It never bothered us anymore.

NASA inspectors checked our work with a magnifying glass. Most of our work was done without magnifying glass. Because we were building quality work, nothing was ever rejected. Full credit for this goes to my co-worker, Isabel Iverson, who had fantastic eyes for soldering. She soldered without any magnifying glass and did it fast. When the NASA inspector came to check it with the magnifying glass, he was stunned. He could not understand how she could do the soldering without any magnification. He never could find anything wrong. That is what training, job skill, and a natural gift does—produce a perfect product.

By now our accuracy, our reliability, and our fame for doing excellent work, was well known in NASA circles. We were only a subcontractor, but they had so much trust in us that we never had to bid for contracts anymore. Our excellent products spoke for us.

We used only special Hi-Rel parts, High Reliability parts. We got the contract for devices for Sky Lab and the Orbiting Positioning satellite. I worked on all of them and on other military projects.

We got the contract for the Space Shuttle at a time before anybody knew there would be a Space Shuttle. We were told by the contractor for NASA that it would be a re-usable device. As was openly publicized later by ADC, it was a system of current sensors under the designation CS-108. It had to be different from what we used in Apollo and it had to be smaller. That was what we always feared. Whatever new project or order we got from NASA, it had to be smaller than before. It had to be designed for smaller dimensions, which meant the parts inside the device were more cramped, and it had to be more protected from the space environment, including vibration.

The re-usable clause was a big problem for engineering. When something was engineered out on the drawing board or the bread board, where parts were actually lined up and soldered together to see if they worked, the contractor for NASA would often ask for a change. The device had to do more than it was originally designed for. They changed the specifications and engineering had to utter that fearful phrase, "Let's go back to the drawing board."

Many times the contractors for NASA asked for fundamental changes. They already knew what the Space Shuttle would be used for and what they wished to do later on in space. They were already thinking of the many labs they wanted in orbit for space research, like the European Space Lab and the many labs with furnaces and freezers and other laboratory equipment. Our devices had to satisfy future programs NASA planned. They were produced with Hi-Rel parts, x-rayed components, and the finished devices were themselves x-rayed.

The re-usable clause was also important in the design and testing of the devices. I believe NASA wanted a fifty year guaranty on these devices. Where could you find electronic devices with this kind of guaranty? When we actually finished the devices, and after the space environment tests, our documentation showed we exceeded all the specifications and could guaranty these devices for at least 70 years. By the way, the space environmental tests for the devices were done by an outside and neutral test lab, in their own lab; and the test results were electronically recorded and printed. All our devices had to pass these tests.

We had delivered our CS-108 for NASA in time and we were waiting for the first launch of Columbia, the first Space Shuttle. In late 1979 the Space Shuttle was supposed to blast off. It was postponed. In the Encyclopedia Americana 1981 Science Annual, page 4, there is an article regarding the postponement:

> At one time the US National Aeronautics and Space Administration (NASA) had hoped to get the space shuttle off the ground in 1979, but repeated setbacks with engine testing and the installation of a thermal protection coating have forced one postponement after another. The shuttle is a winged vehicle to be launched like a rocket, flown in orbit like a spacecraft, and steered to a runway landing like a glider.

And further back in the article, it says:

> The first manned orbital test flight is not now expected to occur before late 1980 or early 1981.

The decision was made by ADC Telecommunication to completely get out of doing business with the military and NASA. My feelings were not considered. I was just a little cog in the wheel. Besides, this was an economic decision by people who knew that our perfect product for NASA would not get us any re-orders for a very long time, and also military contracts have a way of fading out eventually. So I had to close down my work on our military contracts. I wrote my last manual for the test equipment we shipped out to the military and we sold everything in our department that could be sold. Our NASA affiliation was over.

One thing that filled me with joy and delight was when the Columbia Space Shuttle had its first flight. It was only a test flight, but it was successful in every way.

An article in our company paper called "The ADC Communicator" dated June 1981, Volume 32, Issue 3, says on the last page:

Columbia Affirms Technological Prowess

When the Columbia Space Shuttle touched safely down in California's Mojave Desert, huge smiles could be seen on nine faces in Minneapolis, Minnesota. The smiles belonged to nine ADC employees who had cooperatively designed and manufactured the CS-108 Current Sensor, an integral part of the first re-usable space craft.

Columbia's stunning success was certainly an affirmation of U.S. technological prowess and in turn, of ADC's. The tight-knit team that is responsible for custom designing and manufacturing the current sensor are listed: Sig Hoffmann, Production; H. E. DeCambaliza, Material Control; Isabelle Iverson, Manufacturing (now retired); Ron Kurth, Testing; Sheldon Plath, Plastics; Bill Peppel, Marketing Contract; Al Giernett and Vern Baxter, Engineering and Shirley Ponce, Toroidal Winding. The efficient, competent teamwork of each individual resulted in a technically perfect product.

The function of the CS-108 Current Sensor is to measure the current in the power system of the spacecraft in the most reliable and precise manner. The CS-108 Current Sensor measure the current without being physically connected, eliminating the possibility of interrupting the current.

The CS-108 Current Sensor project was subcontracted with McDonnell-Douglas, the company that developed the power system for the Columbia Space Shuttle. "As with any custom project, an immense amount of engineering effort goes into a project like this," stated Vern Baxter, one of the engineers involved in the project. An extremely exhaustive reliability study was made on each current sensor. This entails very extensive testing in a space environment-type test.

In 1962, ADC designed and manufactured the first current sensor, OAO - (Orbiting Astrological Observatory). ADC supplied 26 current sensors to manage the power in that satellite. Since the first space craft was launched, ADC has been supplying various pieces of equipment such as temperature controls, temperature telemetry units and voltage telemetry units. The Columbia Space Shuttle was a stunning success, and ADC is very proud to be a part of it.

Next to the article is a group picture of us nine persons mentioned in the article with our names underneath. Just one comment on the article. It was Magnetic Controls who produced, in 1962, the first current sensors.

It was time for me to change to a different department in our company. The Power Supply Department wanted me and asked me to change to their department. My interest was to improve the testing methods of our industry. So I changed to the Automatic Testing Department, a fairly new department where we tested new methods, mostly computerized, to test electronic devices.

In the beginning, our computers were old-fashioned instruments that our company had bought from other companies. There was still a lot of mechanical testing which was very inaccurate and not dependable. Everybody worked hard and contributed to the constant improvement of the automatic test procedure. New computers designed to do the automatic testing were the breakthrough. We were now testing devices faster and more accurately than ever. The speed of the new computer was tremendous and truly solved our problems. We still had to troubleshoot our devices, and I was good at that. Our only problem left was that we had no containers to put the devices in. We used old cardboard boxes from the Shipping and Receiving Department. There were never enough boxes for our jobs. The reason why I mentioned that will be seen in the next event.

It was now 1982. In 1986, I planned to retire at 65. Up at our weekend cabin, we finally decided to get a bigger house. We had put a trailer house on our lake lot, had dug a deep well, and also had a sewer system dug to comply with the county's shoreland management law. It was s big investment, but Helen and I were working and I had a chance to work overtime.

Soon I was working 10 to 12 hours a day testing and troubleshooting our devices, and I was happy to make some money. Then it happened. I took a carton of devices from the top of a shelf, as usual, for testing. As I brought the carton over the edge, I suddenly felt the heavy load and tried not to drop it. I felt a sharp pain in my back, but I didn't drop it. A fellow employee who saw this helped me to put down the carton. The supervisor who was in charge of placing the devices in the carton also saw this and asked what was wrong. I told him the carton was too heavy and I hurt my back. The devices were instruments, each costing over a thousand dollars. As I went back to my computer bench, I felt a warm pain in my back. I counted the instruments in the carton. The maximum allowed limited in the carton was supposed to be only 20; I counted over 40.

During the day my back hurt more and got warmer. I did not want to go home and lose a chance to work overtime. Over the next days it got continually worse, and finally I decided to go and see a doctor who admitted me immediately to the hospital.

Thus followed a very hard time for me. Weeks of hospital care and the pain got worse. The company took me off the employment list, and I had to apply for worker's compensation. For at least two months I received neither wages nor workmen's compensation. Bills were coming in from the well driller, sewer digger, trailer house payment, and our regular bills; and I could not pay them. After two months, the first payment of worker's compensation arrived. It was $200 for two weeks. I thought I would lose everything I had worked for and achieved during my life.

I had lost all my feeling in my right leg. My doctor said he would operate as soon as I started to lose the feeling in my left leg. In 1983, after I lost the feeling in both legs, I had my back surgery. After surgery came months and months of slow rehabilitation. Whirlpool treatment and swimming in the warm pool of the Courage Center, a treatment center for the handicapped, brought me back a life worth living. The most important thing I learned in the Courage Center was that there were a lot of people in worse shape than I and coping with it better than I was.

As I said, the rehabilitation was very slow. I was considering early retirement. ADC was asking me to come back and work only as much as I could. They said they would make it possible for me to work without strain on my back. They promised me many things and I agreed.

I started to work, with the doctor's permission, three hours a day every other day, with time to relax and lay down. The only place I could lay down was in the women's restroom. I did not want to do that. They created an inspection table for me where I could sit in a soft special chair with back support, looking straight at a lighted glass table. The company did everything I asked them to do just to make it possible for me to work. I could do my inspection without bending.

Slowly I increased my working time to three hours every day till I was working half a day every day. My wage was not enough to help me get out of debt. We decided to sell our house. First we had to get the needed repairs on the house done in order to sell it, and I needed money for that. It was a constant fight to survive.

Despite all my exercise in the Courage Center, I knew I would be handicapped the rest of my life. The back pain was always there. When I got up after sitting for a while, I was limping. The doctor did not know why I limped.

My day of retirement eventually came around. I was interviewed for the company paper. Rumors were that my fellow employees planned a party for me. It was the last day in June 1986. A lot of people were gathering in our department. Everybody stopped working. A lot of my friends from different departments came over to me to shake my hand. Our CEO, Chuck Denny, was there and some of our vice presidents. Chuck Denny spoke. He recounted all the hard work I did over the years and my contribution to ADC's good name. He wished me good luck in my retirement. I also was asked to speak. I did not speak long. I had tears in my eyes.

My fellow employees had collected some money and bought me an excellent fishing rod and a depth finder plus other nice presents. I received a card with at least 50 names on it. I did not know I had so many good friends.

Epilogue

Now that we are retired and living in the winter months in Florida, we often go to see a Space Shuttle launch. Many times now we stand at Cape Canaveral with thousands of others to watch the Space Shuttle go up. Every time the thundering roar of the rocket engines lifts the Space Shuttle upwards, my feelings and my thoughts go upward with the Astronauts and their complex and delicate work. I feel I did my best to make their journey a safe one and to ensure their return. The next Space Shuttle again will carry the system we built for them. Many people who had built the Space Shuttle would probably feel the same way. Every part is critical for a safe journey and return.

I have a wooden plate I received in the POW camp in 1943, with pencil engraving of a POW tower. It was our first Christmas in the United States. It hangs in my den next to a photograph of a Space Shuttle on a launch pad. The pencil engraving on the plate is fading away. It was a long, hard way from the time in prison camp to the time of a Space Shuttle launch. It encompassed a big part of my life.

We gave it our best shot. With Helen on my side, we enjoyed our life and we suffered along with problems life dished out. Along with sickness and accidents, we have survived.

I don't know why I was given so many chances to work on various important projects. My dream was, with these products, to give thanks to the United States for all this country did for me. It gave me back my life and my future. Austria refused to give me any chance to live properly, and the future was bleak. There was no future for my children in Austria. Helen and I gave our children the direction and the moral upbringing. It is up to them to find their niche, their life in the United States of America.

Reference

From:

Geschichte der deutschen Sprachinsel Bielitz

(Schlesien)

Author:

Walter Kuhn

Published:

Wurzburg Holzner 1981

Subject:

Bielsko-Biala (Poland-History)

All pages